Paddle
for Water

Canoeing across America with a Message

And a Man I Never Intended to Marry

Nancy DeWitte Condon

ISBN: 979-8-9859883-0-7 (Paperback)
979-8-9859883-1-4 (ebook)

Published by Nancy DeWitte Condon
https://paddleforwater.net

Edited by Margaret A. Harrell, https://margaretharrell.com
Cover design by Van-garde Imagery, Inc.
Original photo of chapter illustration courtesy of *Billings Gazette*.
Artistic rendering of paddling picture by Katherine McDowell McGough
Map by Gary Condon
Unless otherwise noted, photos were taken by Paddle for Water crew.
For bulk orders, signed copies, or speaking engagement
requests, visit the author's website:
www.paddleforwater.net

To my favorite paddling partner
and devoted husband Tom,
who waited until I had a hankering
to marry him too.

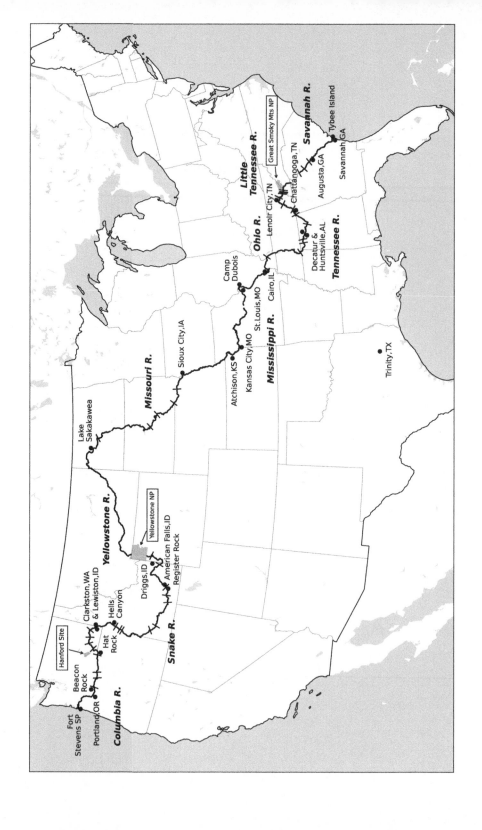

Paddle For Water
Canoe Route

5,000 miles

19 states

9 rivers

13 months of paddling

58 dams (listed here)

Columbia River

Bonneville Lock and Dam
The Dalles Lock and Dam
John Day Lock and Dam
McNary Lock and Dam

Snake River

Ice Harbor Lock and Dam
Lower Monumental Lock and Dam
Little Goose Lock and Dam
Lower Granite Lock and Dam
Hells Canyon Dam
Oxbow Dam
Brownlee Dam
Swan Falls Dam
CJ Strike Dam
Milner Dam
Minidoka Dam
American Falls Dam
Palisades Dam
Jackson Lake Dam
+ 12 diversion dams

Tennessee River

Kentucky Dam
Pickwick Landing Dam
Wilson Dam
Wheeler Dam
Guntersville Dam
Nickajack Dam
Chickamauga Dam
Watts Bar Dam
Fort Loudoun Dam

Little Tennessee River

Calderwood Dam
Chilhowee Dam
Cheoah Dam
Fontana Dam

Savannah River

Hartwell Dam
Richard B. Russell Dam
J. Strom Thurmond Dam

Yellowstone River

+ 7 diversion dams

Missouri River

Garrison Dam
Oahe Dam
Big Bend Dam
Fort Randall Dam
Gavins Point Dam

May every dip of your paddle lead you towards a rediscovery of yourself, of your canoeing companions, of the wonders of nature, and of
the unmatched physical and spiritual rapture made possible by the
humble canoe.

— Pierre Elliott Trudeau

Contents

A Note from the Author

Barely a day goes by that our cross-country canoe expedition doesn't come to mind. This is extraordinary, really, because it began thirty-six years prior to publication of this book. Not extraordinary, on the other hand, because the thirteen months and five thousand miles spent as a river person shaped the future I now live.

A thorough scouring of journals kept by Tom and myself help to straighten memories that may have become embellished or contorted over time. Memory adjusters like daily journals, natural history notes, letters, maps, my personal-thoughts journal—a whole assortment of expedition memorabilia—fill a box that, in case of a house fire, is the first thing I'd save. Tom will have to fend for himself. So the crazy antics and adventures portrayed here actually happened. But, as Alfred Hitchcock once said, "Drama is life with the dull bits cut out." Over the course of those thousands of miles, there are a lot of dull bits (and some exciting bits) that ended up on the cutting room floor. My website, https://paddleforwater.net, shares more of our expedition.

Remember Ektachrome? The pictures herein are digitized versions of Kodak slide film that required mailing away to develop. Instant feedback was futuristic in the '80s and '90s. We received knowledge of light meter problems and operator blunders weeks after pictures were taken. Today's "fix-a-photo" measures were utilized to the best of my abilities.

"Portage," "confluence," and "draw" are commonplace words in my vocabulary, but I've since learned they are not ubiquitous. Therefore, I include a glossary to help bring out your river savvy.

If you look for this book in hardcover, I'm afraid you won't find it. I have chosen to publish tangible versions only in the greenest way possible. Hardcovers are not recyclable. Paperbacks are. I just hope each copy is read and enjoyed until completely tattered.

I write this book as an inspiration and motivation for you, dear reader, who may have that adventure gene gnawing at your innards as I did. Listen to it. There is plenty of challenge to be found in nature. Plenty of beauty. Plenty of opportunities to learn and grow. Plenty of causes to champion. Although I find euphoria ensconced in a canoe on a Class II or III rapid and my serenity complete on a calm pond, your bliss may be completely different. I invite you to seek that part of you that yearns to be in nature. Your grand adventure may be just outside your door.

CHAPTER 1

Commitment

Everyone must believe in something.
I believe I'll go canoeing.

—Unknown. (Not Henry David Thoreau)

Testing What's Possible

Day 1 (June 14, 1986): Wind whips my ponytail, battering my cheeks. Salty spray shears off the crest of two-foot breaking waves continually showering my face and stinging my eyes. I am fighting to maintain our direction, using powerful paddle strokes to make our canoe slice into each wave the ocean is throwing at us.

We are headed straight for the Columbia Bar, the most treacherous section of the "Graveyard of the Pacific." This juncture, where the Columbia River meets the ocean, has sent thousands of boats to the bottom and drowned capable sailors. Not where Tom and I want to be! My paddling partner, in the bow of the canoe, is on the lookout for how to escape this madness.

We've been paddling along this confounded barrier for a half-hour, hoping for an opening, but that seems unlikely now. Tom sacrifices a stroke to point his paddle starboard, toward the jetty of jagged rocks beyond which is the Columbia River. "Pull in over there," he shouts over his shoulder, barely audible in the gale.

"You want to portage over *that*?" I holler back, eyes wide, mouth agape. I know he is suggesting that we land the canoe, unload it, and lug it and all our three hundred pounds of equipment up and over feet-high boulders to the other side of the jetty. But that spot is, like every other spot along the jetty, a huge jumble of angular rocks assaulted by crashing waves.

"There's no other way," he yells.

My heart races. As captain-of-the-day, it is my job to decide between two absurd options. But only this one choice makes sense: risk this short but dangerous portage up and over this stupid jetty.

"Okaaaay," I manage. I decide to put my faith in Tom. He's the more seasoned canoeist and I trust his judgment. Together, we maneuver the boat with strong draws, sweeps, and prying of our paddles. As the crashing waves and wet, slippery, jagged boulders get closer, my dread grows. I ignore my chilly face, numb fingers, and screaming shoulder muscles, concentrating on bringing the canoe, slowly, carefully, parallel to the jetty.

"We'll have to make this fast so the boat doesn't get beat up," Tom shouts as he hops from the pitching boat. Immediately, landing on a boulder, he turns, crouches, and braces himself, using both arms to keep the boat from smashing against the rocks. "I'll hold her away, and you untie the gear and toss it out on the rocks or to me."

Inching along, staying low, attempting to maintain my balance,

I heave gear out of the boat while getting tossed back and forth with each wave. The canoe bangs against rocks repeatedly, but Tom tempers the impact. It's a frantic operation, to be sure, but all the gear is finally lodged behind a rock somewhere on this irksome ridge of boulders.

With no ballast, the boat is pitching madly. I'm grasping the gunwales, spread eagle on my knees, trying not to fall overboard. "Let's haul the canoe to the other side," Tom hollers. "Fast!" Timing it between waves, I spring out of the canoe, nimbly shifting my weight to solid rock. Not waiting a second longer, we lug her—stumbling, slipping, and grunting—over, and down the jetty ridge to the much-calmer water of the Columbia River. Finally, *finally*, we head east on the Columbia River, having sampled the wrath of the Pacific Ocean.

Boulder-climbing while carrying a canoe is something one should *never* do. But having just done so, suffering merely shin abrasions and contusions but no broken leg or sprained ankle, I congratulate myself. The satisfying victory of a problem solved feels good, and my whole body relaxes as we take leisurely strokes up the waveless river.

"I never would have considered landing on those rocks with the waves like that, and then hauling the canoe over that rock embankment," I confess.

"Sometimes ya gotta do what ya gotta do," Tom replies, turning his head over his shoulder to throw his voice back to me.

"It just didn't strike me as a thing that could be done."

"Well, we may have to make some mental adjustments."

What other notions am I going to obliterate on this venture? Testing the extent of my capabilities is part of why I'm here.

I come back to the tangible. "We should have put in on the other side of that thing."

"Yeah, that's pretty obvious," Tom says in an almost, but not quite, cynical tone. We decree, right then and there, that "should of" (or any grammatical permutation thereof) will have no part in our vocabulary. We'll make the most sensible decision we can in the moment and proceed with no regrets.

Our earlier examination of the map of Oregon's Fort Stevens State Park showed a curious line separating the Pacific Ocean from the Columbia River. This line extended beyond the end of the map, with no indication what it was or how far it went. We now understand that this line indicates the 6.5-mile South Jetty built to prevent the Pacific from depositing piles of shifting sands in the river mouth. The price of wanting to dip our paddles in the Pacific Ocean to begin this journey is now paid.

The Columbia hardly looks like a river here. The mouth measures four miles across and we can't see the other side. It's dotted with islands, ocean-going vessels, and small craft. We stick to the south side and paddle only about a half mile before, succumbing to weariness, we stop for the night at the nearest beach. It is beyond disappointing to learn that we are still in Fort Stevens State Park.

When I finally lie down in the tent with my life jacket as a pillow, I reflect upon our first day of this expedition.

It was only three or four hours ago that I lay sprawled in the salt grass, lungs heaving, legs shaking, and arms limp. Tom, flopped beside me, was also trying to recuperate from the fifteen-mile portage we just completed. From our campsite at Fort Stevens State Park to the nearest ocean access was a mere three miles. Three trips— first to scout while carrying handheld items and lunch pack, second with personal backpacks and paddles, and third with the canoe and kitchen—had put my muscles in a state of shock. We hadn't even set our canoe in the water, and already I was spent. I remember rousting from my reverie for a moment to look over at Tom. Smiling, I said, "We made it," to my sprawled-out partner.

"Yeah," he said, opening his eyes to look at me. "I hope this will be the hardest portage we'll ever have to do." I smiled and nodded in agreement at the time.

I chuckle to myself now. That hope has already been dashed.

I vaguely hear Tom fussing around outside the tent, but I tune the present noises out to reminisce about how in the world I ended up here on this preposterously exhausting day.

The Promise

February (four months earlier): Tom and I stood against the wall in the back of the chapel at YMCA Camp Cullen. This camp is about a hundred miles north of Houston in the little town of Trinity, Texas, on the northern shores of Lake Livingston. Here Tom and I work as environmental educators for the Houston Independent School District (HISD). Camp Cullen is one of two Outdoor Education Centers (OECs) in the area that host all the fifth graders in the largest school district in Texas. For four days, these inner-city kids immerse themselves in the piney woods of East Texas, where armadillos wander among the palmetto fronds at night. Our charges not only learn science but mingle with students from other districts.

Environmental Education (EE) is a hands-on approach to teaching and learning that builds a greater understanding of ecological processes; nourishes a respect for land, water, air, and earth's inhabitants; and develops an understanding that humans are an integral part of the natural world. EE cultivates skills and inspires involvement in local and global issues. Environmental educators integrate science, math, art, history, and language arts and regularly teach outdoors. They work in zoos, parks, nature centers, wildlife agencies and in association with school districts, like here at Camp Cullen. The aim of EE is to create a more sustainable world by cultivating ecologically literate, civically engaged citizens who live in healthy, environmentally mindful communities.

Like most every Tuesday, this night the staff performed a puppet show for a standing-room-only audience of laughing kids, who arrived by the busload. The hall buzzed with excitement. Amaryllis, the red-yarn-topped bratty girl puppet, had just heaved two perfectly recyclable soda cans into the audience and will soon get a talking-to by Sebastian, the environmentally aware spider.

As we watched, propped up against the back wall, Tom leaned over to whisper in my ear, "Peter asked me if I wanted to go on a cross-country canoe trip." Tom had never been much on lead-ins.

"Whaaaat??" I turned to glare at him. The look on his matter-of-fact face revealed that Peter's was no mere hypothetical question. Scruffy and bearded, his pale blue eyes hidden behind coke-bottle glasses, Tom is a rugged guy who, I knew, split firewood for fun. He can free a breached canoe from a rapid, no matter how firmly rushing water has it pinned against a rock. A wizard with knots, he can tie a sheet bend or trucker's hitch with eyes closed. It was easy to see why Peter invited this confident, knowledgeable outdoorsman.

"Canoe from coast to coast?" Did I hear him correctly? I got a little nod with a raised eyebrow. Looking away, I stared at the floor to let this idea sink in. I've always been game for a paddling trip, *but this*? It's big time. My adventure gene immediately kicked in and said, *just do it!* Unequivocally, I yearned to go.

Here in Texas, working my first job far away from home, I had a newly adopted "just do it" mantra. Not original, I know, but it helped me embarrass myself without remorse, attempting the Texas two-step at the bar in town. It helped me get my Saturday job as a wrangler, guiding horseback rides from 5 a.m. to 3 p.m., despite the measly thirty-five-dollar-a-day pay. It was a good mantra for an introvert like me, as I urged myself to try new things.

A play-it-safe; do as I'm told; don't ruffle feathers kind of person up till now, I'd always gotten good grades, gone to college, didn't drink or smoke or do drugs. Then got a job—I had done everything right. Here was my opportunity to rattle the cage of conformity. I loved clanging.

As I stood in the back of that room, Tom's statement went straight to the heart of my mindset. It triggered an intense yearning. I didn't think: *This is exactly what I want to do.* No, this unmistakable longing didn't erupt because of any specific thought process on my part. It was a deeply seated feeling, logic resistant. It was an ache. It was a need. I *had* to go.

"Who all is going?" I looked up at him abruptly. I'm not as straightforward as Tom in voicing my gut feelings.

"It's Pete's idea. Mike's going too," he said. "We would talk about it all the time when I guided in Maine." He stopped and feigned attention to the puppet show. I, on the other hand, stared at the floorboards again, brow furrowed.

Peter was my boyfriend. The vexing question was, "Why didn't Peter invite *me* on his canoe trip?" Secrets of this magnitude tend to put a hex on a relationship.

Peter was a modern-day John Muir—the type who would throw a little bread and beef jerky in his rucksack and head off into the wilds. He never traveled without his mandolin. He might neglect to bring a shovel to dig a cat hole (for an outdoor potty), but his ability to listen to his inner self and express it through music and art inspired me. That part of my brain doesn't work very well. I envied how he could just speak his mind. I couldn't do that. My thoughts were always ultra-censored through the "should I say it?" "How do I say it?" "When should I say it?" "Will it hurt his feelings?" filters, until I'm struck silent, with nothing to say at all.

His "you control only yourself" attitude was new to me. With his influence, I believed I could climb out of the prosaic station in life I felt I was in. Freed from social convention.

Maybe Tom sensed my yearning, as he popped the much anticipated question, "You wanna go?"

My mind reeled. Again, I couldn't bring myself to voice my true feelings. I tried to picture myself undertaking such a tremendous journey. This was the stuff of extreme outdoor adventurers—stories you read about in *Outside Magazine* or *National Geographic*. I didn't think I was that caliber of person. Yet, I couldn't dismiss the idea as I would have if asked to go cliff diving or bull riding or something outrageous.

"How long will it take?" I asked.

"I figure about a year," Tom replied without hesitancy.

His tone was so calm and matter of fact, but inside, he must have been enthused. As for me, the idea checked every box of who I was and who I wanted to be. My favorite sport is paddling; I long to travel and see the country; an unknown adventure is super intriguing to me; accompanying my friends would be the best; and doing something notable and unique is my aspiration. I'm totally in!

"Yeah . . . ya know . . . I would," I said falteringly, smiling and nodding at Tom, masking my enthusiasm. Struck with the confidence and speed it took to make such a weighty decision, I immediately felt the heady rush of saying it out loud. I knew it wasn't the final word because it seemed like I was being invited to a party by one of the guests. "Would it be all right? Do you think Peter or Michael would mind?"

"No, I don't think they'd mind at all. Four is a good number. We'd prob'ly go two solo boats and a tandem. Safer that way."

"Why didn't Peter ask me himself?"

"I dunno," he said with a shrug.

"I'll ask 'em anyway," I said, "both of them."

Day 1 (July 14): I am roused from my musings by a clanging of pots and the whooshing sound of a camp stove Tom is firing up as he prepares supper. A contented smile overtakes me as I turn over, close my eyes, and recall my conversation with Michael.

(Late February): "Sure, Nance, it's fine by me," he answered without giving it any thought.

"No, I mean, really think about it. I wouldn't cramp your style, infringe on a 'men only' type-a-deal or anything like that?"

He laughed. "No, it'd be fine. Really."

And with that, I believed him. Michael is the king of "laid back." He could get me screeching with laughter over a stupid, witty joke. Other times during intense discussions his profound insights would test my philosophical beliefs. To him, life was deep *and* funny. To broaden my perspectives and lighten any mood, I would love to accompany Michael on such an expedition.

If only it were that easy with my boyfriend, Peter. Our conversation about how invitations had gone out was not pretty, but he was open to me joining the expedition. We talked and pondered for days. We'd be putting ourselves into a very nontraditional dating situation.

To weather any course correction this more intimate situation might take us, we'd better be strong enough friends first. Tricky business. As we sat in his car in the parking lot at the end of our weekly Dairy Queen run, Peter proposed his idea. "Let's make a formal commitment to each other about this trip. 'Yes' means you're in. 'No' means you're not."

"Fair enough," I agreed.

"How 'bout we exchange notes on Friday."

"Friday, then." I gave a snappy nod, delivered a quick kiss, then ran off to my cabin nestled among the pine trees. That gave us almost two days. Enough daydreaming and wishful thinking. *Am I up for the physical demand, the interpersonal relations, the unknown, unforeseeable trials?* Peter's idea was sound. A commitment on paper had that added bit of authenticity.

Being an environmental educator at a residential camp is an all-consuming affair. Teacher by day and nanny by night, I had eight to twelve girls as my responsibility twenty-four hours a day, week after week, during the school year. The lifespan for a front-line educator here is about two years, precisely my tolerance. I was nearing the end of my second year, resigned to move on at its conclusion. To where? I hadn't a clue, but it would be in environmental education. It had been a respectable job, to be sure. Savings accumulated easily, with no time or place to spend it. Working outdoors with like-minded colleagues forged lifelong friendships. I loved it, but it was draining. The timing of a once-in-a-lifetime adventure couldn't have been more appealing as I looked for my next step in life.

Two days flew by, but it was time enough to give this whole situation some consideration. No rent. No mortgage. No utility bills. No vehicle. I smiled at the thought of living on the fringe. I had some savings—not much, but it should do.

Physically, I had some shaping up to do. I wasn't flabby but I was no honed athlete, either. I prescribed push-ups for myself every night. I would also have to take up dreaded running again. Years of running track in high school and college drained all the running desire out of me. Nevertheless, I knew I'd be grateful for it.

While my girls slept the night before decision day, I sat on the edge of my bed in our shared cabin and turned my thoughts inward. What would it look like if I didn't go? How would I feel? As I thought of not going, I immediately flushed with regret. I felt aimless, worthless, envious, but most decidedly regretful. My whole being yearns for the intrigue and excitement of doing something noteworthy in my life. I will honor my gut reaction.

The next morning, I woke contented. I felt I had more than a scrap of paper with the word "yes" written on it in my back pocket. I knew I had done the right thing. I had confidence in myself to carry out the commitment I made in my heart. It was hard to keep from betraying my inner satisfaction with a visible smile.

The noise of over a hundred children soon filled the dining hall. I saw Peter excuse himself to come over to the table I shared with my girls. *Good, he had already decided too.* We passed notes wordlessly like schoolchildren. I tried to determine the content of his message from the look in his eyes, but all he wore was the neutrality that we had all perfected around the myriad of fifth graders continually surrounding us.

"Ohhhh, Peter gave Miss Nancy a love note," one of my girls said to all the rest of her cabinmates. The table burst forth with jeers and speculations. I indicated with an admonishing look and a half-smile I was not happy about them meddling in my affairs, but this passing of notes was, I admit, a funny school-girl prank.

"Do ya like him, Miss Nancy? He's SOO cute!" another chimed in. My half-smile turned into the best frown I could muster, but I knew I couldn't quell the pestering. Letting the conversation diverge into which one of the male staff was the cutest, I put the note directly into my pocket.

Back at the cabin, I accompanied the girls to the bathhouse to brush teeth and use the restroom. Taking advantage of the lack of attention around me, I pulled out the note. It was folded about as many times as a piece of paper could be. My heart thumped a bit faster. If this note said, "No," the trip would vaporize into nothingness. He was the one who had brought it all together. He was the kingpin for us all. Please, please, please say *yes*.

I unfolded the paper and breathed a contented sigh of relief.

Preparations

(**Early March**): Preparations began in earnest. The four of us—Peter, Michael, Tom, and I—agreed to get together often to dole out duties, gather equipment, throw out ideas, and have fun doing it. When our jobs at Camp Cullen OEC concluded in mid-May, we would begin the venture. That left only two and a half months to transform this group of idealistic environmental educators into a well-outfitted, organized expedition.

One doesn't just set out across the country in any old pig boat. We needed quality "tripping" canoes, paddles, suitable life jackets (what we call "Poofduhs" or PFDs, short for personal floatation devices), water-proof camera cases, water filters, and all the other odds and ends needed for extended canoe camping. Among us, we had cooking gear, stoves, questionably adequate sleeping bags, and tents. We counted heavily on the generosity of sponsors to supply us with additional equipment in return for publicity, which we would happily provide.

As we deliberated over potential sponsors, Michael fell suspiciously silent, then got a goofy expression. I saw him scribbling away on a piece of paper, sometimes smirking. *What's this jokester up to now?* Finally, he interrupted. "Okay here, Nance. I've got it." He handed me the paper, and I read it out loud:

> *Hey, MAN—Me and my friends want to go canoeing across the country. Now, we ain't got the dough so's we wants yous to give us a couple of boats or maybe some cash.*
>
> *Now my main man "Tommy C" He's real good at canoeing. He canoes white water and everything. My Bro Pete "The Madman" C—is also real good & went canoeing a lot. Yours truly has been canoeing a little but as you can see, I has a way with words, oh yeah, & ya see I could maybe write a story or two & mention ya.*
>
> *The chick, "Nancy D" is comin because she wants to and we all happen to like her. Heyyy not like that man, she just gives us a little class. And I hope this don't offend you, 3 guys & a broad cohabitatin in a canoe for 3,000 miles— It's all on the up and up—If ya know what I mean.*
>
> *We are gonna start around Oregon & pick up some rivers east for about 7 or 12 months. Ending up in the Atlantic somewhere. So if ya can spare it, we could use your help. And if not thanx for nothin.*
>
> *Be Free,*
> *Michael*

I wrote one we could actually use.

Tom took control of the canoe search. As he had built a fiberglass whitewater boat several years earlier and was familiar with the intricacies of form and function, the properties of various materials, and the reputation of canoe manufacturers, the rest of us let him have that job. We needed lightweight touring boats, capable of carrying all our gear, easily repairable, sturdy, and easily portaged.

Tom decided on the Sawyer X-17. Its combination of Kevlar for strength, and fiberglass for ease of repair made it the perfect choice. Plus it was affordable and came with the terrific assistance offered us by Harry Roberts, Sawyer's vice president in charge of sales.

One of my jobs was to talk to a veteran canoeist, who could offer advice on equipment, teamwork, what to expect on big rivers, and anything else we didn't even know to ask. Peter gave me the number of Valerie Fons, the wife of paddler extraordinaire Verlen Kruger. Verlen and partner Steve Landick canoed the famed Ultimate Canoe Challenge, a 28,000 mile, three-and-a-half-year expedition in and around the U.S. and Canada from 1980 to 1983. Valerie was a notable canoeist in her own right. She paddled the Baja peninsula section of the trip with Verlen for three months. A year after that, in 1984, Verlen and Valerie broke the world record for canoeing the Mississippi River. They completed this 2,348-mile venture in 23 days, 10 hours 20 minutes—beating the previous record, set by a British Royal Air Force team, by 17 days!

When I got up the gumption, I called my canoe hero.

I managed to spit out what we were embarking on, indicating that I would be the only woman of a four-person team, and she quickly, confidently launched into useful pointers. "Take turns being the captain," she said. "Be the boss on alternating days." She told me I need to be a "full, involved, and intimate part of the trip." She also advised that I take time for myself, maintaining a balance between my own needs and group needs. *Good advice for us all*, I thought.

Then I learned she and Verlen were to embark on a new expedition themselves. They would begin a Two Continent Canoe Expedition, a 21,000-mile journey from the Arctic Ocean to Cape Horn around the same time we would set our paddles to work in the mouth of the Columbia River. When I hung up the phone, I felt inspired, motivated, and comforted—knowing that while we paddled, others were doing the same on a journey much grander than our mere 5,000-mile venture.

At our third planning meeting, Peter proposed inviting a couple more friends. Tom thought this was getting a little large and didn't like adding unknown elements. Peter took offense and disagreed. Tom was afraid personality conflicts could result, but Peter felt confident this would not be the case. Michael and I sat silently, watching this uncomfortable exchange end with no conclusion. I left with a tightness in my chest.

On this first Friday of March, camp was quiet. The students were bussed away. Time to relax and unwind. Only the prospect of a jog ruined the luxurious thought of a weekend of freedom from 24-hour-a-day kids. Procrastinating, I headed for the staff lounge on the off-chance Peter was there in hopes of discussing the group's rift with him. As luck would have it, he was there, all by himself.

"Ahh, great, I found you," I said cheerily, waltzing through the door. He was sitting on the edge of the couch, elbows on knees, hands clenched, fingers intertwined, staring at the floor.

"Nance, I can't go on the trip."

I stopped short. My mood plummeted. I felt my face flush—intensely aware of my heartbeat.

"What . . . what do you mean you can't go?"

He sat back, looking up into my eyes and straight into my soul. "I've prayed long and hard, and now I know that I just can't go on the trip." I heard no sorrow, no room for doubt, and no apologetic tone. It scared me.

"But . . . you decided before," I stammered. The heat from inside me was starting to boil over. "You made a promise."

Peter fed me some explanations about his long, deep soul searching—that he was now absolutely sure he had made the right decision. My brain was filtering all the hateful words I felt like spewing, but they stayed swimming in my mind: *How could you wreck it now? How dare you take this trip away! What does the word "commitment" mean to you? Have you thought about the rest of us?* Instead, I stared at him, dumbstruck.

I tried to listen as long as possible, but I heard nothing that made sense. When I could bear no more, I had to escape. I charged out the back door, feeling a slight relief from the solid slam. Now I felt like running—a fast and brutal run.

Energized by anger, I ran hard. When the blow of feeling betrayed overwhelmed me, I limped nearly to a stop, panting, holding back tears. *How could he do this to me? To us!?* Without Peter, I knew Michael wouldn't go. For the first time, I felt the firmness with which I held onto that trip. I ran every dusty trail in that piney, palmetto-strewn camp in fits and starts, letting my emotions do what they would with my body.

With that, our relationship crumbled. No use trying to convince him. I knew no one could undertake such a strenuous expedition without heart and soul behind it. Eventually I calmed down and accepted that Peter couldn't buck his feelings. Somehow, I hoped we could bridge this chasm, but I should have known better. Dropping the canoe trip was an emotional bomb for me, and it made me look at him in a new light. He saw me differently too. We were through.

I was miserable for days.

One thing was certain: I realized how ardently I yearned to go on this trip. There is no better way to feel the value of something than when it's lost. How strange. I mourned the loss of the expedition more than I mourned the loss of Peter. So I was not fated to be with Peter. The same was not true of the expedition. The urge to undertake this challenge gnawed at me and did not let up.

The following Tuesday evening was the first time I ran into Tom to commiserate. He sat on the couch in the staff lounge with an ankle on a knee, leafing mindlessly through an old magazine. I plopped down next to him, which made him bounce. "Are you as bummed as I am?" I said.

"Worse," he said, likewise seeing it as a missed opportunity. I think he was surprised at my persistence, even after my boyfriend backed out. Closing his magazine, he looked my way, "Do you still wanna go?"

I hesitated, not fully grasping the meaning of his question. It was he who said four would be better than three, and now we had only two. "Of course, I want to go, but it's a moot point now, isn't it?" I was still in a gruff and grumbly mood.

"Well, we could rethink it, and just the two of us go."

The idea had never occurred to me. I fiddled with the thought a bit. Tom and I together for a whole year? That scenario didn't fit into my current thinking.

"No, I don't think so. It wouldn't be the same."

"No, it wouldn't be the same, but it could still work with one canoe."

His offering felt as cruel as giving a starving person plastic fruit. *What about his previous safety precautions with three boats? And just Tom and I? Really?*

"Naw . . . I don't think so," I said as I got up to leave.

"Well, think about it anyway," Tom said. I gave him a backward glance and nodded.

Tom and I

(**Mid-March**): With the expedition infiltrating my every thought, I couldn't help but consider the "Tom and I" scenario. His proposal lit a flicker of hope, but I needed a sounding board of the feminine sort. That evening, when my girls were asleep, I snuck next door to Lauren's cabin and tapped lightly on the window by her bed.

Lauren was an environmental educator like me, a kindred spirit—a lover of the outdoors, always seeking to do new things. The two of us ventured off together on a weekend canoe trip a few months back.

She came out into the beautiful moonlit night and joined me on a log between our cabins.

"It's about the canoe trip, isn't it?" she said.

"Yeah, you know Peter pulled the plug."

"Oh yeah. Everybody knows."

"Well, Tom is proposing that just he and I go."

"What's the matter with that?" Lauren asked flatly.

I looked at her. "Well . . . ah . . . not quite sure."

For the next forty-five minutes, I felt like I was in therapy. Lauren threw in prompts and questions and let me do all the talking. She was neither judgmental nor opinionated. As I spoke, it became increasingly evident that the trip was still firm in my mind, and this was an exercise in clearing away the doubts—gaining a new vision. She didn't even blink at the impossibility of Tom and me as a feasible team. I left Lauren that night not only with bunches of hugs and a dozen thank-yous but feeling like this turn of affairs might be the best answer, after all. It was so clear to me now. The trip was back on!

There was one complication that needed addressing. One man plus one woman, twenty-four hours-a-day for one year equals—well— a relationship that I was not interested in. I was confident in my ability to maintain our relationship's status quo, but Tom needed to abide by the same rules. I didn't want this trip undermined by any private agendas. I would have to address this and make sure he would agree.

In a few days, the two of us were alone. We had been the first of our crew to call it quits after a fun night in town. I drove us home. This was my opportunity. His trivial banter filled numerous breaks in the conversation, but finally, after getting up enough gumption, I claimed one of the silences.

"Now, there's something I need to make clear to you about this trip," I began, trying to pick confident-sounding words.

"Okaaaayy . . . ," he said.

"I want to go just as friends . . . like we are now . . . just friends," I stammered.

I stole a glance his way to find him looking straight at me. "Oh?" he said.

"Yeah, you know, if two people end up spending a lot of time together like we're going to, a relationship would tend to develop."

He turned away from me to look out his side window. "Oh," he said again, his deflated tone revealing volumes. I could feel my face flush in the realization that he had feelings for me. I pressed on.

"I think it's best if we keep it a friendship, okay?" I glanced his way to assess his reaction.

He was still staring out the side window. I managed to detect a slight shrug of the shoulders. "Okay, whatever you want."

Good. That's the end of that. Phew. I give him a little nod. My shoulders relaxed, my grip on the steering wheel loosened. I breathed normally. I'm such a baby when it comes to adult conversations. I let it drop.

My teaching assignment for this semester at Camp Cullen OEC was the S.O.S. lesson—Save our Spaceship. "Spaceship" refers to Earth. During the three-hour class, the kids slogged in the pond, looking for aquatic creatures; learned about how coal, sun, water, and even their muscles could create electricity; and toured the camp's wastewater-treatment facility. It was there while teaching about water purification that the idea struck me.

"This water came from the toilets?" The incredulous little girl gathered up the braided ends of her cornrows, holding them back as she leaned closer to examine the jar of clear effluent from the waste-water-treatment plant that I held.

"Yup," I said in my proper educator vernacular. "This water has traveled all over since our Earth first formed. Where can water be found on Earth?" I entertained all the usual answers (such as clouds, oceans, underground, glaciers, lakes, trees) and added others.

"Maybe a dinosaur drank it and peed it out millions of years ago." I let the "*ew*'s" die down before continuing. "The amount of water here on Earth's surface and atmosphere is basically no more or less than what was here millions of years ago," I said. "We can't go anywhere else to get more. Earth has all the water we need, but we have to take care of it. Not only that, animals and plants and people all need *clean* water, so of course we have to clean it after we use it."

At this moment, as I let this concept of environmental steward-ship sink in, the idea dawned on me. I tuned my students out as I toyed with my realization. *Paddling a canoe across the country would be the perfect forum to spread a water message.* We could tout water-conservation techniques and let folks know that we shouldn't be taking such a precious resource for granted.

The prospect of reaching more than just Houston fifth graders was my dream as an environmental educator. This trip could serve a greater purpose in addition to my personal growth. I was stunned by the realization of this perfect marriage.

"Miss Nancy?" A little girl stirred me from my reverie.

"Huh? Oh, yes. Uh, let's go see how the dirty water gets cleaned."

The next time Tom and I got together, I proposed my idea. Tom was as much of an environmental advocate as I and thought that utilizing the trip to promote clean water was a perfect idea. We decided the trip needed to be named appropriately. "Canoeing for a cause," "Canoe for clean water," "Clean river canoe," "Rivers run clean," "Water watch"—the brainstorming was getting us nowhere. We continued to throw words out into the air, hoping the other could make a catchy theme. "Paddle your boat," "Paddle, not row your boat," "Paddle a stream," "Paddle for a stream."

Finally, "Paddle for Water." We both stopped right there and stared at each other. That was it—the perfect summation of our trip.

It took a few more nights to devise a flyer to circulate among reporters and interested folks.

Below a line drawing of the United States, outlining our route, is a quote long attributed to Chief Seattle, leader of the Duwamish and Squamish peoples of the Puget Sound region. Chief Seattle was a great orator, but long after penning our flyer, I learned this attribution is a fallacy. Nevertheless, unknowingly yet ardently, we spread the sentiment: "All things are connected. Whatever befalls the earth, befalls the children of the earth."

Then the mission:

Paddle For Water is Tom Condon's and Nancy DeWitte's attempt to bring a simple but important message to America. The uniqueness of a cross-country canoe trip, we hope, will help inspire people we meet to conserve our water resources. The trip we've planned will take us not only to some of America's most beautiful areas but also through the heart of working America.

Our route follows. Then, an appeal:

Take a minute to think about the items you use every day. Most, if not all, require water to grow, produce, or package. Could you live without some of these items? Are there similar products on the market which require less water and other resources to produce?

Today, America's natural environment needs all of our help. Here are some ways that you can make a difference:
- *Know your water source—where it comes from and how it is cleaned.*
- *How much water do you use daily—can you cut back?*
- *What potential threats are facing your water source— industrial discharges, toxic wastes, acid rain, inadequate sewage treatment, excessive demands?*
- *Practice good conservation techniques:*
    If you must water lawns, do so in the evening to reduce evaporation
    Repair dripping faucets and leaky pipes quickly
    Use water-saving showerheads and toilets

> *Wash your car with a bucket or hose and noz-*
> *zle. Better yet, do it on your lawn.*
> • *Reduce your own negative impacts:*
>   *Dispose of solvents, household cleaners, used*
>   *engine oil, and potentially harmful chemi-*
>   *cals properly*
>   *Use garden pesticides and fertilizers carefully*
>   *Keep from dumping trash in or near water*
>   *sources*

We finish by listing and thanking our sponsors. It was spiffy for an amateur job. Most importantly, it spoke my heart.

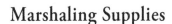

Marshaling Supplies

(**Early May**): Tears, hugs, well-wishes abounded that morning of our departure. Summer break was upon us. Tom and I were among several who would not be returning that fall. Sue, my direct supervisor, gave Tom and me twenty dollars toward our mission. I was so touched but overwhelmed by the tearful emotion in which it was bestowed. The support of my friends gave me a sense of responsibility and the comfort of not being in this alone.

A small group of us shared one last camping trip to the Ozarks before going our separate ways. Afterward, to pick up our canoe directly from the Sawyer canoe manufacturing plant, Tom and I skedaddled up to Oscoda, Michigan. There, "Uncle Harry," aka Harry Roberts, warmly received us into his canoeing family. A highly regarded canoeist himself, he authored the book *The Basic Essentials of Canoe Paddling* and many articles, plus having been the recipient of the American Canoe Association's Legends of Paddling Award. What a privilege to be taken under his wing.

After a tour of the assembly area, Uncle Harry introduced us to our pride and joy. It felt like visiting an adoption agency. We took her out to the river for a test run. A beautiful thing—sleek, unblemished white with graceful contours—with what ease she sliced through the water! I had a good time playing with the sliding-bow tractor seat. Tom tried all the adjustments for the foot brace in the stern. Feeling like proud parents, we ran her through some paces—drawing, eddying, turning right and left.

Uncle Harry was not done with us yet. He arranged for a reporter and photographer from the local paper to cover our story. After the photos and interview, Uncle Harry hooked us up with Grade VI Expeditions for a dry bag and a spray skirt. A spray skirt covers the gear and even cinches up around us—like a skirt—to prevent rain and big waves from filling up our boat. We had not thought of it, but Uncle Harry had. We also made a long-distance acquaintance with Dwight Rockwell, our publicist.

Dwight lived in the New York City area. We never met face to face, but it wasn't necessary. With our initial call, I liked him right away. He talked and joked and made affable banter as if we were the best of friends. He also laid down the plan. We were to call him at least once every week so he could send word to the media of our pending arrival in upcoming towns. He would also identify our next mail drop to send us a list of the media folks he contacted. I thought that sounded just dandy.

When all the business was taken care of, we requested one more favor of Uncle Harry—to sign our Norse thank-you paddle.

We had two beautiful white, extremely sturdy paddles from Norse Paddle Company. Tom had the idea of making one a "thank-you paddle" and the other a "publicity paddle." We would remember all the people who helped us along the way from their signature on our thank-you paddle. Newspaper reporters and other media folks would sign the publicity paddle.

A feeling of gratitude enveloped me as I watched him sign "Uncle Harry" with a flourish in bold red permanent marker, in keeping with his personality. After only one visit, he did indeed seem like an uncle. We left, determined all the more to achieve our goal and make Uncle Harry proud.

The Fam

(**Mid-May, one month earlier**): "Nance, you're not experienced enough to do this," Dad says, shaking his head. He is standing against the refrigerator, where most family discussions take place. Generally happy and ever ready with a joke, Dad is in an unusually somber mood tonight. This, in itself, puts me on edge.

"*You* taught me how to canoe, Dad, a long time ago. I'm a whole lot better than that day I crashed us onto the beach on Fish Creek Pond," I banter back, hoping this comical memory will lighten the mood. I hop atop the counter above the dishwasher, sitting there—legs dangling, more to put space between us than to rest my feet. It isn't a huge kitchen, and I feel hemmed in by the close quarters and the grilling. My comment didn't seem to change the ambience. I push forward. "That was what? Fifteen years ago? I've canoed a lot since then. I'm competent in a canoe." I try to sound convincing, but the truth is, I harbor my own reservations.

"Those rivers are big out there," my brother Dave chimes in as he hoists himself onto the countertop opposite me. Mom, nervously fiddling with the fringe of a towel hanging on the oven door, purses her lips with worry.

"What do you know about those rivers?" Dad continues.

"Well, yes, they are big. Big enough for us to avoid the ocean-going vessels that will be on them." I try to sound confident, but after I say it, I realize that I just planted a new concern in their minds. This isn't going well.

"What about the dams?" Dad asks.

"We can lock through, like any other boat." I bring to mind the huge chambers where water levels are raised or lowered, enabling vessels passage around a dam.

"How?"

"I don't know the details yet, Dad"—my voice is rising. "We'll find out when we drive out there."

My family has never ganged up on me before. My only advocate is my absent sister. "There's a lot we don't know yet," I concede. "We can't possibly research everything. We'll have to figure it out as we go."

"And we don't know much about Tom." Mom finds her voice.

"Well, he's a good guy *and* a competent canoeist and outdoorsman," I say. Going away in a canoe with a guy for a whole year is too much for my family to swallow.

I can see I'm not convincing them. Once again, Dad slowly shakes his head, which I read to mean, "She's always been so sensible. What's happened to her?"

"I know there's a lot of concerns," I blurt out. "There's a lot of things we don't know, and yes, I don't know if I can do this. But this is something I *really* want to try. For the first time in my life, I have a strong feeling about something I want to do. I'm committed, and you can't talk me out of it." Acting like a belligerent teenager, I hop down and storm past Dave and Dad, ending any further discussion.

Tom and I planned to spend two weeks at our respective homes, attending to our self-assigned tasks. Tom would spend the third week at my house, during which we would conduct a shakedown trip, check and double-check equipment, and make final preparations.

It was my job to arrange for one-way transportation to get out west, canoe and all. A driveaway company would be our best bet. I hoped to locate a car whose owner had moved west and would appreciate our driving his car out to him.

Tom had to outfit the canoe with kneeling pads and skid plates, and he had to figure out a way to rig it up for fuel bottles and journal box carriers. He would assemble a first-aid kit and make a few modifications to my Eureka Timberline tent. His mom offered to be our trip manager, so she and Tom needed to set up a bank account through which she could pay our bills. It was a race against time. With each accomplishment, the dream became more tangible.

Shakedown

(May 31, 1986): We needed a dry run, or "shakedown," to see if all our stuff fit in the boat, see how the loaded canoe paddled, see if we forgot anything, and discover what we hadn't thought of.

My friends Steve and Diane heartily agreed to join us for an overnight trip on Keuka Lake, one of the Finger Lakes south of Rochester, New York. Diane and I had shared a house in Naples, New York, for a year while we worked together at a nearby nature center soon after I graduated from college. I was pleased to befriend such a strongwilled, adventurous soul. Steve also worked at the nature center. A generous, warm-hearted farmer, he charmed his way into my heart and stayed there for two years before my move to Texas brought the romantic aspect of our relationship to an end. Both Steve and Diane knew the definition of friendship as well as adventure.

Our boat held everything we wanted it to, but Tom was surprised by how full it was. The canoe cut through the water like a newly sharpened knife, powered by our new bent shaft Mitchell paddles. We left poor Steve and Diane in our wake, as their aluminum Grumman couldn't compete, not even when powered by the strong hay-bale-throwing arms of Steve. The second day, on the way back, we met wave action.

Tom and I were so taken with what the canoe could do that we powered out of sight of our companions. Turning back, we searched both shores and finally found them at the dock of a nearby bar, having surrendered to the waves.

"You're just too much of a beast," Tom chided.

"Me? No, I'm just paddling. It's the canoe. It goes so easily."

"I still think you're a beast."

"Yeah, well, you're no less to blame . . . you . . . you . . . brute!" Hence our new nicknames, Beast and Brute.

As a result of the shakedown, we felt confident in our equipment and the enhanced possibility that we could make this trip. But we were abashed at what poor paddling partners we turned out to be for Diane and Steve. Nevertheless, they had two T-shirts made for us. On the front, one said, "Paddle" and on the back "For Water." The other vice versa.

With equipment stowed in the back of the gray drive-away sedan we were to deliver to its rightful owner, and the canoe tied snuggly atop, I was anxious to go. When departure morning finally arrived, my folks saw us off with hugs, kisses, and well-wishes, but to my immense relief, no tears, urges of reconsideration, or heart-wrenching emotion. Tom's dad sent him a letter earlier in the week, informing him that his mom was having trouble sleeping and had eaten very little because of worry. Tom tried his best to console her. We promised our parents we would phone weekly.

Nancy and Tom ready for launch

Settled into the driver's seat, I backed out of our suburban driveway onto our quiet street and headed west, with one last wave to my folks, standing together at the top of the driveway.

Hightailing it Westward

(**June 5, 1986**): We planned to drive westward as quickly as possible to do some river research while we still had wheels.

We drove 814 miles the first day. On the second, we got waylaid.

"Look at that bank of clouds ahead," Tom commented. It was rather hard to miss. It rolled down the road like nighttime eating up the day.

I pulled onto the shoulder of the divided highway to get a photograph. Getting out of the car, I lined up the shot. As I did, a trucker speeding eastward ahead of the storm yelled to us out of his cab, "Get off the . . ."—trailing off into unintelligible garble as he roared past. The intent was unmistakable. His urgent warning instantly converted my fascination to fear. We directed our attention from gawking to preparing for the storm about to engulf us.

Speeding up, we raced for the next exit, but it was too far. Just in time for a collision with the wall of rain, blackness, and violent wind, I angled onto the highway's shoulder. With the big sailboat-like canoe tied on top, our little sedan was mere folly for what seemed like ten linebackers ramming us broadside. Eyes wide, with hands clenched around the steering wheel, I hoped the tires held fast to the road as we rocked back and forth.

"I should turn into the wind, right?" I looked over at Tom. Outside, I could see nothing but torrents of water and darkness, so the road edge was mere conjecture.

"I don't know." Tom's shaky voice was indecisive, revealing his own distress. Then a pounding surge lurched the canoe with a screech, giving us a good jostling. That was my answer. We could do without rolling over or having the canoe break free and launch into the air.

"Yeah, that's what I'm gonna do." Driving blind, I inched the car back, assuming no one but us could possibly be moving on the road at this time, and then forward, and back, and forward, until we faced the storm head on. The wind then assaulted the aerodynamic contours of both canoe and car, and the beating was less severe. So we sat, helplessly watching the water batter the windshield and listening to the ferocious wind try to pry our canoe from the roof. All we could do was depend on Tom's knots.

Rain soon led to hail. After ten minutes, the rain and hail suddenly abated. Darkness vanished, as if someone had flipped a switch.

I hesitated to get out to join Tom in the inspection, fearing hail damage or worse to the vehicle. I desperately wanted to return this car to the owner in perfect shape. I finally opened the door.

"Oh no—what should we tell the owner?" I commiserated with Tom as we inspected a broken antenna. The shifting canoe had bent it over.

"Just tell him what happened. It can be fixed," Tom replied as he loosened the ropes and readjusted the boat to the center of the car.

"You do tie a good knot," I remarked. "I'm surprised it stayed put as well as it did." The boat shifted maybe two inches from its original position.

"I don't know how people can go through life without knowing knots," he replied. Ever the Boy Scout.

I looked around. The sky, rinsed of all impurities, was fresh and beautiful in the approaching sunset. Birds had emerged from their mysterious hiding places to search for food once more over the vibrant green carpet of prairie. Even reflections on the pavement created a mosaic of blues and blacks that contributed to the overall sparkling effect of Mother Nature's scrubbing. On this, the second day of our travels, we covered 750 miles.

From here, our pace slowed as we sought answers to some questions: How do we lock through a dam? Will roadmaps do for navigation? (Turns out "yes.") Will we be overrun by barges or cargo ships? How the hell do we paddle *up* Hells Canyon? Beyond the reservoirs on the Snake River, can we still muscle our way up the mountainous river? And other tidbits we investigated that either allayed or added to my trepidation. But nothing deterred my resolve.

Six days after departure we reached my cousin John's house in Yacolt, Washington. He had readily agreed to help us deliver the driveaway car to Bellevue, near Seattle, then feed us into the mouth of the Columbia.

I won the coin toss for John's waterbed that evening, feeling only a tiny bit guilty. After all, it was—as John reminded me—the last of that luxury I'd enjoy for quite some time.

The following day, June 12, John came with us to Bellevue. Luckily, the owner—just pleased to have the car back—disregarded the broken antennae as a minor matter. I heaved a great sigh of relief, at last responsible only for ourselves.

On June 13, John drove all our gear and us up to Fort Stevens State Park.

Fort Stevens is an earthen and wood structure completed in 1865 to protect the mouth of the Columbia River from Confederate forces and the British Navy during the Civil War. Its strategic location on the Columbia River, where it meets the Pacific Ocean, made this fort important during the Spanish-American War, World War I, and World War II. Now only vacationers invade this 4,300-acre state park to camp, swim, hike, bike, and tour the fort itself. It was a logical spot to launch our expedition except that, the campground, it turned out, was a disappointingly long ways from the water. Paved bike trails and roads made the ocean easily accessible—to those with bikes and cars—but for us poor suckers who would have to walk, carrying three hundred pounds of gear and a canoe, the distance was formidable.

Mark, from the *Daily Astorian* (Astoria, Oregon), was at the park, looking for us, when we arrived. Dwight had sent him a press release, and we followed up. Cousin John stayed until after the interview. We waved until both trucks were out of sight.

"So that's it. We're on our own." I turned to Tom.

"Yep, it's all up to us now." He looked at me.

"It's exciting." I shrugged as a smile overtook me.

"The adventure begins," he said. "What do ya say we take a walk out to the ocean after supper? We'll head out tomorrow."

"That's the plan."

The Route

Tom first began to dream of paddling cross-country years ago while he guided Boy Scout trips in Maine. He and fellow canoe guides would sit on the porch in rocking chairs, discussing their ultimate canoe trip. What rivers provided the best passage? What dams, waterfalls, rapids, and lakes would be encountered? How long might it take? He had the route all worked out.

His plan—now our plan—entails starting west of Astoria, at the mouth of the **Columbia River**. Going upriver, we will get assistance from this dam-harnessed electricity-producing workhorse of a river, locking through dams from lake to lake like transport vessels. We will travel the Washington/Oregon border on the Columbia to the Tri-Cities in Washington—Kennewick, Pasco, and Richland—where the Snake River joins the Columbia.

From there, in an ever-upward push toward the Rocky Mountains, we will continue eastward up the **Snake River**, again using human-made lakes. We probably won't be able to paddle all the way up to the headwaters of the Snake in Yellowstone National Park, but we will go as far as we can. Then, either hoofing it or catching a ride, we intend to cross the Continental Divide, where water drains toward the Pacific Ocean if it falls on the west side, or toward the Atlantic Ocean if it falls to the east. Then we will put our paddles to work north of Yellowstone National Park in the **Yellowstone River**.

This river will be our first opportunity for downriver travel.

Following the Yellowstone across Montana, we will let it feed us into the **Missouri River** where Montana meets North Dakota. Continuing down the Missouri, we will pass through or alongside six states by the time we reach St. Louis. Just north of the city, the Missouri and Mississippi rivers converge.

After a short couple hundred miles on the famed **Mississippi**, we will exit onto the **Ohio River** by Cairo, Illinois—the turn Mark Twain's characters, Huck Finn and Jim, missed on their raft trip down the Mississippi.

Our travels will start uphill again and continue when we veer eastward off the Ohio to chug up the **Tennessee River** near Paducah, Kentucky. Tennessee Valley Authority lock and dams will make uphill travel on the Tennessee possible until its confluence with the **Little Tennessee River.**

On the Little T, we will head southeast toward the Smoky Mountains to meet the second of two mountain ranges we will have to surmount. Here, the Eastern Continental Divide separates two major watersheds, with water destined for the Atlantic Ocean falling to the east as water headed for the Gulf of Mexico falls west of the Appalachian Mountain chain.

When we can no longer paddle or pole or drag up the Little T, we will be forced to portage over the mountains. Then we will put into the **Savannah River** drainage in South Carolina, following her all the way to the **Atlantic Ocean.** The End. By then, we will have paddled, by our count, 4,946 miles.

One very cool thing about taking this route is that we will follow in the "footsteps" of the famous Lewis and Clark expedition. In 1803, President Thomas Jefferson commissioned his personal secretary, Meriwether Lewis, to form an expedition to explore the newly acquired Louisiana Purchase. Lewis asked his former army friend, William Clark, to co-lead this monumental project. West of the Mississippi River, much of the land was uncharted. Sold by France for fifteen million dollars, the Louisiana Purchase stretched from the Mississippi River to the Rocky Mountains. All or part of fifteen states were eventually carved out of this expanse, doubling the size of the United States.

Jefferson tasked Lewis and Clark with documenting the plants, animals, and geography of the territory, establishing friendly relations with the indigenous peoples, and seeking a water connection to the Pacific Ocean. (By the way, there isn't one; the Rocky Mountains are in the way, separating the eastern and western watersheds.)

Over thirty members comprising the Corps of Discovery— including army volunteers, officers, boatmen, and even one Newfoundland dog (Seaman)—departed Camp River Dubois on May 14, 1804. Near the confluence of the Mississippi and Missouri Rivers just north of St. Louis, Missouri, it marks the beginning— and end—of their twenty-eight-month expedition. The Corps of Discovery returned to a hero's welcome in September of 1806.[1]

As a result of this expedition, the stage was set for big changes. The U.S. strengthened its hold on the West. Maps and documents provided much-needed information about the geography and inhabitants of the region. The fur trade expanded, greatly impacting wildlife populations. Native Americans received the brunt of the impact in the mid-nineteenth century clashing with settlers and military. The two centuries between Lewis and Clark's expedition and ours have wrought profound changes.

I'm looking forward to following in Lewis and Clark's wake, seeing what they saw, and noting how different our river experience will be from theirs. One difference is we will start at the Pacific Ocean, where the Corps' westward travels ended. So, our route follows their return trip. Also, we will follow the whole Snake River; they did only a portion of the lower Snake. And once we head east of St. Louis, we'll be in territory well-known in 1803, not part of their journey.

Ugg—It Has Begun

Day 1 (June 14) continued: Tom rousts me out of my reverie. "Supper's ready."

Man, am I sore, but I'm also ravenous. I would have sat bolt upright if my back only let me. I crawl out of the tent on my hands and knees, my Therm-a-Rest chair in tow. "Great. What have we got?"

"Fried potatoes, mac and cheese . . . and wine."

"Wine?!"

"Yup, I brought it along to celebrate the beginning." I hobble over to where he is sitting by the stoves in the sand. I collapse with a groan onto my chair, then take the plastic cup he holds out.

"To the start of a great trip," he toasts.

"To a great trip," I repeat. We tap cups, drink, and eat greedily.

"You really impressed me today," Tom says between mouthfuls.

"Yeah?"

"You really are a beast."

This I take with gratitude and pleasure, in the spirit of the compliment for which it was intended. "Yes, well, you're not so bad yourself, you Brute you." We clink again (as well as plastic can clink), sip, and gorge.

"You hauled the canoe further than I did today," he says.

"You don't have to tell that to my back," I say, rubbing. "Besides, I couldn't stand the grunting and groaning anymore."

"That boat has to weigh ninety pounds," Tom says, shaking his head and rubbing his neck.

"We could have taken out all that extra stuff," I mention, although I said that a couple of times earlier today. We have two journal boxes strapped in behind the bow seat, four full quart fuel bottles tied on to the stern floatation chamber, and a camera tripod tied onto a thwart. That added a lot to the stripped-down sixty-pound canoe.

"That's a 'should-of,'" Tom points out.

"Yeah, yeah," I concede.

As I crawl into our little Timberline tent, twitches, twangs, spasms, and aches originating in my back manifest themselves as groans and jab-induced barks. Tom too produces a repertoire of pain-induced noises. We are a sad and sorry lot. Backrubs are in order. I lose the coin toss and have to receive first. Therefore, I have to roust myself to massage Tom after I am nicely relaxed.

"We 'should-of' brought Lauren with us," I say, trying to put what she taught me into practice on Tom's back. I'm fully cognizant of my use of the forbidden phrase, but Tom doesn't call me on it.

No matter how much lotion I use, Tom winces and twitches when I hit a knot or snarl his copious back hair. I can't help it. I'm trying my best just to stay awake.

CHAPTER 2

Paddling with the Big Boys

Believe me, my young friend,
there is nothing—absolutely nothing—
half so much worth doing as simply
messing about in boats.

—Kenneth Grahame

Reconciling the Body

Day 2 (June 15): Tightness, twitching, general achiness, and an occasional spasm—that's my back talking to me. Apparently, you cannot abuse a back one day, provide a mere inch of padding between it and the hard ground overnight, then expect it to be hunky-dory the next morning. My muscles loosen up as I waddle around, hunched over, but they don't quit complaining. I just have to suck it up. My motivation rests in the assumption that today can't possibly be worse than yesterday.

Today, we've got to get well east of Astoria, Oregon, which is still about five miles further east. That marks the point at which we begin to follow the Lewis and Clark Expedition on their return trip back to St. Louis.

After a hearty pancake and eggs breakfast, we load up and head out. I am in the bow. Tracking our progress, I keep my eye on a distant pier. We paddle hard as minutes multiply. That blasted pier doesn't get any nearer. I paddle harder. The bow of the canoe is slicing through the oncoming current like we're flying along. The sandy beach to our right stretches forward and back as far as I can see, offering no point of reference.

Heaving with exertion, I finally holler over my shoulder to Tom, "Why aren't we moving?"

"Yeah, I know," he says between gasps. "Let's pull over."

We nose the canoe onto land. I hop out and hoist the boat securely ashore, allowing Tom to disembark. I take a few steps downriver, holding my crybaby back, stretching backward and then forward when I spy something in the sand.

"Hey, here's some footprints." This is a curious sight along this desolate strip. I put my foot next to one. "It's *my* footprint!" I straighten up and look around. "This is where we put-in forty-five minutes ago, isn't it?" I give Tom a wide-eyed, mouth-agog-in-disbelief look.

"Yup," he says, checking it out. "You're right." He doesn't seem to be as aghast as me. "The tide is making us stand still. We'll just have to wait." I realize he suspected the tide to be a problem, even with the wind pushing us from behind. We concede to the powers of nature. There is nothing to do but hunker down on the beach and wait until 1:00 p.m. when the tide comes in.

The Columbia is a commercial river, with millions of tons of goods passing in and out of ports. There are no dams between the

Pacific and Portland, so once on the river again, we see ocean-going freighters from Japan, Germany, and other far reaches of the globe. I am concerned about the tremendous wakes these multi-ton behemoths may produce. Will they toss us about like a cork on the ocean?

We adopt the strategy of taking refuge behind islands, but the time comes when we cannot escape the inevitable massive container vessel passing nearby. We pull to shore, yank the canoe up, and wait to see what type of wake this ship serves up. We watch as a huge gentle swell rolls toward shore. Another comes, well separated from the first, followed by another buxom bump, and then another. "These are just lazy rolling hills," I say to Tom.

"Yeah, these aren't going to be a problem at all." From then on, we look forward to riding the distant wake of a passing vessel. We rise to the crest and surf down the back of each swell into the spacious trough as we sing the *Hawaii Five-O* theme song.

Over the next few days, we get into the groove of putting in miles. We encounter steelhead anglers, otter, osprey, nuclear power plants, log booms, and paper mills. I particularly enjoy our passing conversations with anglers. It often goes something like this:

Angler: "Where you folks headin'?"

Me (or Tom): "The Atlantic Ocean."

Angler: "No kiddin'," or "Ya don't say," or "You shitting me?" By this time we've glided by and are out of earshot.

Bewildering anglers becomes my favorite pastime.

Before we reach Portland, Tom gets a brilliant idea. His folks, he recalls, are familiar with the owner of the Portland Marriott Hotel.

The thought of renewing our bodies for a couple of nights makes me drool. It seems a bold request, but Tom places the call.

Without hesitation, the owner reserves a room for us that weekend at no charge. Glory hallelujah, it worked! I dance a little jig and hug Tom. But first, we have to pay our dues with six more days of hard paddling.

"Good morning," Tom says. It is pleasant to wake up to his voice. As I wrench my eyes open, I see him smiling at me in the greenish-yellow hue of the Timberline tent. I can't understand how he can be so perky the second he wakes. He can't understand why it takes me so long to get moving. "Did you sleep well?"

"Mmmm," I mutter, trying to move sore muscles. "You?" I manage.

"Yup, I didn't wake up once," he replies. "Did you have any dreams?"

"Not that I remember," I murmur sleepily. "You?"

"Yeah, as a matter of fact," he replies. I can tell this is what he is trying to get at.

"Mmm, great." I figure I can lie in my sleeping bag for the extra few seconds it takes for him to tell me about it. "What was it?" I close my eyes again.

"I dreamt a whole bunch of naked people came to our campsite and wanted us to join their commune. They said we could play volleyball or swim or whatever, but we had to go naked."

"Oh, I know where that came from," I say, opening my eyes to look at him. "Did we?"

"No, we escaped in our canoe."

"Disappointed?" I ask him.

"Definitely," he says with a wink. "Now get up sleepyhead." He gives me a shaking. "And you don't even have to get dressed. After all, when in Rome . . ."

"Oh, stop." I thump his chest with a weak fling of my arm. "What time is it, anyway?"

"6:48 and time to get up. We've got to get to Portland today."

Yesterday, an angler told us our choices for camping that night were limited: a wildlife refuge that prohibited camping, or private land. When our twenty miles had exhausted us and we needed to stop, we couldn't find any private signs on a reasonably flat, desolate beach we liked, so, we set up camp. Enjoying a beautiful sunset after supper, we discovered we were not alone. A solitary man, leisurely walking the beach at dusk, didn't even see us way back by the trees. His presence did, however, confirm that we were not camped in a wildlife refuge. From his profile, it was evident this man wore only a shirt. We went to bed, wondering whether more clothing-deprived people would materialize and speculated whether the angler had set us up. Private land, indeed! Apparently, anglers can play this bewilderment game just as well as we can. Touché.

By the time I revive—and dress—my weary body, I'm anxious to leave the nudist colony and end Tom's "when in Rome . . ." teasing.

By late morning we paddle into the Portland waterfront. After tiresome inquiries at a marina, we finally meet a couple who will allow us to moor our canoe in their slip. Once the canoe is spray-skirted against the inevitable rain, we take off, backpacks in tow.

Via foot and bus, we find the Portland Marriott. The hotel is downtown, on the waterfront. The lobby is grand, more impressive than I expected—with glistening chandeliers and oriental rugs. Smartly dressed businesswomen in heels, carrying the latest handbags and with perfectly coiffured hair, pass through the grand entryway. Men in their power suits and buffed shoes hustle in and out, briefcases in hand. We make our way over to a well-manicured woman behind the desk. I can tell by the faces of the clerks and the sidelong glances of other patrons that not many scraggly river people with backpacks check in here. Tom merely has to mention the owner's name, asking about our reservation.

"Of course, Mr. Condon. Your room is ready. Your reservation is for two nights." I can barely contain my grin.

Our room is lavish, and the colossal bed luxurious. Much of our time, however, is spent in the hot tub, jets kneading aching muscles. One day and two nights in this posh hotel are all I need to make peace with my body again.

From here on, my muscles concede to the work required of them with hardly ever a complaint. Hereafter, my legs show only major contusions, not the nineteen bruises I tally at the hotel. The tender blisters I now have on my hands will harden into calluses and protect me from further blisters. By the time we leave the hotel, mind and body are ready for any challenge this river can dish out—I think. Whatever is in store, I'm in the mood to meet it head-on.

Learning the Rhythm of the River

Day 13 (June 26): Three days after our Portland respite, I wake to munching, snorting, and stomping just beyond the thin nylon walls of our tent. Tom lies beside me. He looks at me. I know this sound. Simultaneously we state the obvious: "Cows." Tom climbs out, chases them a safe distance away and rights the kitchen that one overly curious cow knocked over.

We make a compact campsite, with a little green tent, an overturned white canoe, and a plastic-bag-covered kitchen pack when we turn in for the night. Our kitchen is a self-standing external-frame backpack from Tom's younger Boy Scout days. It serves the purpose quite well—holding stoves, food, spices, utensils, and miscellaneous necessities, like a sewing kit and repair kit. After grocery shopping, the kitchen could weigh sixty pounds or more.

Tom in the kitchen

Tom is always up and out first. It not only takes me longer to rev up my body, but that way, I can dress in privacy and use the whole five-foot width and four-foot height of the tent for myself. Tom starts a feast of burritos, our favorite after-shopping breakfast. I wander off to pee, take my toiletries to the river to wash my face, and brush and rebraid my hair. I find the Pippi Longstocking style of two French braids more suitable than one fat braid. Two braids hold my short hairs in place and are more comfortable to sleep on.

I return to stuff the sleeping bags, roll up the mattress pads, and take down the tent, by which time Tom has breakfast ready. We indulge in stoking up our internal fires before sharing the task of doing dishes, packing the kitchen, and walking things down to the water. It is usually two hours from wake-up to our first stroke.

"So, what time is it?" Tom asks as we hit the river. Tom has the only watch between us. I look around to get a feel for the quality of light, thinking of how our routine may have been slowed or speeded up, and give my prediction.

"Nine-twelve," I say.

"Wrong, nine-thirteen," he replies.

"Rats."

"Close, but no cigar." In the days ahead, I increase my number of 'direct hits' in this guessing game. Today, I am pleased to realize that after having been on the river for only thirteen days, I am already in tune with the rhythm of the sun. Out here, I am not a slave to a clock or hidden from the elements by a roof and four walls. It is a risky thing to give up the security blankets we build around us in modern society, but I find the rewards commensurate with the challenge.

Beacon Rock, an ancient volcano core, now a black monolith of basalt, is our first stop for today. It towers above the Columbia River on the Washington side. Indeed, it sticks out like a beacon. In his journal, Clark made note of "Beaten" rock (perhaps misunderstanding what Lewis said) when the Corps passed by in 1805. Lewis, in 1806, referred to it as "the beacon rock."[2] Later it was dubbed Castle Rock. When Henry Biddle purchased it in 1915, he requested its original name be restored. Biddle went to extraordinary lengths to build a trail to the top, which the Civilian Conservation Corps has since rebuilt. We couldn't let such a landmark go unexplored. Landing and tying the canoe securely ashore, we set out to hike up the 848-foot rock. Our legs got a much-needed workout along this mile-long trail as it zig-zags to the top.

The peak affords a terrific view of today's canoeing challenge: Bonneville Dam. In 1805, Lewis and Clark first noticed the influence of the tide at Beacon Rock. Once past this westernmost dam on the Columbia, our first of many, we will no longer be affected by the tide.

An angler told us that Bonneville's small lock creates a bottleneck of towboat traffic. He suggested portaging around. Scouting from atop Beacon Rock, we see tall fences, rock buttresses, cement barricades, and a steep riprap (boulder strewn) shoreline, with no road access anywhere. Scrap portaging!

Back in our canoe, we discover that water released from the Bonneville hydroelectric plant creates fast current and turbulence. Either by sneaking up behind islands and making use of their eddies or by paddling close to the rocky shore, we cover the distance. A steady pace of powerful strokes coaxes the canoe to make headway. Facing this unyielding current, I am secretly thankful for my self-imposed endurance training. When our forward momentum equals or is less than the backward force, we get out and "line" the boat along the rocky shoreline, that is, manually pull the canoe along by the bow and stern painters.

Closing in on the dam, we paddle up to a congregation of anglers; they stand shoulder to shoulder high above us atop a wall. With immensely long fishing poles outfitted with heavy-duty monofilament, they are trying their luck at catching sturgeon. Out beyond their lines, the deep cold-water current is far too swift to paddle against. We need to ply the shoreline eddy. But fishing line in front of us lace a monofilament fence across our course. Tom has an idea.

"Hold your poles out!" Tom shouts between heaving breaths, hoping the anglers can hear. "Hold them out," he repeats over and over like a guy selling popcorn at a baseball game. It works.

The lines become vertical, not angled, and out far enough for us to pass between them and the wall. I adeptly navigate us through this narrow corridor, and we steadily inch along. Even so, I paddle hunched over and hope no one reels in. Hey, we're doing it. Suddenly, I feel a tug on my life jacket. Then something lifts me a tiny bit. My eyes go wide.

"Tom, *stop*! I'm caught!" Immediately he quits paddling but works to keep the boat within our tiny confines as I squirm about to free myself.

"Slack! Slack!" I holler, hoping the unseen angler who has snagged me hears. I twist this way and that, contorting myself to locate the huge hook embedded in the back of my PFD. Fiddling frantically, I somehow manage to wiggle it out without stabbing myself.

"OK, I'm good," I holler to Tom as I pick up my paddle and dig in hard. We shift from reverse to forward and continue our corridor crawl. Tom continues to yell, "Hold your poles OUT," more fervently now. The rest of the anglers oblige, but I can just feel the swearing going on up there.

After slow and arduous effort, we finally arrive at the small craft pull cord hung from the entry wall of the lock. Tom gives it a tug and shouts into the air, "We're in a canoe and would like to lock through." The answer comes over a loudspeaker.

"It's too dangerous to lock through in a canoe. It will be one and a half hours before I can lock you through with a towboat."

The word "dangerous" did nothing to soothe my already existing nervousness. It is our first dam to lock through, and although we have done our homework, it is rather unnerving. Now, we have an hour and a half to dwell on it. Resigned to wait, we pull our canoe up on the riprap embankment.

After an hour of rocks for a seat, I can hardly feel my butt. We perform a few gluteal awakening exercises and climb in the canoe to sit on our seat pads for the last half-hour. Right on time, the towboat *Tyee* emerges from behind the downriver gate, pushing a barge loaded with wheat. After securing the barge and returning for another load, the captain shouts over to us.

"Want to lock through?"

We reply with thumbs up, head nods, and an enthusiastic "yes, please." Having consulted via radio with the lockmaster, the captain invites us to ascend aboard the *Tyee*. We paddle into the far end of the massive lock, as instructed. I feel like a small mouse trapped in a corner as the big cat creeps in after us. Once the *Tyee* is secure, we tie up to her starboard side and are hoisted aboard by strong, friendly hands of the crew.

Tom and I join the two men and one woman in the galley. They offer us some juice and slivers of avocado, and we swap river experiences while we eat. From his bridge, the captain keeps a keen eye on our canoe, radioing to convey her seaworthiness to the lockmaster. The captain is concerned our canoe will not be able to withstand the full fury of maximum water intake. When the tainter valves are fully open, the water surface is turbulent in this old lock, so the lockmaster only partially opens these pivoting gates that control the flow. The captain says their twelve-minute ride will now take closer to an hour.

Both Tom and I realize with a mixture of guilt and gratitude what they are doing for us. We peer over the railing. Driftwood and dead fish are stirred up in one whirlpool after another. Proudly we watch our buoyant canoe take it in stride. Eventually, the captain reports, "Open 'er up all the way! She's floating like a cork." The sixty-foot ascent ultimately takes only twenty minutes.

Bonneville was the first dam and powerhouse built on the Columbia River. Authorized by President Roosevelt, it was constructed under his New Deal program. The impetus was to get people back to work during the Great Depression as well as to provide hydroelectric power to the northwest. Finished in 1938, the dam, like all those that the U.S. Army Corps of Engineers operates on the Columbia River, provides hydropower, irrigation capabilities to farmers upriver, and a safer navigational waterway.

Bonneville's backwater—Lake Bonneville—now covers a stretch of treacherous whitewater that boats once had to portage around or risk disaster by running. What was once Cascade Rapids, William Clark called the "the great Shute." He wrote of the river flowing "with great velocity foming & boiling in a most horriable manner" (his spelling) October 31, 1805.[3] Over most of the four-mile stretch, traversing slippery slopes and rocks, the men had to drag their heavy boats and lug equipment. For us, the rapids are a thing of the past and the dam marks our location as 145.5 miles from the Pacific coast.

The navigational lock at Bonneville Dam became operational in 1938. It was suitable for its time, but today, powerful towboats ferry numerous barges up and down the river. Some towboats make up to five trips back and forth to lock their full contingency of cargo through. A new, larger lock was built in 1993 to remedy the situation.

One tiny lock is all we've got in 1986. We are fortunate to be able to share a trip with the *Tyee*.

Over the next week or so, the *Tyee* is a familiar, welcome sight on the lower Columbia. When we see her, we wave our arms and maybe a paddle in a non-alarming way. The captain always spots us and responds with two friendly toots. Our little canoe has a big boat friend!

Our Nemesis the Wind

Day 16 (June 29): Gusty wind jars me awake. It shakes and shoves the tent we pitched on a flat open spot. I peek out to see the river covered with whitecaps, spray blowing off each crest. By the time we move up to a more secluded spot, have breakfast, and break camp, wind is less severe, waves less high. But the river is still intimidating. We need to make a decision.

"Oregon State Park is not too far upriver," Tom says.

"That would be a better place to wait out wind," I reply. "And the wind will be at our back, not blowing against us."

"Yes, but we don't really have to go, you know. We could hang out here for another day. But you're the captain today."

My shoulders slump under the weight of my commission. I don't want to waste time hanging out, but I don't want to make a regretful decision. I have to decide.

"I'm willing to go if you think we can manage these waves," I say.

"Oh, the canoe will ride these waves fine. If it gets too hard, we can always pull out."

Yes, we can always pull out. Sounds reasonable enough. We load up the boat, don life vests, snap on the spray skirt, and head out. My push-up-trained arms soon get pushed to their limit in the stern.

Wind wants to push the canoe broadside—which would be most unsatisfactory, presenting our broad surface to a single wave, lifting one gunwale on the crest of the wave while dropping the other gunwale in the trough. That would be great if we wanted to overturn our canoe.

Seasoned paddlers would say we are not trimmed correctly, meaning the weight in the canoe is not distributed properly. About the only thing we can do about this is slide the bow seat to compensate, but this has no effect. It doesn't offset the tremendous bulk of gear in the middle. Instead, we use paddle power to make sure the stern slices each wave as it comes upon us. The wave will travel along from stern to bow, only affecting a small section of our boat at a time. When the stern is on the crest of a wave and the bow is in the trough we surf, getting quite a boost. When on the crest of a wave, I use the wave as a pivot point, steering rather handily.

My mind is analyzing these discoveries at the same time my muscles are straining to obey. *One wave at a time*, I keep thinking, trying to shut the consequences of a broadside hit out of my mind. Even being a little cockeyed gives us a taste of how easily a wave could toss us over. My mind visits the flipping scenario. My heart rate shoots up as if it is actually happening. *Just don't allow it*, I tell myself. *One wave at a time.*

"DRAW," I yell to Tom. These little woman's-push-up arms are no match for this incessant wind. I see the wind blowing spray off the crest of the white-capped waves and think: *What in the world are we out here for?* My energy is draining. I can't let myself get fatigued. I want to pull out, but the shoreline is an inaccessible boulder field. We keep going. Steep banks of nothing but rocks line the river as far as the eye can see. After a good ten minutes more, I make a decision. "Pull over!"

I remind myself that we've taken our gear out on riprap before. We can *do* this. This *can* be done.

We pull the boat alongside the piled-up loose stone; Tom jumps ashore and steadies her for me to climb out. We both push the boat out to keep it from pounding against the boulders. Together, we heave each piece of gear out, one at a time. I grab each, swing it around behind, heave it as high on the wall of riprap my squirrely arms can manage, and prop it between a couple of rocks. Finally, we pull the empty boat up to higher rocks. Only then do we take a moment to look at what we've been paddling in.

Spray is blowing off every wave; we estimate the waves are three feet high. The wind must be forty miles per hour. This is not your typical canoeing weather. We hunker down on the riprap to while away the time.

Riprap hunkerin' is not an easy way to spend a day. A pile of rocks does not a comfy seat make. Nevertheless, we eat lunch, read, and journal. Wedging oneself between chilly boulders for any length of time tends to make one cranky and crampy. After two hours of irritating boredom and rock-squished butts, that river doesn't look so bad. We decide to dare the wind and waves again.

A higher power sends a different message. Just as we are sliding the boat back in, a gust knocks me to the ground. "No, Tom, we can't do this again!" I am adamant. My better judgment is taking charge. We bag it.

This wind has to let up. There is no place to camp here. This place is no place at all. There is only this steep rock embankment that leads up to a busy railroad and Highway 14 at the top, barred by a fence. No place even resembles a spot to sit comfortably, much less set up a tent.

"What are we going to do?" I ask Tom. I have no ideas at all.

"Well, we can't camp here." Tom starts with the obvious. "We'll have to head out eventually, before it gets dark."

"Yeah," I moan, like a reluctant teenager. I'm mad at myself for deciding to venture onward when we obviously should have stayed at last night's campsite. It was a poor decision. Tom knows this too.

"I would have stayed at the campsite," he says. I snap him an angry look.

"Yeah, well, you might have offered that opinion at the time!" I bark. "Besides, that's a 'should-of.'" Now taciturn, each of us glowering in our own regret, we stare at the river.

"See that treed area on the Oregon side?" Tom breaks the silence. "If we can just get over there. It's not very far."

I look skeptical, sufficiently humbled and intimidated by the force of the wind and waves. Reluctantly, I agree. We can't stay here.

We head out, this time with Tom in the stern.

Now he gets a taste of steering in this maelstrom. "Draw . . . HARD . . . now FORWARD," he barks. Like a bully, the wind tries to rip my paddle from my hands the second it comes out of the water. I fight back with diligent feathering and a deathly grip. One thing is for sure—we are flying!

"We can't cross this!" Tom yells. I nod in agreement. The park across the river whizzes by.

"Look at the waves around that point," I holler, referring to the jut of land we would have to paddle out around. "I don't want to do that!" This situation is looking a mite grim as waves routinely roll over the bow, deflected only by the spray skirt cinched around me.

"Neither do I."

There is only one solution. Once again, we guide our frolicking steed toward the rocky embankment. We've got this routine down pat now. Upon finding somewhat secure footing on a very steep boulder, I hold the boat at bay while Tom jumps out. He hurriedly unclips one pack at a time, shoving each toward me while desperately trying to fend the canoe off. I heave the big packs onto my back, small ones over my shoulder, clamber up a few feet in search of a sturdy rock to wedge each behind. Trip after grueling trip, I rack up nothing worse than a few bruises. As the merciless waves bash the canoe rhythmically against the rocks, Tom gets shoved onto his butt a couple of times but scrambles back up to finish the deed. Finally, we climb and stumble with the canoe up the riprap hill to clunk her down behind a log that is well out of the water and stable enough to secure her.

Now what? Here we sit—again—on a hill of boulders. One thing is certain—we can't be out on the river anymore. We've got to hike, no matter how far, to a place to stay.

Each hoisting a pack onto our backs, using hands and feet, we crawl up the rocks to the top. Yahoo, no fence! Across the railroad tracks, over the highway, down a little dirt road, we find a lovely, secluded spot with a beautiful little waterfall. I discover a small, flat area with negligible wind suitable for our tent. This is our spot. God is watching out for us; there is no doubt.

If only I knew then what I learned years later. Collins Point, the point with the wicked wind-kicked waves, was the last location where two seasoned canoeists, trying to cross the country in 1978, were last seen alive. They ventured out in high waves and wind. *Just like us!* Fatal decision.

What accounts for our success and their failure? Physical endurance? Adeptness at canoe handling? Not likely. We did see fit not to venture far from the safety of the shoreline. Perhaps this accounts for the critical difference, as they were last seen out in the middle of the river. I would probably never have set out on the waves at all today had I known the story of Tim Black and Peter Macridis.

Then again, maybe I would have been unwilling to take the necessary risk of paddling in high waves at all. Refusing to paddle significant waves would have put a halt to our trip very early on. Crossing the whole country by canoe without encountering choppy water is impossible. Perhaps it was best I didn't know of these two young men at the time. Yet when I read of their fated exploit, I felt an instant kinship with their cause and an intimate connection to their spirits, known only to the few who have battled such conditions in a humble canoe.

Wave Vocabulary

Day 17 (June 30): I have heard that Inuit and Yupik people, who live in the Arctic, have forty to fifty words describing snow. Other languages have even more.[4] Since this aspect of their environment affects their culture tremendously, they need to speak of snow in very specific terms. Waves influence our lives. They abide with us constantly. We cannot possibly describe the day or speak of weather without defining them. After a few weeks of living with waves we come up with our own, extremely satisfying, dictionary of terms.

Glassy Smooth (or GS) condition—The water is wholly undisturbed. The surface reflects a perfect mirror image of surrounding objects. If we ever encounter this, it is usually in the early morning. Paddling in this water is one of the great pleasures of canoeing. Watching the canoe's prow slice into the stillness and, with a glance behind, seeing the ever-widening "V" of our wake. There is a feeling of how tenuous this stillness is, to the point where one feels compelled to not even talk, lest we disturb it.

Placid Piddles—These are tiny ripples on the water's surface. They are not waves as such, but they break up a glassy smooth condition. They result from a trouble-free cooling breeze.

Lollygaggers—These are the smallest wind-induced waves, no more than three inches in height. They lap the shoreline gently with peaceful, rhythmic music. Under their influence, the canoe may begin to feel the cadence and dance a little bit, but they are harmless.

Tossers—The canoe is in full dancing mode on top of these waves. They can rock us from side to side. These can range from four inches to a foot high.

Paytentions—These pushy waves, one to two feet high, force us to pay attention. They give the stern man a decent workout. You want to slice these suckers with the bow or stern.

Bowlickers—As their name implies, these lick over the top of the bow when rocking us end to end. It is prudent for the bow person to don the spray skirt, as it is common to end up with a lapful of water. We don't get broadside to these waves, which can reach from two to four feet, handily capsizing a canoe.

Tsunamis—No one in their right mind should paddle these waves.

Being more than four feet high, they come in over the bow or stern. You're done for if you get broadsided. If paddling in them, you need a full spray skirt, but the best advice by far is to not go out in them in the first place.

Rollers—Boat wakes create these surges. There are two kinds. Freighter Rollers are big, well-spaced swells. As in a gentle amusement park ride, they're a blast to ride up one side, then gently toboggin down the other. Small Motorboat Rollers are jostling annoyances. They're small but close together and send us bouncing as if sitting in the saddle of a trotting pony.

The next day is contrastingly mellow. We put in early to rack up miles the following morning. Around lunchtime, we make it to the city of Hood River, Oregon, and navigate around windsurfers languishing in the mediocre breeze. We pull into a riverside park, where wetsuit-clad beach bodies mill about.

After a telephone conversation with Dwight, we know that Mike, from the *Hood River News*, is due shortly. In the meantime, we want to find out what this crowd is all about. I confidently approach a young blond, muscular couple strapping windsurfers onto their car.

"What's going on here?" I inquire. The girl diverts her attention to us and starts to strip off her wetsuit.

"A windsurfing competition took place yesterday," she says. "I took sixth and he took ninth," she adds with a glance at her partner. She flashes me a forced smile and a shrug, obviously having hoped for better. According to her, yesterday was awesome, but today is a total bust. Windless days in Hood River are apparently rare.

As I reflect on how our canoeist's point of view is precisely the opposite, I notice a man wandering the parking lot, dressed in a suit. We take our leave of the couple and turn to intercept Mike.

Our discussion with the reporter centers around beneficial river relations. Mike said these windsurfers make a significant contribution to the Hood River economy. After all, Hood River's nickname is "The Windsurfing Capital of the World."

The Columbia River has carved a deep canyon—the Columbia River Gorge—through the Cascade Mountain range here. Cool, moist air to the west and the hot, dry air to the east create an air pressure differential. The Columbia River Gorge acts as an equalizer, funneling air from west to east. Cities within the gorge are seldom windless.

I am by now convinced that this day has been granted by divine benevolence to allow us to pass this wind tunnel safely. Accepting the gift gratefully, we wrap up our interview and hop in the canoe to take advantage of this windless blessing.

John Day Dam and Jim

Day 21 (July 4): Today, like every other day except that God-given day in Hood River, is windy. Today we tackle the John Day Dam. First, a trip to Maryhill State Park—right next door to our camp—for a twenty-five-cent six-minute shower. This little luxury gives me the boost I need to tackle what looks like another perpetually rough few hours.

Three-foot bowlickers are the norm today. Every so often, a tsunami rolls over the spray skirt—the size we decided not to paddle in just last week. These waves are further apart, and it isn't gusty today, so the paddling is easier. At least that's the rationalization.

Paddling the waves gives me the opportunity for reflection.

Today, as the bow person, I just paddle unless my captain orders otherwise. I concentrate on feeling "one" with the boat and the waves. One must master a Zen-like connection to succeed in these waves. Rock with them, roll with them. As if riding a horse, move with them, don't fight them. Me, Tom, the canoe, the waves, we are all connected, and if I can get in sync with the rhythm, the flow, the motion, I'll surpass fear and come to a comfortable balance, literally and spiritually, with our constant companions.

Amid my inner thoughts on conquering my fear of what could happen, I am happy that I started push-ups months before this trip. My once weakling arms come through for me now. They get tired paddling hard for a long time, especially with the heavy Norse paddle, but afterward, they aren't sore. I'm relieved that neither Tom nor I need backrubs as we did at the beginning.

The river and Route 84 are hubs of activity. Paddling along the shoreline near the highway gives rise to all sorts of diversions. Truckers honk their horns, sometimes at my request with a wave of my paddle but often with no invitation at all. They must have seen *The Dalles Chronicle* yesterday with a big color photo of us on the front page. We pass our friend the *Tyee*. We wave; they toot back. All sorts of people and goods are traveling from here to there, living life and seeing to their personal and professional business. I feel like a tiny speck, observing it all yet welcomed by the friendliness of people. Our canoe is a little piece of this picture of life.

Nearing the lock, Tom spots a towboat with barges making its way upriver toward the dam. The downriver doors are opening for it. If we hurry, we can save a whole lockage of water if we accompany the towboat. The trouble is, we need to cross the choppy bowlicker-ridden river to the lock on the opposite shore in another typically wind-whipped day.

On your mark—get set—GO! Paddle, pull hard, steady. Come

on arms, pull, concentrate, balance, pull harder. The towboat is coming closer. We can make it. Think *one with the waves*. With the wind gusting, we have to yell to communicate. We are almost there when a motor boater comes bouncing like a bucking bronco to within shouting distance. "Hey, are you guys okay?" We motion we are fine. With the way his bow crashes down in each wave trough, I was hoping he'd be the same. I see why he came over. He thinks we're nuts.

We make it—sort of. The towboat is almost here, so we opt not to cross over to the other wall, where the pull cord must be. Instead, we wave frantically to the towboat as it slides by. The captain can radio the lockmaster and hopefully invite us along. No one notices. We yell and wave our arms some more, but they must be too busy lining her up to enter the narrow lock. We paddle furiously over to the wall to yank the pull cord. Where is it? It's not on this wall. We turn around and see it on the wall we just came from.

Another furious paddle back from where we just were reveals the cord blowing in the wind. The blasted thing is blowing out of my reach. I have to stand up on my seat, stretch my canoe paddle out to block it, and reach for the frayed ends. For some seconds, I get the feeling of what it is like to be a surfer, or maybe a bareback rider standing on a galloping horse. I meet each peak and trough with shock-absorber knees to keep upright. Finally, I trap the rope and yank. This sets off the buzzer, and the lockmaster knows we are here. I'm relieved to sit on my tush again and not fall into the drink.

"Hello." The lockmaster's voice comes over some hidden loudspeaker.

"We're in a canoe. Can we lock through with this boat?" I yell into the air.

"This is a hazardous lock. You'll have to wait forty-five minutes for the towboat to get through first," is the reply. Ugh. I droop—all that effort for nothing. The only thing to do is to pull out on the rocks and eat lunch on a piece of driftwood. No matter how many times we hang out on riprap, it's still horrible.

John Day lock gate inviting us in

Sure enough, after forty-five minutes—no more no less—the massive vertically hung door rises and invites us in. In thirty minutes, we ascend 106 feet—the highest vertical change made by a single lock in the U.S.. Surprisingly, the enclosed chamber provides no refuge from the wind. The top presents even windier conditions. Right around the corner of the exit is a dockage. We paddle over, survey the wind situation, and unanimously decide to hang out on the dam for a while. We tie the canoe to the moorings and climb out.

The summoning of my bladder urges me to seek modern facilities. We venture off, laughing at the way we have to lean into the wind to get anywhere. On the way to the visitor center, we happen into the lockmaster who just came on duty—Jim Peterson.

"I was wondering when you would come through," he says. He saw the newspaper article and knew he would encounter us at the dam. "How about a tour?" This guy turned a wind cursed anti-canoeist day into a fantastic warm memory.

Jim is a refreshing mix of knowledge, courtesy, and free spirit. Probably in his mid-fifties, he is tall, graying, handsome, and charming. He worked as a superintendent for two dams further upriver, consulted in Brazil on hydropower, raised three kids of whom he is very proud, and mined for silver in Northern Idaho in younger days. I am instantly drawn to this remarkable, generous man.

At my urging, our first stop on the tour is the bathroom. That concluded, we go to Jim's truck, as this monstrous place requires travel by vehicle if we are to complete a tour today. I am the one sandwiched between Jim and Tom on the truck's bench seat. Sliding over to my middle spot, I pick up two flashlights, a flag, and a clipboard, holding them on my lap for lack of a better place and returning them to the seat each time I slide out.

In the control room, we meet Boyd. Things seem to be very well in hand here; at least it is pretty laid back. Jim brings me a can of pop and Tom a coffee, and we both accept a scrumptious sweet roll. With that fare, we chat about life. Boyd reminds me of an older Michael, a sort of philosopher with probing questions. We talk of human nature and foreign relations, but ecological issues and energy top the list.

Boyd and Jim politely get their opinion across that the general population lacks common sense about wildlife protection, clean water, and power production. Today's lifestyle demands power, and today's technologies offer several ways to get it, each requiring certain sacrifices. Hydroelectric plants are controversial now and forever will be.

Compared to coal-fired and nuclear power sources, hydropower provides a clean, highly controllable, endless source of energy. Here in the Northwest, rivers are power sources. But capturing the energy of falling water alters a river's character: flowing water becomes still; oxygenated water becomes deoxygenated; cold water becomes warm. The fishing resources have been the hardest hit. Our next stop is the fish ladder.

Artificial currents attract fish going upstream to the fish ladder. From the outside, you can see two of these stairstep affairs zigzagging up to the water level above. Little do the fish know (or care!) that at one of those steps alongside the powerhouse, there is an underwater window. On the other side of that window, observing them, a woman sits in a small, dark room. She is the fish counter. At a glance, she identifies the type of fish passing by her window. To her count, she adds any fish that makes forward progress and subtracts the backward-moving ones. As she explains her work, I can tell she takes pride in what she does. Jim explains the bigger problem is getting the fingerlings down.

So the baby fish don't have to be twirled through the turbines en route to the ocean, a forty-million-dollar fingerling bypass project is in effect. Jim estimates a mere 4 percent mortality rate, even if they did go through the turbines. He says gulls account for a much higher percentage of the take. The Army Corps has installed wires over the gates to lessen the impact of gull predation on fingerlings. I depart, wondering if we can ever truly figure out how energy production and wildlife can coexist.

Next, we go inside the powerhouse, which contains sixteen enormous turbine generators stretching out of sight. Jim says seven are running today, spinning at 90 RPMs to create 60-cycle electricity. A wild array of gauges and meters and switches accompanies each turbine generator. Overhead, massive scaffolding suspended on tracks dangle gigantic hooks designed to lift any generator out for repair. I feel miniaturized here.

After an exclusive tour of the visitor center—closed to the public today—we head up to the lockmaster's booth because Jim received notification on his beeper of a boat requiring lockage. While Jim perches on his seat in front of the control panel, Tom and I squeeze in behind him. Were it not for the window surrounds, I'd feel pretty claustrophobic. He works the controls that open valves while keeping an eye on the Cleo Brusco tug as it rises up from Lake Celilo to Lake Umatilla, like we did a few hours ago. The three of us munch down cantaloupe, doughnuts, cheese, and chocolate chip cookies—a fine dinner indeed.

By 8:00 p.m., our tour complete, Jim drives us to the canoe. I head toward the boat to get our thank-you paddle for Jim to sign. Jim follows.

"Here, you forgot this," he says to me and holds up one of the flashlights.

"Oh, that's not mine. It was in the truck."

Jim looks me in the eye, and with a twinkle in his, and a touch of a smile, he says, "You may need it sometime."

We have Jim sign our paddle and bid our good-byes. Under much calmer conditions, we leave John Day Dam that evening with a cantaloupe, a banana, a flashlight, and new knowledge, delighted at having made a new friend.

CHAPTER 3

A Job to Do

Thousands have lived without love,
not one without water.

—W. H. Auden

The Canoe Gets a Name

Day 26 (July 9): "That's it!" I blurt out. I am reading about our whereabouts in our handy river sourcebook.

"That's what?" Tom responds, looking up from his journal writing. Like me, he is sitting on his PFD at our campsite for the night, the two stoves chugging away between us, heating water for supper. Our beautiful, secluded site is without cows this time. Just us, nestled next to the river, where nobody ever ventures. I am reading a book we happened upon during one of our town stops—*Cruising the Columbia and Snake Rivers* by Sharlene P. and Ted W. Nelson and Joan LeMieux. This second edition, written for boaters "as well as others who enjoy the rivers and want to learn more about the environs and history," is our river guide. The information on marinas, boat ramps, amenities, distances between landmarks, and the history of the area has been particularly helpful.

"Our canoe's last name, *Wallula*, means 'many waters.'"

"*Memsochette Wallula*?" He pronounces it out loud to see how it sounds. He puckers out his lips and furrows his brow as if it takes considerable concentration to determine whether he likes it or not. Tom suggested *Memsochette* earlier in the trip. We already decided it would be a part of her name. "Memsochette" is the English spelling of "traveler" in the language of the Lenape of the Delaware Nation, a tribe from the Eastern United States. For me, this isn't enough. Like "Cher" or "Madonna" or "Sting," it leaves my eyebrows raised, waiting for the rest of the name. We agreed an appropriate last name should be of West Coast origin, preferably also Native American.

"It's perfect," I say. "And it says here the name comes from the native vocabulary.

"What tribe?"

"Hmmm . . . doesn't say."

"Could be Umatilla or Yakima. They have reservations around here. Why does it mention it?"

"It's a town, the second oldest in Washington, near the mouth of the Walla Walla River, where it dumps into the Columbia. Most of the original town is underwater now, thanks to McNary Dam."

"What's Walla Walla mean?"

I scour the paragraph again. "Hmm . . . doesn't say. It's a town too—the oldest in Washington—thirty miles up the Walla Walla River. Hey, we've achieved boilage." I point to the pot of now-boiling water. He unceremoniously dumps in the macaroni and dogs. It has been a week since we visited a grocery. No matter. Mac and cheese and hot dogs last a long time unrefrigerated—which is slightly scary. We try not to think about it. If there's no visible growth, we consume it. "Anyway, what do you think of *Memsochette Wallula, Traveler of Many Waters?*" I ask expectantly.

Tom nods in approval. "We'll have to call her *MW* for short."

I smile with great satisfaction. Like having a puppy for a month without a name, it is inappropriate and awkward, referring to our canoe as just an object. She has already displayed character and inspired confidence. And, I venture to say, is showing her personality. Equal in worthiness to any troller, schooner, tanker, tug, or dog, she has earned and deserves a name. We have no champagne, and frankly, I don't want to break anything on her. We vow to get some stick-on letters the next time we stop in a town so she can display her name proudly on her stern.

Tom declares dinner fully cooked. He slaps the dogs on the buns I hold out; he stirs the powdered "cheese" in the mostly drained macaroni, then dishes it onto our plates. We sit back in our cozy Therm-a-Rest chairs, stuffing ourselves with comfort food and gazing on our river.

Hermits or Celebrities

Day 27 (July 10): The problem with isolation, among a myriad of other obvious hardships, is that one cannot conduct a media campaign that way. Therefore, the trip took on a bipolar flavor, with periods of isolation and solitude followed by media blitzes. One day I skinny-dipped in complete seclusion. The next day our pictures (perfectly clothed, mind you) might be plastered on the front page of the local paper. The polarization from one day in civilization to the next in seclusion can be extreme. If I had my druthers, I'd choose quiet isolation. But an upcoming city or sizable town is not only our opportunity to speak out on the purpose we undertook this trip to promote but is also necessary to stock up on supplies. So, populated areas are not only tolerated but, in fact, a welcome stop.

Being an isolationist makes it challenging to keep up on news-worthy matters. It is convenient to grill the reporter, who comes to interview us. We can keep up with the summer fires in Treasure Valley, discover what oddball people have captained small craft in these parts, or hear of foreign despots scheming insane terrorism plans. Reporters know these things, and I often learn more than I want to know.

From the very beginning, we planned to coordinate the publicity with Dwight, our publicist. In weekly phone calls, we would announce our next mail drop so he could send us a list of all the press he'd contacted in upcoming towns. Good thing he let us call collect because, among his other endearing qualities of refreshing humor and appealing charm, he sure was chatty. In theory, this strategy sounded feasible. After all, he was the man with connections. In practice, it seldom worked as planned.

There was not always a letter from him at the post office when we arrived. He was not always available when we called. In that case, we just picked up a telephone book and dialed the local papers on our own. After we got directed to the correct reporter and explained what we were up to, the reporter's usual response was something on the order of, "I'll be there in ten minutes." Two loners abandoning society for a life on the river is a human-interest feature that reporters can't resist. Only one paper turned us down—for lack of staffing on a Sunday. And I think they were sincerely disappointed.

With the publication of any article comes the ensuing mini celebrity standing. After our interview with the *Daily Astorian*, truckers

along I-84 would honk when they saw us on the river, sometimes several days after publication. Anglers would remark, "So you're paddling
that all the way cross country?" A woman in the campground, after
having spoken to Tom, went back to report to her husband that they
were "camping next to celebrities." My ultimate favorite was another
woman's comment after the *Oregonian* article entitled, "Two Teachers
Paddling Across Country" was published. Upon recognizing us, she
remarked, "Oh, you're the paddling teachers!" which I suppose is not
untrue, but it sure sounded like we spank children regularly.

It takes several encounters before we get reasonably competent
in steering the interview toward our message of environmental conservation. Our first interviews reflected the excitement of setting out
on such an enormous journey. Reporters asked us everything short of
how we pee in the woods.

Steering a reporter away from the novelty of the expedition and
toward our message proved to be a challenge. Each with our own
agenda—the reporter has a human-interest story to cover, and we
have a message to get out—communication was awkward. An interview might go something like this:

Reporter: "So why are you canoeing across the country?"

Nancy: "To raise awareness about the importance of water conservation."

Reporter: "That's great. Now, where did you start, and where will you
finish?"

Tom: "We started at the mouth of the Columbia River, and we'll
finish up at Tybee Island at the mouth of the Savannah River. I hope
that we can meet people and find out what they think about our water, and the condition of our water resources."

Reporter: "And how many miles will you cover?"

Nancy: "About five thousand miles. One of our major objectives for this trip is to make people aware of their impact on the environment, specifically water."

Reporter: "That's great. And how much gear do you carry?"

Tom: "Food, packs, and gear are about three hundred pounds. Our boat weighs another sixty pounds. Here's our brochure that tells why we're doing this."

Reporter: "Thanks. And where do you sleep at night?"

And so it goes. But invariably, our message finds its way into each article. Later in the interview, we don't have to push it so hard. The reporters have to get their curiosity satiated first, and then we can plug our message.

We had arranged for a mail drop at the little town of Umatilla, Oregon. Little did we know that when we pulled into Umatilla Marina, we would receive the opportunity to exercise the purpose of Paddle for Water. There, some folks hanging out on a sailboat greet us. Pat, the owner—and, impressively enough, builder of the beautiful sixty-foot sailboat, *Bald Eagle*—invites us aboard. There we meet Pete, Sheila, and son Shawn Overlie. They are sailing the *Bald Eagle* from Pasco, Washington, downriver to Portland, where the Overlies will disembark. Here Pat and a guy named Dick will sail the *Bald Eagle* down the California coast and out to Hawaii. Right now, however, the *Eagle* had landed. The crew is waiting for a diver to come check out the propeller. The motor started clanking soon after they locked through the McNary Dam just upriver, necessitating a tow to this marina.

We are anxious to get to town. Pete said he'd watch MW for us and, with a wink, said he'd sell her only for a good price.

"Paddle for Water's here!" the postmistress hollers to an unknown entity in the back when we inquire about our general delivery. We walk out of the Post Office and park ourselves on a nearby bench. What a haul! Tom's mom sent a package of our safety knives, a letter for me from Lauren, and a hundred-dollar money order. We are down to thirty dollars, so this is a welcome relief. My doting Grandma sent us a package, which included T-shirts, lifesavers, brownies, and her traditional Fourth of July flag cookies. Like undisciplined children, we devour every single flag cookie and half the brownies with giddy delight. Few things in life are as marvelous as a mail drop.

Our Hi-Tec lightweight-hiking boots finally catch up with us here. Since we were well underway before receiving the boots, they have been chasing us from two previous mail drops. I parade mine around the bench like a kid at Christmas. Tom follows with uncharacteristic delight. I'm sure Hi-Tec wasn't counting on lunatic spokespeople.

Finally, a call to the local paper, the *East Oregonian* results in Ray Linker saying he'll meet us at the marina in ten minutes. With the help of a gracious driver who saw us previously at the marina, we are back with the Overlies on the *Bald Eagle* when Ray tracks us down.

"Rivers were the water trails or highways of the past, and we feel we can get closer to our land by making this canoe journey," I'm quoted as saying. Daily paddling distance, type of canoe, our route, and the lifestyle of river people dominate the article, but our environmental message is weak. Overlies will change that.

After the reporter leaves, the *Bald Eagle* crew insists we join them for lunch. We feast on banana bread, bananas, doughnuts, chocolate cake, candy, and pop—my kind of lunch. Pete commences to tell us of the nuclear-waste dump at the Hanford Site in the Tri-Cities area.

Leakage would not only contaminate the groundwater and surrounding soil, but once in the Columbia River, radioactive waste would affect living things from there to the coast and beyond. He and Pat ask that we speak up about the dangers of toxic waste leakage when we arrive in the area.

The Hanford Site is a 560-square-mile federally owned reservation in the desert of eastern Washington, just north of the Snake/ Columbia River confluence. It had a significant influence on our world history, so it deserves a moment of back-paddling.

Nearly forty years of plutonium production took place at this location, where, in 1943, the U.S. Army Corps of Engineers established Hanford Engineer Works. Although it was not heavily populated, it displaced two towns and the local Wanapum people to accommodate a massive industrial complex. The remote location, suitable soil, abundant power, rail lines, and ready water supply from the Columbia River were ideal for working on the top-secret Manhattan Project. Its goal was to make the world's first atomic bomb.

Ultimately, 51,000 workers came together at Hanford to build and operate a facility to fabricate, test, and irradiate uranium to isolate plutonium. The process created far more waste than product. Over twenty years, workers built 149 huge underground tanks to accommodate the radioactive and toxic liquid byproducts of plutonium production. The resulting plutonium served as the core of "Fat Man," the bomb that destroyed Nagasaki, Japan, in 1945. With the bombing of Hiroshima three days prior, World War II came to an end.[5]

Plutonium continued to be produced here throughout the Cold War with the Soviet Union in the 1950s, requiring the construction of more underground tanks to store waste. Many leaky tanks have allowed liquid effluent to contaminate soil and seep into the groundwater and into the Columbia River, seven miles to the north and ten miles east.

Twenty-eight additional double-shelled tanks have since been built to accommodate waste pumped from older, leaking, single-shelled tanks.

Today, all the Manhattan Project reactors and buildings have been decommissioned. The impetus is on cleaning up the staggering amount of contaminants generated during decades of plutonium production. Billions of gallons of highly radioactive liquid waste, contaminated buildings, spent fuel rods, polluted groundwater, and more make for a colossal job that will take decades and perhaps a century to remediate.[6]

As for Tom and I, our mission is to encourage residents to make noise about wanting a clean environment and to ensure that officials step up with a cleanup plan, stopping further contamination and remediating what has occurred.

In 1989, three years after our visit to Pasco, the U.S. Environmental Protection Agency, U.S. Department of Energy, and the Washington State Department of Ecology signed the Tri-Party Agreement. This contract establishes an action plan for cleanup and regulatory compliance at the Hanford Site. I wish I could say this resulted from our visit, but that's far too bold.

Before lunch, Pete shoved two dollars into my hand, instructing me to send them a letter upon completion of our trip. I remarked that a stamp was only twenty-two cents, but he huffed me off. After lunch, Sheila shoved a twenty-dollar bill into my hand.

"No, no, no, no—we're not collecting money," I say adamantly, shoving it back at her.

"I know," she says, staring insistently at me. "Just have yourself a nice meal—on us," and she closes my hand around the bill and will hear no more.

Bidding farewell to our new friends, we make our way through bowlickers to McNary locks on the other side of the river. There is hardly any wait, as a motorboat had already pulled the cord; the green light gives us the go-ahead to enter the recently opened gate.

While we paddle to our mooring spot, the motorboat guy takes a photo of us, accompanied by the comment, "I gotta get this—if you're crazy enough to come in here." I think he said "brave" but Tom insists he heard "crazy." We shrug it off. McNary being our fourth dam, we feel comfortable locking through by now. I tie a bowline in the bow painter and toss the loop over the mooring pin when we get close. Now it is just a matter of maintaining our position while the water lifts us to the top of this concrete monstrosity.

When we have risen apparently to within shouting range of the top of the lock, a familiar voice yells down to us, "We've made arrangements. Meet us at the dock." It's Pete. I look overhead to see waving hands. Pat and the Overlies had come to see us ascend the lock.

I look at Tom. "Did you and Pete make some sort of arrangement?"

"No, I don't know what he's talking about."

Up top, the Overlies introduce us to a friend they just met—Bill Stein, from Pasco, Washington. We all agree to go together to the fish-counting room. The seven of us somehow squeeze into this tiny, dark room illuminated with only the light from the underwater window. The wildlife biologist gladly gives us a thirty-five-minute spiel on the status of the fisheries in the area. About a week and a half ago, Tom and I heard much on this topic from Jim Peterson at the John Day Dam. Fish passing through here are primarily Chinook salmon and steelhead, a few lampreys as well. The counter identifies each at a glance, adding them to the count.

It is getting late. We have to find a campsite before dark. The fish counter recommends a U.S. Army Corps of Engineers park. "It's closed," he says, "so no one will bother you." We take that as permission to camp.

Just before departing, I spot Tom and Bill conspiring. It turns out Bill wants to put us up at the Pasco Motor Inn for Monday night, three days from now. Ahh, the arrangements.

Plush campsites like tonight's site don't come around too often. That Army Corps sure knows how to build a park. Clean restrooms, running water, picnic tables, trees, lush green grass, and no one else around. The only drawback is dodging the sprinkler system.

We set up camp in an area that had already been watered. Just in case, to avoid an unexpected drenching, we cover nearby sprinkler heads with upside-down pots. I run around barefoot in the luscious grass. That done, taking a shower, nibbling on our mail-drop candy, I finally sit down to reminisce with Tom.

"Do you know Bill gave me ten dollars today?"

He chuckles. "No, but I'm not surprised. He's a generous man."

"He insisted. That's thirty-two dollars and thirty-five cents we got today, not counting our money order from your mom."

"Ten from Bill, twenty from Sheila, two from Pete and—"

"Thirty-five cents from can returns at the grocery store," I remind him.

I close my eyes to contemplate how yesterday's strangers have become today's friends. *They believe in us.* The warmth such thoughts create inside me is as real as drinking a cup of hot chocolate.

"Now, tell me again what you guys set up," I ask Tom. I want to make sure I heard right.

"Bill is going to put us up for a night at the Pasco Motor Inn."

"He's going to put us up there?"

"Yup. And he's going to contact the local TV station to interview us too."

"How 'bout that?" I shake my head in disbelief. Bill is determined to be our surrogate grandpa. But I have a tiny, little concern.

"I'm a little leery about the camera thing," I confess to Tom.

"Oh, it'll be fine." Tom dismisses my worry.

"No, really, what if I freeze or can't think of the words or something?"

"Just be yourself. It'll be fine."

I still have camera doubts, but I allow myself to forget about it for a while. We have three days and forty miles before that reality strikes.

I Prefer Solitude

Day 28 (July 11): We paddle only six miles the next day. Constant wind and bowlickers that leap over the top of the canoe, rocking us end to end, whip us into submission until we reach Hat Rock State Park, seven miles up from McNary Dam. A curious basalt tower sits atop a nearby hill. The pillar itself is fenced off, but a pond where an old couple is tossing bread to mongrel ducks and geese provides adequate entertainment. After I greet them, the woman graciously hands me four slices of day-old bread. Knowing the bread is not good for the birds and having ulterior motives, I throw only tiny tidbits. Soon birds quit soliciting me, deeming my offerings too meager to bother with. Finally, after the couple departs, I forsake the begging birds and abscond with bread for our supper.

The Corps of Discovery also saw this seventy-foot-high volcanic monolith. Clark noted its location and its "resembling a hat" in his journal, naming it Hat Rock on his map. It is indeed an impressive top hat. While they maneuvered rapids here, we paddle Lake Wallula, McNary Dam's backwater.

The river takes us north into the interior of Washington State. Wide-open spaces give way to a narrow corridor as the stunning

Horse Heaven Hills rise around us. Horse Heaven Hills formed fifteen million years ago when volcanic fissures deposited so much lava the crust sank, causing the accumulating basalt to compress, pushing the hills upward. The dry soil doesn't support any trees, but plenty of grass—heaven for a horse. The indigenous people preferred more productive valleys for their homes, but these hills served as a boundary between tribes. The Corps of Discovery were their first encounter with Europeans. It looks hot and dry up above, but for us down on the river, a cooling westerly wind blows at our backs, making paddling extremely pleasant.

Paddling through Wallula Gap, the narrowest passage in Horse Heaven Hills, we pass by a pair of jagged, crested rock buttes that stand out from the rolling landscape like sentinels. Several names have floated around for these geologic curiosities, including Two Captains (it was not mentioned in Lewis' or Clark's journal), Chimney Rocks, Cayuse Sisters, Two Sisters, Hell's Smoke Stacks, Two Virgins, and more. Finally, the U.S. Geological Service bestowed the formation its official name: Two Sisters. The Cayuse tell the origin of these basalt towers:

> Coyote, that notorious trickster, fell in love with three sisters who came to build a salmon trap by the river each day. He destroyed the trap each night. Each day, the sisters came to rebuild it. One day, Coyote saw them crying and went up to ask why. They said they were starving because they've been unable to catch any fish. Coyote then made a deal with them. If they agreed to marry him, he would let them fish.
>
> They agreed, and lived happily for many years, but eventually Coyote grew jealous of them. He turned two into these rock pillars, and the third into a cave

downstream. Then he turned himself to stone so he could watch over them all the rest of time.

Today, since I am captain, I dub the pillars "Two Paddlers."

Never a day goes by when we don't see fish, sometimes jumping clear out of the water for insects. I'll try to catch one today. I must employ a handless trolling method if I am to paddle. I tie the line to my seat, then bring it forward around my knee. There is no rod or reel to complicate matters. In this way, my knee registers the tug—if I were to get a tug—which I don't. I never do. Today I even lose the fishing line. But I measure success on a different scale. My efforts produce a blue frisbee plucked from the weedy waters. It's a good consolation prize.

Two days later we make landfall in Kennewick's Two Rivers Park, referring to the Columbia and Snake Rivers. It is a nicely maintained swimming and picnicking park right on the bank of the Columbia. On this beautiful Sunday in July, more and more people come as late morning turns to early afternoon. I give our picnic table to picnic-basket-laden folks, searching in vain for an empty. "We can easily live without," I explain to Tom when he returns from buying a newspaper. So we sit on the ground, reading the paper and watching folks. Flat-bellied girls saunter up and down the beach. Saliva-inducing barbeque aromas waft in our direction. We could even get a free puppy.

Right about the time our fried spam is done, the pleasantness ends, as young guys at a table near us suddenly start cussing each other out. This erupts into a fistfight; two other fellas intervene to pull them apart. With the rest of the park now wide-eyed and silent—I know I am—other guys join in hurling threats and curses. Clearly now, two separate factions form behind the brawlers. A fight is afoot. Gawking, I watch gangsters twirl knives loosely in their grip, musclemen punch their palms with brass knuckles, and others tap clubs in cupped hands, threatening the rival gang to make the first move. I finally come to my senses.

"We've got to call the police," I whisper to Tom.

"I see a phone over there." But before he can move, we hear police sirens getting louder and closer. The police, brandishing pistols and rifles, storm the picnic area. A number of uniformed and plain-clothes officers run in hot pursuit as the hoodlums scatter. Three officers stay within sight to "secure the scene."

"Get in your cars and go home," one shouts to the rest of us picnickers. "The park is now closed."

"Oh no," is my immediate response. Our stoves are chugging away, and our stuff strewn about. I can see other picnickers just throwing their ready-made food into picnic baskets and heading for the parking lot.

"Take it easy," Tom reassures.

"Time to go home, folks," the officer barks at us directly.

"We came by canoe," I attempt to explain.

"We'll be out of here as soon as we can," Tom says coolly. The officer seems to get the picture and permits us to gather our belongings. I watch as officers handcuff a girl after she picked something up from the ground in what is now a crime scene.

After hastily throwing our stuff in MW, we paddle across the inlet to a tall, flowered field. Here, we figure, our tent is out of sight. It's not too far, however, to be able to come back for the appointment we made earlier with the TV folks for 9:30 tomorrow morning at what is now a crime scene.

I like being mouselike. Being able to paddle off and disappear is comforting for me. No one can find us here. I'm not even worried about the hooligans. There's a body of water between the crime scene and us. Tonight, I wash my hair (I've got to look good on camera tomorrow) and enjoy the beautiful sunset before crawling into my sleeping bag.

"It sure was an exciting day today, huh?" Tom asks.

"It's not exactly the reception I was expecting," I admit, "Nerve-wracking is a better word for it."

"I'll say," he chuckles.

"So, did you have a favorite thing today?" This question, along with our usual morning conversation, was becoming customary.

"The guys drawing knives on each other, that was pretty memorable."

He turns to look at me with a smile. "Seeing young, muscular, macho, guys—that was your favorite?" he teases.

"Naw," I smile and worm my way closer to him in my sleeping bag. "My favorite thing is right now, feeling safe with you."

"You go for the hairy little guys over big macho men?"

"Naw, you're just warm."

He put his arm around me, and we fall asleep feeling safe and secure in our own little world.

In the thirty days we have been on the river, I have become aware he has not given up trying to win me over. Frankly, it is nice lying beside him in the tent. It is nice waking up beside him in the morning. I am definitely slipping.

The next day, Two Rivers Park is calm and peaceful. No gangsters in sight. Our television interview, arranged by our new friend Bill, is to take place here.

Thom, the cameraman's laid-back style helps calm my camera shyness a bit—but I have an abundance of jitters. I answer our lifestyle and trip-related questions fine but leave the environmental advocacy, including the Hanford toxic-waste issue to Tom.

Upon the interview's completion, Thom graciously drives me to town. He even transports me back to the park. As he and I exchange goodbyes, the pay phone near us rings. I look at Thom and he at me. We both shrug. I wander over and answer. It is the *Tri-City Herald*. Arrangements have been made for Tom and me to meet a photographer at the Port of Pasco in one hour, which puts it at noon. According to Thom, this is four miles away. We'd have to boogie. I bid farewell to Thom, the TV guy, and go down to the water to join my own Tom, who is staying behind with the gear.

With that, we hop in MW and head out. We don't know where the Port of Pasco is precisely, but we can gauge four miles reasonably well.

After what we think might be four miles, we pull into what turns out to be Water World Marina.

"You passed it," the marina guy says in response to Tom's inquiry. Tom and I swap glances.

Quickly hopping in MW, we get back on the river just in time to see a motorboat zoom toward us, carrying an equipment-laden photographer. After brief introductions, the photographer gets down to business. He instructs us where to go. He instructs his boat driver where to go, and exactly how fast. We paddle around the railroad bridge and up the river and down the river. He aims his telephoto lens, his wide-angle lens, and who knows what else at us. I never know when to smile. After twenty minutes of this, in the marina, he snaps some more. Finally satisfied, he and his driver zoom off from whence they came.

"How many pictures do ya think he shot?" I ask Tom.

"I don't know. I hope he'll be able to find one good one out of all those zillions."

"I'd hope so."

All this fanfare is exciting. The folks at the marina allow us to moor MW there for a couple of days while we take our much-anticipated hiatus in Pasco.

The Pasco Motor Inn is no Marriott, but it is no little green tent either. The man at the desk greets us warmly and ushers us to room 218. No sooner do I jump into the shower than we receive a message to call the *Tri-City Herald* reporter. Since there is no room phone, we go out and call from the reception desk to conduct a phone interview.

Now famished, we treat ourselves to lunch in town. On the desk clerk's advice, we mosey over to Station 1 restaurant. Grandpa Bill soon shows up. He squeezes my hand tenderly and refers to us as "my canoers," excitedly showing us the publicity blurb he wrote up and distributed to KEPR and the *Herald*. The part that says, "They have some equipment sponsors but are helped along by well-wishers" makes me pause. I don't know where he got that idea, but he sure is going out of his way to help us along.

Despite my urging, he doesn't join us for lunch, but has made "arrangements" to pick up our lunch, dinner, and tomorrow's breakfast checks. A bigger heart could never be found.

That evening at six we watch ourselves on TV. I thought it would be just a little human-interest blurb, but nooooo, we have a regular two-minute feature spot. Due to the interviewer's prompts, we strayed a bit outside of our prearranged roles. We each came across as pragmatic but without conveying much emotion. I thought our message lacked urgency.

"It sounds like we don't care," I complain to Tom.

"It's okay," he reassures. "It's our first TV interview."

"Yeah, well, it could have been better." I realize I am falling into the forbidden "should have" mode and shake out of it. "You were good, though. You came across well on the Hanford issue."

With that, we accept our moment in the spotlight and hope our message had some meaning.

CHAPTER 4

Snake River Trials

What sets a canoeing expedition apart
is that it purifies you more rapidly
and inescapably than any other travel.
Travel a thousand miles by train and
you are a brute; pedal five hundred on
a bicycle and you remain basically a
bourgeois; paddle a hundred in a canoe
and you are already a child of nature.

—Pierre Elliott Trudeau

It Starts So Well

Day 32 (July 15): I figured that the Snake River got its name from its meandering course. It would be appropriate but not true. Our U.S. Army Corps of Engineers friend told us otherwise. Among the Snake's early travelers, the river got a reputation of being like a snake in a trail. You travel along merrily until you turn a corner; then POW—it strikes, sending adrenalin surging through your arteries. Likewise, the Snake River could spring dangerous rapids, odd currents, or sudden upwellings on an unwary boater, more so back in the day rather than now with four dams to calm it. Other origin stories attribute the name to misinterpretations by early European travelers. When the newcomers met Shoshone people, for whom this river had been home for thousands of years, sign language was the only option for communication. The Shoshone moved their hands in an undulating fashion to convey where they lived—near the water, where there were fish. The intruders, however, thought they were being told the name of the river and interpreted the motion to be that of a snake. It is also thought that the Shoshone were speaking of basket weaving with the winding arm motion, and again, "snake" was the interpretation. Any way you look at it, Snake is a good name for this river.

From its origins in Yellowstone National Park in Wyoming, the Snake loops around the southern part of Idaho, until it heads north and forms the border between Idaho and Oregon. It continues along the boundary of Idaho and Washington—splitting the towns of Lewiston, Idaho, and Clarkston, Washington. It is not hard to figure out who these cities were named after.

By way of historical reference, the Corps of Discovery arrived here in dugout canoes in the fall of 1805. They had paddled down the Clearwater River to its confluence with the Snake, where these cities are now. The Snake then took them to the Columbia and the Pacific coast.

Much later, a gold rush in 1860 brought a surge of prospectors to this area, and Ragtown and Jawbone Flats quickly became established. As quaint and befitting as these names were, by the turn of the twentieth century, name changes were in order. Ragtown became

Lewiston, and Jawbone Flats was thankfully renamed Clarkston.

From there, the Snake heads west, joining the Columbia River at the Tri-Cities of Richland, Pasco, and Kennewick, Washington.

Our journey calls for going in the opposite direction of the flow. Four dams on the lower Snake, between the Tri-Cities of Washington and Lewiston/Clarkston, provide lakes where we don't have to paddle against a current. After that, where the inland waterway ends, the river will present us with new tribulations.

With the *Tri-City Herald* tucked under his arm, Grandpa Bill escorts us to breakfast like a proud father. Tom and I made the front page in full color. With strawberry Belgian waffles and whipped cream in our tummies, Grandpa Bill drives us to our canoe. It is hard to leave him. His enthusiasm for life and carefree sense of humor can hardly be equaled. I hope we encounter more like him in our journey, but I doubt we will.

On our own again, we are curious as to how much of the roughly 1,036 miles of this river's length we can actually paddle. Ahead lie the Grand Tetons, a part of that enormous obstacle called the Rocky Mountains. How far can one paddle up a mountain stream? We shall soon find out.

I'm also intrigued to judge for myself how much of the Snake's original temperament remains. I expect most of the rapids that surprised early river travelers lie drowned under dam-formed lakes. Will she have different tricks in store for us?

Ice Harbor Lock and Dam is only thirteen miles upriver from Grandpa Bill. The procedure, we now have down pat: attach our bow painter to one of the floating mooring pins. I must emphasize the importance of tying up to a *floating* mooring pin. Tying to something stationary like a ladder rung would be disastrous. As water in the chamber rose, the poor tethered boat would slowly get engulfed, sinking, drowning, disappearing. Oh, the horror! Likewise, it would be unnerving not to be tied off at all. In the surge of water filling the chamber, a canoe would swirl about like a rubber ducky in a flushing toilet. We assume our usual position at #7 mooring pin and wait.

Soon the door clangs shut, leaving us in this giant chamber, waiting calmly for millions of gallons of water to surge in. No problem. We're getting good at this. Here at Ice Harbor, the lockmaster let us have it. He opened all the valves, and we rose five feet in the first twenty seconds. We rise 103 feet in twelve minutes. We depart now on Lake Sacajawea.

Tom is in a good mood. We are camping tonight at Wingate Park—legally, I might add. Jim, the park attendant, has struck up a conversation with Tom, and before I know it they are out fishing together. I stay at our site—writing and reading. I start reading a book Tom recently finished called *Entropy* and promptly fall asleep.

"Hey, Nance, look what I got!" I spring awake, but it takes a couple of seconds to get my bearings. "Oh, sorry, did I wake you?" My bewildered expression is not lost on him. Tom proudly holds up two little salmon. Jim, right behind, presents me with one more fish.

"Here's a little cornmeal to coat them with. Fry 'em up in lots of butter," Jim instructs. "Nothin' like fresh fish for supper," he adds as he takes his leave after providing us with some lemon juice, celery, and carrot sticks. Wow—a wholesome meal of fresh-caught salmon! I soon realize it's not a dream. Tom gets busy cleaning the fish. I think he's whistling.

Lower Monumental Lock and Dam is three miles away. The next day Tom is still riding high on his catch and is trolling with the corn and worms Jim sent off with us. His mood is not to last, as the current below the dam is intense. There are no eddies to help us out here. Eventually, we make it to the lock-entry wall and the pull cord. This dam has a vertical lift. After a fifteen-minute wait, the gate lifts, the horn sounds, and the green light indicates we can enter. The massive door above us drips onto our heads and looms intimidatingly, so we don't linger. Up we go to Lake Herbert G. West.

Little Goose Lock and Dam awaits us at the end of Lake Herbert G. West, and by the time we ascend through the lock, we find ourselves on Lake Bryan. We have now risen 637 feet up from the ocean.

"Come on in, Nance!" Tom yells. Tom has a hankering to "do" the Snake before the moon rises. "The water's just right!" Now is as good a time as ever, and I want to wash off today's sweat.

Somewhere on the Columbia, we made a pact to skinny-dip in every state on our route. It's just something that must be done. As canoeists, we thrive on ritual. Tom told me that when he did white water, he and his fellow canoeists would pee in the river at the beginning, then again at the take-out. No reason—just ritual. Since we are on a clean-water mission, I forbid it. I deem skinny-dipping an acceptable alternative. I charge into the water when Tom isn't looking, exhilarated but shocked by the cold "just right" temperature.

"Yikes!"

"Took you long enough. Now I'm cold. I'm getting out."

"You're such a wiener." I swim around by myself, yell echoes off the canyon walls, and relish our seclusion until I am a little chilly.

"OK, I'm ready to come out!"

"So?"

"Go away! Turn around!"

"You're no fun." I run for my clothes while Tom complains about my prudishness.

Beyond these lakes and atop the basalt bluffs, thirsty hillsides rise and roll off into the distance. It strikes me funny to see parched land of dry grass and sagebrush sitting right beside these large, deep lakes filled with the liquid of life. They call this Palouse country, where mile after mile of bunchgrass is occasionally interrupted by a wheat field. We pass a grain elevator, where a barge is filling with wheat. At times, we see an orderly patch of verdant green. Sometimes these patches are peach orchards; sometimes irrigated cropland where the U.S. Army Corp of Engineers produce forage for game species.

These wildlife-friendly spots mitigate habitat lost as a consequence of these dammed-up lakes. Sometimes these patches are recreational parks, thanks to the Corps again. Many have tent and RV sites, which are not necessarily to our liking. If there is a fee for camping, we lurk on the outskirts, waiting for the cloak of darkness to pitch our tent. Paying for a campsite is contrary to our nature. "Sleep for free" is one of the many challenges with which we burden ourselves.

The river has sliced most of these distant hillsides to reveal fantastic basalt cliffs. An outcropping on a hill up from Lake Herbert G. West carves its way through the surrounding rocky swells like a ship. Captain William Clark named it "Ship Rock." Today, known as "Monumental Rock," it lends its name to Lower Monumental Lock and Dam. Volcanic eruptions occurring between fourteen million and six million years ago deposited this sea of basalt, this outcrop being more resistant to erosion. As we paddle by Monumental Rock, I contemplate the disparity of this river's landmarks—resilient basalt over six million years old versus human-made dams such as Lower Monumental completed in 1969. New to Earth, we humans are quick to alter our surroundings. But Earth can far outlast our constructs.

The water in the Snake lakes is scummy—the bottom a combination of sand and hard, slimy muck. Some of this muck floats on top. Water sitting in these lakes of the lower Snake, backed up by the huge energy-producing dams, has plenty of time to warm up in the hot sun. As July turns to August the heat of the Idaho desert is upon us.

Despite a bit of floating water scum, heatstroke-prevention plunges become routine as 104-degree days follow 102-degree days. The sternsman has a distinct advantage in the surprise plunge. After a jolt of the boat and a big splash, I look back from my bow position to find Tom no longer on board.

I soon catapult myself up and out to follow suit. Landing in bathtub-warm water does little to refresh, and the negligible wind provides meager radiant cooling afterward. But continually basting with Snake River water prevents us from cooking to a crisp. Fortunately, the U.S. Army Corps of Engineers maintains several parks and landings along the waterway, complete with shade trees for lunchtime respite.

Tom beats the heat by playing troll.

Eventually, the heat forces us to change tactics. We knock off miles during morning and evening paddles only. Midday finds us under the shade of a park tree or hunkered under a bridge overpass like a couple of transient trolls.

Tom pursues his fishing savvy, which consists mostly of accepting fish donations from actual anglers. I can't say precisely when the craving hit me, but I could not let go of the notion to try the fish we see every day—carp.

This large-scaled primitive-looking fish has been our companion above all the dams on the Columbia and lower Snake. Their arched backs breach the water, dorsal fin blowing in the wind, while they lazily slurp and gulp the surface scum. For wild creatures, they are amazingly lackadaisical and oblivious. It is not uncommon—without even trying—to hit them with a paddle.

Sometimes MW plows into one. This, of course, instantly snaps the carp out of his stupor. With a crack on the water, his tail sends a plume into my face, and I swear I hear a sort of fish expletive in that instant of startling realization. No matter how I prepare myself, and I always see it coming, his explosive response never fails to send me an inch off my seat with a scream of my own. Tom tells me to stop shaking the boat. It is times like these when I start to think about eating one.

The opportunity presents itself below Lower Granite Lock and Dam. The water level, having dropped suddenly, left a throng of carp flopping around in puddles. We pull into the newly exposed shore and slog around in the mud. I wonder if they are all destined to die before the water level rises. Might as well harvest one if that's his/her destiny.

"Here's one," I say, pointing out my pick like you would a lobster in the grocery-store tank.

"Okay," Tom says, surveying my fish. Gripping the Norse shaft with two hands, he raises the paddle high over his head like an ax.

"Stand back." I didn't need to be told. With a grunt, he whacks the fish's spine with the edge of the paddle, resulting in a loud thud.

"He's still flopping around," I observe.

WHACK WHACK WHACK. It's still flopping. "This sucker's a friggin' rock!" Tom huffs and whacks some more.

"Oh, stop!" I plead. "I thought it would be quick and merciful." My thoughts race between a humane way of harvesting this creature and breaking the paddle.

"I need a different method," Tom concedes, getting a little perturbed. I am glad to see his brain starting to have some influence over his brawn. He pulls out his knife. I turn my head, now feeling like maybe I don't need to try carp.

"Please don't torture the poor thing," I beg, hands clenched to my chest. "Do it fast."

At this point, Tom's manliness is at stake. I hear a few choice words as the slimy fellow escapes his attempts to pick it up time and again. More grunts and expletives. Eventually, Tom and the fish go for a walk away from the water, and soon he comes back with a couple of big fillets.

I don't recommend eating carp. Nothing magical happens to the scummy stuff it ingests before it becomes oily meat.

I prefer plant delicacies. The discovery of cattail root fried up with potatoes and carrots (forever after known as "Tuber Delight") tops my list. Many a dinner gets washed down with rosehip tea. Berry bushes are cause to back-paddle without question. Dandelion and sorrel leaves provide natural salads loaded with vitamins. We even find a lone apricot tree. Upon occasion, I join an assortment of critters—birds, raccoons, skunks—in raiding mulberry trees. For days afterward, Tom and I have mulberry pancakes, mulberry tarts, mulberries by the handful, and mulberry-stained fingers. We don't get too exotic collecting from nature. No experimenting. Wild good-ies provide a refreshing additive to our overprocessed, prepackaged never-spoil staples.

I prepare cattail root for a meal of tuber delight.

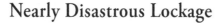

Nearly Disastrous Lockage

Day 40 (July 23): Being a glass-is-half-full kind of person, I see Day 40 as a kind of fortunate wake-up call. On this day, we lock through Lower Granite Lock and Dam, the last of the western inland waterways on the Snake. It is our eighth lockage. The next major lockage won't be until the Tennessee River in Kentucky, over 2,000 miles away. No more free rides for a very long time. From here on up, we portage dams.

After a typical twenty-five-minute wait, the gate opens, and we paddle over to our usual #7 mooring pin. This positions us close to the upstream gate and on the side of the lockmaster. Tom, in the bow, tosses the looped painter around it. With a resounding clang the doors close us in. The water rushing toward us is exceptionally turbulent. The twirling water pushes MW about. From the stern, with gentle occasional correction strokes, as is my custom, I keep us away from the wall. To catch her nose on the wall as we ascend would be a very bad thing. I don't at first take note of how taut our tether is against the mooring. Incredulously, I watch as, like a Lipizzaner stallion bowing, MW's bow begins to dip.

"Oh my gosh!" I scream as gallons of water dump in around Tom. He hollers something but a whole lot less restrained. Like in a fast-speed film, within the next brief few seconds we accomplish many panicky actions. I grab my PFD and zip it up and yell at Tom to do the same. With grand arm gestures, Tom motions the lockmaster to stop the filling while I instinctively take a stroke forward to release the pull on the rope. Relieving the tension this way does the trick. MW's bow resurfaces, but by then, water fills MW to within four inches of the gunwales.

"Bail, Nance, BAIL," Tom yells. I go to work frantically with the bailer while Tom does the same with his hat. We throw water overboard in a carefully balanced frenzy. MW is underwater, but upright. And any weight shift would make a lousy situation desperate. No amount of frantic arm waving by Tom slows our ascent at all. We keep bailing as we rise.

By the time we make the top, we have less than an inch of water left in the bottom of the boat. MW maintained her upright attitude admirably during the precarious situation. Afterward, I thought this extremely fortunate. I've played around canoes enough to know how easily a swamped boat can tip and turn. Her broad-beamed hull, our good sense of balance, and the steadying hand of God all must have played a part in averting this disaster.

It is our custom, always, to clip gear onto a thwart. Were we ever to topple, our equipment would be attached to the canoe so that it wouldn't sink to the bottom. But it sure would weigh MW down—better than an anchor. I don't know how we would hoist that kitchen up when it was trying its best to bring MW to the bottom. Luckily, we didn't have to experience that scenario.

Finally, at the top, while the gate opens, the lockmaster comes over to check on us. While I sponge out the last of the water in MW and gather my wits, he explains he certainly understood what Tom's arm flailing meant, but he did not slow the filling after Tom's urgent request because, he said, it would have taken five minutes to close the gates and he would have brought us up fully swamped anyway.

Three miles upriver, the green oasis of Wawawai County Park provides the perfect spot to spread out all our stuff for drying. Gallon-size, freezer-strength zipper bags are a canoeist's staple. Packing belongings in these inside a backpack not only helps to keep things organized but also dry in events such as this. That is, until they've seen forty days of continual use. It is now easy to determine which bags have holes. In our case—most of them.

Wawawai Park is beautiful. We make it a bit less beautiful as we lay a colorful patchwork of clothes, foodstuffs, dishes, and first-aid supplies all over the verdant green grass and nearly every picnic table. Fortunately, the intense Idaho sun makes quick work of drying. My panties dry in no time. Rice and noodles get trashed. Once things dry, we load up and hit the water again, having been instructed not to camp here. Five miles further, we happen upon an even better spot. Cherries, perfectly ripe for the picking, dangle from trees. I feed my face and fill a pot. We sleep out under the stars because the evening is so pleasant, but primarily because the tent is still waterlogged.

Our next obstacle upriver is Hells Canyon, a stretch of whitewater below Hells Canyon Dam. Hells Canyon, with Class II, III, and some Class IV white water rapids, is a popular place for thrill seekers to bump, bounce, and career down rapids in rubber boats, hooting and hollering, getting drenched and laughing about it. We can't paddle up this. It requires portaging.

Tom brews up a brilliant plan on how to bypass Hells Canyon: catch a ride with a whitewater outfitter transporting clients for a day on the river. Where there is runnable whitewater, there are entrepreneurs to provide the service, and Lewiston has them. Tour companies run rapids with rafts, jet boats, and dories. A dory, by the way, is a wooden, flat-bottomed boat with high sides that is maneuvered with oars. Curiously, I don't see canoes. Any of these companies will be headed where we want to go—above the rapids—and has the means to carry MW too. We delve into the phone book. With a lot of telephone time and a good sales pitch, Tom finagles a ride with the generous folks of Grand Canyon Dories.

While we sweet-talk outfitters in Lewiston, we also finagle an overnight stay at Hells Gate State Park. Here we'll spin evening campfire tales of cross-country canoeing adventures in exchange for free camping. It all worked!

Hells Canyon forms a sixty-mile boundary between Oregon and, to the east, Idaho. According to the Nez Perce tradition, Coyote, the trickster and mischief maker, dug the canyon in one day to protect the people on the west side of the river from the evil-spirit devils living in the mountain range to the east. Geologists have determined that the walls, uplifted by mountain-building processes, are of volcanic origin. The Snake River continues to work tirelessly to erode its chasm.

Idaho's rugged Seven Devils Range to the east of the canyon is part of the Nez Perce National Forest and Payette National Forest. On the western Oregon shore is Hells Canyon National Recreation Area with accompanying Wallowa-Whitman National Forest. This, North America's deepest gorge, reaches a depth of 7,913 feet seven miles downstream of Hells Canyon Dam. The Snake River north of this dam was designated a National Wild and Scenic River in 1975.

On Monday, we find ourselves in a van with Grand Canyon Dory clients. We head south into the Wallowa Mountains. Although the cool ponderosa pine forest brings a smile to my face, the twisty-turny mountainous roads bring another, threatening, queasy feeling to my throat. By the time we get dropped off at Hells Canyon Park, I feel a minor victory in not having tossed my cookies.

Here, on the slack water a good ways behind Hells Canyon Dam, we are 180 road miles upriver from our campsite in Lewiston.

"Well, here we are," I state with a shrug while finishing up my Tuber Delight with mushrooms. "We got around it."

With a bowed head and emotionless agreement, Tom replies, "Yeah, it worked out." He lifts his plate to his mouth, shovels food into it, and takes a moment to chew. "We saved bunches of time.

I think we covered a hundred and five river miles today." Ever the logistics officer.

I continue, "I feel bad we haven't even seen the canyon," wondering if I read him correctly. "I'd like to see if it's all it's cracked up to be." I reach for the pudding pan and ladle almost half onto my plate.

Tom raises his head to look at me. "Yeah, me too." Some brightness is coming back into his voice.

"It's stupid to paddle the Snake River and just bypass Hells Canyon without even seeing it," I continue.

"You don't have to twist my arm." Tom is now downright perky. With that, I pass the lemon pudding with smooshed banana, and he happily slurps it up.

The next morning, with lunch, cameras, and raincoats in hand, we manage a ride from the first vehicle that comes by. It is a small truck. We hop in the bed next to a big strapped-in gas tank. The guy says he provides gasoline for Hells Canyon Adventures jet boats. Those sixteen miles take five years off my lifespan. This madman of the mountain runs the Grand Prix on this twisty-curvy road. He passes cars on blind curves, and I swear we are on two tires on some of those turns. I hold on for dear life, eyeing that big fuel tank. On the verge of hysteria, my rational angel whispers in my ear: *This gas tank is not my enemy. It's my savior. When we crash, we will all be blown to kingdom come and never know a thing. No suffering. No struggling through life in a mutilated state.* The thought of instant death calms my nerves, and I no longer contemplate hurling myself out of the vehicle. Miraculously, we arrive at Hells Canyon Dam in one piece.

The beauty of Hells Canyon is just the tonic I need to bring my heart rate and blood pressure down. Beautiful ponderosa pine-covered mountainsides reach down to a boisterous river. It is not all sheer cliffs to the water. Some spots are flat and open enough for even an abandoned ramshackle of a house, which we curiously find on our hike. It probably isn't proper, but as this is public land, we make off with a wire, a fire extinguisher clip, and a nail that may be just the ticket for our current canoe repairs.

We watch a tourist-filled jet boat, three rafts, and a kayak navigate down through the rapids. On the tiny fraction of river we can canvass by foot, Class II and III rapids, negligible eddies, and a definite lack of take-outs provide us the satisfaction of a troublesome spot avoided. We manage a ride back home with three adventurous ladies we befriended on the trail. Much to my relief, four tires are always in contact with the road.

As we paddle out of the Wallowa Mountains, I can usually be found slathered in sun lotion in my swimsuit. To protect him from the relentless sun, Tom, shirtless, has his coating of hair. Off the water, a continuous din of snaps and crackles fills the air as thick swarms of grasshoppers hurl themselves about. Moses must have raised his staff. This was an outbreak of plague proportions. Like making a splash in a puddle, grasshoppers spring out from under every step. It's like being inside an air popper. The vermin nibble my journal pages, land on my face, squiggle around in my hair, and launch themselves into the cooking pot. Chukar partridges pay no heed to us, busily gorging themselves on the abundant insects. I'm glad others are benefitting from them. They drive us mad.

Dam Portages

Day 46 (July 29): The dry, grassy hillsides roll right down to touch the plentiful water in this big river. This doesn't make sense to me. Vegetation should be along the shoreline, taking advantage of the water there. I conjecture that water-level fluctuations from the Brownlee and Oxbow Dams upriver do not allow anything to establish itself. The only trees and significant vegetation are in gulches, which cleave the hills, ushering what little runoff there is ever so curvaceously down to the river. This landscape is not very conducive to flat tenting spots, but no matter. It is much more pleasant to sleep out under the stars in the cool night air.

Why erect a tent when it's not needed?

The water above Lewiston and Hells Canyon Dam is no better than it was in the lakes behind the big dams on the lower Snake. Algae thrive on the water's surface in clumps. Some large globs look like pea soup. Other small particles, perhaps pollen, are in suspension in the first foot or so below the surface. Despite this apparent algae bloom, the water seems clear, and when not blocked by algae globs we can see eight feet down. Gone are the days of the big lakes. We are paddling against oncoming current most all the time now.

Because of constant hard work, frequent heatstroke-prevention plunges, and dry air, my hands are a chronic disaster. No matter how much lotion I use, an array of cavernous slits afflict my thumbs and fingers. To avoid sore spots, I hold the paddle in slightly different ways, causing blisters and tender spots to pop up in new locations. To top it off, each morning I wake to fat sausage fingers. My knuckles are stiff and arthritic-like. Once I get paddling, they loosen up, giving way to a tingling sensation. The tingling leads into all-out numbness of my whole hand, which no amount of shaking can diminish. Within an hour, all those sensations abate, and I forget about the entire chain of events until it begins the next morning.

Two days after leaving Hells Canyon Dam, we arrive at Oxbow Dam. Just downriver, a hurried current, turbulences, whirlpools, and eddy lines toy with MW. The Snake is giving us a taste of her former self.

Having struggled and fought our way up, we find ourselves at the powerhouse. Idaho Power Company dug a tunnel across the oxbow and put the powerhouse at the end of that tunnel, where water reenters the river. The dam is further upriver.

Signs warn vehemently of the irregular, automatic fluctuation boaters should expect. We paddle past the powerhouse, around the oxbow, and take out on the rocks below the spillway of the dam. A steady rising water level chases us up the rocks, requiring gear-shuffling spurts until we hit the level of a beached raft. From there, a switchback dirt road is our stairway to the top. Tom noisily hoists MW, and I lug the kitchen for our first trip. I keep my mind off my burden as I listen to Tom's grunts, groans, curses, and assortment of odd noises.

"You'll have to learn to ignore my noises," Tom mutters as a sort of apology, I suppose.

"Have you always been this vocal on portages?" I ask.

"Nope—arrrrgh!—I had to appear manly before—ugggghhh!—and be able to take it—ahhhhhhhh!—Around you—mother f*****—I don't have to do that."

"Oh." Trying to make sense of this comment occupies my mind during the rest of the grueling procedure. Does he have to act "manly" around men, but not women? Are grunts and groans his twisted way of impressing me with how much burden he can bear? Isn't he aware that the kitchen weighs as much as the canoe? Not wishing to pursue the conversation, I fall back and file his comment under "weird compliment."

Tracy, a high-school summer worker and canoeist godsend at Brownlee Dam, gave us a ride in his truck around that obstacle. Oxbow and Brownlee Dams are now behind us—but so is their slack water. Wordlessly, we muscle our way upriver. Tom tends to the steering today while in the bow I provide "go power." Leaning forward, I dip my paddle in front of me, pulling back steadily and forcibly for about the zillionth time. Abdominal muscles help pull. Despite my push-up prep, there is never enough muscle power in my arms to propel us. Upon the return, I slice through the wind, feathering my paddle, as I reach forward to plant my paddle vertically in the water for yet another stroke. I have to keep a pace that is sustainable for several hours on end, for several days on end.

This sort of paddling firms up my belly, puts definition in my back, and replaces girly limbs with brawny ones. Tom says the muscle definition in my back "would make a marine proud." A stranger even complimented my back muscles recently. Comments about my body in a swimsuit normally make me feel awkward and vulnerable, but seeing as this came from a woman, I instead stood tall and nodded my thanks with a slight smile. I feel proud to bear the name Beast.

I'm amazed how MW gobbles her way up this river, despite the incessant current. Plant, pull, feather; plant, pull, feather; plant, pull, feather . . .

"Hey, did you see that?" I indicate a beer can floating by.

"That's the second one I've seen," Tom says. Then a third bobs down the river. I sacrifice a stroke to snatch this one out of the water.

"Where are these coming from?" I voice out loud, getting agitated. Litter is a pet peeve of mine. I cannot understand how people can go to a beautiful place—or even a not-so-beautiful place—and feel they have the right to violate it with their excrement of laziness. Just then, the answer to the beer-can origins becomes clear as another can flies into the river. I scoop this new can up as it floats to within reach and add it to my collection. I begin to hear men's voices as a break in the trees along the shore reveals the litterbugs.

A half-dozen young men leaning against their cars, drinking beer, come into view. When we are opposite them, I stand up in the canoe and heave one can and then the other back up the bank at them with my brawny arm. "Hey, I think you dropped this!" I shout in my cynical but polite fury. I don't hit them like I want to. In the passion of the moment, I didn't think to weigh the cans with water for better distance. I sit down to resume paddling. We are already slowing. Neither of us wants to allow the current to prolong our stay.

The loafers do nothing but stare. No expletives, no questions, no comments, and certainly no thanks. In their drunken stupor, they are probably dumbfounded that the river would throw beer cans back.

"I can't believe you did that," Tom says, once out of earshot of the inebriated litterbugs.

"Well, I'm sorry I couldn't hit 'em."

Tom laughs. "Me too." It was out of character for me to be so aggressive. "Sometimes you surprise me," he says, shaking his head and smiling behind me.

"Yeah, if I had time to think about it, I 'probly woulda wimped out."

"That was great, though. I'm glad you did it."

"Yeah, me too." I sacrifice a stroke to turn around and accept his approval with a smile.

Paddling Ever Upward

Days 55–58 (August 7–10): We find ourselves paddling a river corridor known as Treasure Valley. This stretch, due west of Boise, supports crops like hay, corn, a legume that might be soybeans, onions, and of course, potatoes. Fierce electrical storms have been plaguing Treasure Valley this summer, starting numerous wildfires. If the name "Treasure" refers to soot, it is aptly named; otherwise, I'm afraid many treasures are going up in smoke.

Rain may or may not accompany these storms. Late one afternoon, such a windstorm suddenly attacks us from the front, nearly snatching my hat off my head. Rain immediately commences by the bucketful. By the time we pull over, hurriedly scrounge for and don our raincoats, we are already drenched, and the cloudburst has passed. The sound of a fire engine heading south on Route 201 to do battle with a new blaze fills the air. This storm would end up sparking seventeen separate fires. Farmers lost winter feed as well as cows from fire and drought and grasshoppers. All we can do is push on.

For days the sky rains soot. Pieces of burnt grass float down, covering the surface of the river, landing on our hats and clothes. Only once is a range fire visible. Its smoke makes the setting sun brilliant red before blocking it out completely. Treasure Valley is burning up. Rain, and plenty of it, is the only real treasure it needs right now.

Now we begin our long, sweeping turn from south to east following Idaho's general shape. The Snake will lead us to the mountains—eventually. This part of southern Idaho is strictly cattle country. Barbed wire fences extending out into the water attest to it if the actual beasts do not. Most of the time, MW chalks up another unusual canoe feat—fence hurdling. She does it with ease. Fences extend down the banks, continuing into the river—submerging deeply enough that we can glide over the top. Sometimes an unusually high fence forces us out into faster-moving water. Occasionally we round a corner and meet our terrestrial comrades.

Cows seldom see canoeists on their river.

Moments before, they were leisurely standing in the river. Suddenly, when one becomes aware of us, all heads swing up, drinking and peeing cease, and for a moment, every ear cocks in our direction. Then the stampede begins. Stumbling and splashing, the startled cows clatter up the embankment to the safety of a flat field as we slide by. I glance back to find them standing in a row, eyes and ears still tuned on us, wondering what manner of interruption this is.

The Snake, like all rivers, is irresistibly lured toward the ocean. With fewer taming dams here in southern Idaho, progress requires continuous work as we force our way against the current in this curvy, snaky river. We like water on the inside, or short side, of the curves, where the flow is slower, but it can be too shallow to get a good bite for the blade. Then again, deeper water toward the outside of the curve allows effective strokes, but the oncoming current is too fast. There is a sweet spot in the river where the water is just right—deep enough to paddle yet slow enough to make progress. With focus and fortitude, we entice MW up this very fine line.

In flatwater, the stern person steers and the bow person could mentally (not literally) drift away while providing forward momentum. In moving water like this, bow and stern coordination is crucial to keep the canoe always pointed directly into the current. Obstacles and directions need to be conveyed from the paddler with the best view—the bow person—to the stern. The bow person's instructions might go something like: "Get out some. . . I'm touching . . . blade length . . . half a blade. . . move right . . . more right . . . better . . . see those sticks? . . . go between them . . . good . . . right here . . . keep on this heading . . . now left of the stump," and on and on and on. The bow position is physically *and* vocally exhausting.

Then there are the Love/Hate islands. In the eddy that islands create behind them, water is generally moving upriver to fill the void created by the obstacle. This, I love. The eddy gives us a little reprieve from our toils. Then, we sneak along the shoreline, where water flows a bit slower than in the main stem of the river. Then payback time. A pillow of gushing water roils at the head of the island. This, I hate.

All the water diverted from its path by this impediment gangs up to challenge us. Heads down, legs braced, paddling in synchrony, full of momentum, we power MW right through the torrent. The bow paddler must correct MW's wavering at the slightest hint. Care must be taken to keep her bow pointed directly into the oncoming current, or she will be persuaded to join it despite our intentions to convince her otherwise.

In this way, we sneak and power our way up the forceful Snake River. Sometimes I paddle so hard my arms start to feel like overcooked spaghetti noodles. Numerous Love/Hate islands allow for eddy breaks to let the lactic acid in my muscles dissipate. Physically and emotionally, this river wears on me. Sometimes, besides fighting the current, I fight to hold back tears.

Often, there is no eddy in sight, so we get out and line MW over shallow spits or rocky shorelines. Jumping out into the water the first ten times is a welcome respite for my upper body. It allows my lower half to get some exercise. But once it gets to be twenty or more times a day—in and out and in and out—then both my body halves complain. The skin between my toes is raw. Uncalloused spots on my hands still form blisters. Plus, there's the toll on my wet shoes. Only a few resolute threads hold the front uppers to the sole, allowing my toes to cavort with rocks. The back heels are ripped to shreds, and the shoelaces are a tangle of knots. It won't be long before those tenacious threads give way, my sole wantonly flops about, and the rocks have their way with my toes.

While we are standing roadside, thumbing into Nampa, Idaho, for some groceries, water, mail, and maybe even fun, Tom makes an exciting discovery.

Nancy's wet shoes still serve their purpose.

"Hey, here's some sneakers." On the shoulder of the road, he points out the discarded shoes.

I pick up each sneaker for inspection. There's mud, a few surface tears, no tread, and only one knot per shoelace. "Wow, they're in pretty good shape!"

"Superb shape next to yours."

Unfortunately, they are about five sizes too big. I salvage the laces, and we continue to try to hitch a ride.

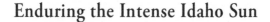

Enduring the Intense Idaho Sun

Day 64 (August 16): We paddle into the Snake River Birds of Prey Natural Area. High basalt cliffs, some looming 600 feet above us, make a natural nesting place for prairie falcons. A large portion of their entire population nests along this stretch of protected river. We keep our eyes alert, but a nighthawk and a great blue heron are the closest we get to birds of prey, which isn't close at all.

Hawks, owls, falcons, eagles, and vultures belong to the lot. With their acute eyesight, sharp arched bills, piercing talons, and (except for vultures) powerful gripping feet, these birds are well equipped for hunting and eating meat.

A preponderance of burrowing mammals find the grainy soil and dense vegetation irresistible on the plateaus above. Raptors likewise find the little furry creatures irresistible. Fifteen species and more than eight hundred pairs nest here, making it the highest concentration of birds of prey in North America. Unfortunately for us, the best viewing occurs in mid-March, May, and June. Birds seem to hunker down in their nests in April. After July, high temperatures coax ground squirrels to stay below, and with the kids fledged, most raptors go on hiatus. By the time we arrive, they have all flown the coop.

If we were up on top, we would be aware of the miles of trails, a visitor center, educational programs, and observation lookouts that the Bureau of Land Management (BLM) operates on this 482,000-acre preserve. But down here in the gorge, people are recreating just like us. We stop for lunch across the river from a parked raft, watching as the six clients and a guide return from a hike downriver. Complete with tablecloth, they set up a table and feast in style—too far away to notice our drooling, covetous faces. I don't know what they're eating, but it isn't what we're eating for the sixty-fourth day in a row—PB & J sandwiches. They must have noticed us inching upriver because as they shove off, the guide stands up, faces us, gives us a snappy salute, then heads in the direction *sensible* nonmotorized craft go—downriver.

In 1993, Congress designated this eighty-one-mile stretch of canyon a National Conservation Area, recognizing its importance in protecting habitat for raptors. In 2009 the area underwent another name change to Morley Nelson Snake River Birds of Prey Conservation Area, in recognition of its ardent proponent.

Nancy frogging

The intense midday sun continues to torture us, so we adopt the habit of paddling in the morning, late afternoon, and evening. We expect to fight our way up Class II whitewater, but the river throws us different challenges now. Monstrous boulders protrude from the shoreline. They force us out into the tumult of deep, rushing water.

It is all we can do to inch up such an onslaught with quick, powerful, synchronized strokes. Every muscle in my body, from fingers to toes, is working hard, especially my cardiac muscle. Plus, lurking below the surface, "thieves" plot to snatch my paddle. Rocks and squirrelly currents try to yank it from my grasp, but hooking a thumb under my Norse paddle's "T" grip prevents many a snatching.

To get to a better route, we sometimes turn MW's nose at a slight angle and allow the rushing water to push MW across to the other side of the river. This is called a ferry. We have to do two things: 1) maintain the proper angle so as not to let the river have its way with us and 2) propel ourselves forward—frantically, I might add—so as not to lose too much ground. In this current, we lose ground. Sometimes a lot. Sometimes the other side isn't better at all. Sometimes we get out and walk MW up through the shallows—a technique called frogging. We use MW for balance as we stumble along the stone-strewn bottom, slogging against knee-deep water intent on knocking us over.

Just ahead, Swan Falls Dam is a welcome sight. Behind it, we are in store for some slack water. After paddling with all my might or dragging a burdensome MW up between rocks through which she may not fit, I am *so* ready for a dam.

I don't even care how long the portage is. It can't be much worse than the struggle against this current. As we near the dam, we are ready for the usual stares of disbelief and angler's comments: "You're going the wrong way, ain't ya?" or "You're going *up* river?!" But already, since this intense current started just twelve days earlier, I feel my arms getting ever more powerful. While paddling toward the dam, I hear a crash and smash of dislodged rock coming towards us from the cliff above.

"Paddle!" Tom yells, and I somehow pour on more power. In three seconds, the hefty rock smashes into the water, a foot directly behind MW—and Tom's head. Its pounding, crashing descent from high above, and the final gulp by which the river swallows it, says all we need to know. This was no pebble. This substantial boulder, hell-bent on our trajectory, could have severely damaged the boat and us. We paddle onward in silence, trying to quell thoughts of what could have been: flipping or fracturing MW, or worse, smashing into Tom's noggin. I am thankful for my powerful arms and quietly let God know I appreciate His looking after us. Soon, we come upon the inevitable angler access that provides an easy portage up to the lake.

Swan Falls Dam gives us about eight miles of relatively trouble-free, slack water. Then it's back to heaving, ferrying, lining, and frogging. As unpoetic and unromantic as I am, I cannot help but spill my feelings for this river in my journal:

Oh Snake River
Sometimes you make me toil
My muscles strain
My lungs heave
In this you make me strong
Oh Snake River
Sometimes you make me cry
I can't push against you
My body is too weak
Yet we go our separate ways
In this you teach me endurance
Oh Snake River
Sometimes you make me smile
Sweeping by majestic cliffs
Doubling their beauty
In the reflection of your flatwater
Snatching it as your own.
In this you teach me serenity.

123

MW Takes a Solo Run

Day 66 (August 18): Returning from today's three-hour siesta to escape the scorching heat of midday, Tom and I wander back toward our canoe and stop by the shore. With a quizzical look, he asks the burning question, "Didn't we park MW here?"

I scan the deserted shoreline with a growing sense of alarm. "Yes . . . yes . . . this is the spot."

But the canoe containing all our belongings is nowhere to be seen. With my stomach in a knot, I realize she shoved off without us. The water had risen so high it set her afloat. Dropping all but his PFD, Tom starts running downstream like a madman. We run on the bank, straining to see her in an eddy or around the next bend. I hear Tom cussing himself out for not tying her up. It is not like us to leave her unfettered, but the lack of hitching posts or even sticks to sink into the mud forced us to haul her up as far as we could and leave her at that.

We tear through underbrush, get scratched by the needle-sharp seed heads of teasels, leap over rock beds, jog cow paths, and founder through muck that sucks off my shoe. Yanking it out and putting it back on puts me even more behind. After about ten minutes and no sightings, I am plumb tuckered. "Tom, stop . . . wait . . . I can't keep up."

Tom waits for me. He is visibly more irate than tired. We had covered about a mile to a big bend we frogged MW around earlier. The water here is fast, not fast enough to flip MW, but fast enough to give her a vigorous boost. From our vantage point, we cannot see her in the half-mile visible to us downriver. "We've got to get a boat," Tom said, "and fast."

I am glad he is working on Plan B rather than outracing her.

Bent over, hands on knees, I try to catch my breath. I think I voice his mind when I gasp, "At least we know MW can only go as far as the dam."

Looking around, we spot a farmhouse on the other side of the field. We clamber over the fences and jog over to introduce ourselves to the Johnstons. I politely yet desperately explain our plight. I cannot say what they thought of two exhausted people wearing life jackets happening in on them on foot, but our story must have been believable. They say they do not have a boat and are just visitors but will be glad to drive us down to the dam.

The Johnstons decide to make a family outing of it. Soon all six of us are in the four-wheel-drive vehicle. Eva, the mom, sits in the back with us, asking us all sorts of questions and providing commentary about the countryside. Her son Sam is at the wheel. He is donned in a white age-thinned T-shirt, sporting a full beard and work-worn hands. Sam's wife, Sandy, sits up front with their fourteen-month-old daughter Shannon.

I soon conclude that this offer of theirs is more than just a drive down the road. We head out an old road along the river, but it soon peters out, and we have to turn back. It is a twenty-mile drive to the dam, only a third of which is paved. As we bounce along small farm roads, the dust flies in through the open windows. I breathe through my bandana. Eva continues with her guided tour, interspersed with questions about our expedition. I answer and try to be sociable while trying not to get carsick. Heading down yet another bumpy, dusty road at long last, we arrive at Swan Falls Dam. The road leads us across a bridge to a locked gate.

I eagerly hop out and jog over to the Idaho Power Company office to find someone to open the gate and inquire about a motorboat. The haggard man on duty first remarks that we shouldn't have come in from that way. However, having determined extenuating circumstances, he goes down to open the gate and let the Johnstons through. We drive over to a small cluster of houses to see if we can find anyone with a boat. The Johnstons wait to see if we connect. After knocking on the doors of a couple of houses, we find our man. Steve is a friendly guy, a motorboat owner. After hugs and our profuse thanks to our rescuers, the Johnstons depart via the "legal" route.

Steve listens to our plight and, without hesitation, makes the necessary arrangements to motor us up the river. He is only one of two in town who owns a powerboat, so we luck out to find him. He gives us each a huge cup of water. I devour mine immediately. Tom downs his even faster. Soon we hop in his boat and zoom upriver. Steve works at the dam, as do all the folks who live in this little community, which I figure is somewhere in the realm of twelve. He seems happy to help.

During our boat ride, Steve advises us to check with Idaho Power Company in Glenns Ferry for river information. He thinks the dams above here have the potential to cause us more trouble. It was C. J. Strike Dam, our next hurdle, which was the culprit of our mishap. It was releasing during our midday break.

I keep my eyes peeled on one side of the river and Tom the other side. I have conflicting hopes. I don't want to see MW too soon, as that would mean redoing hard-earned mileage. Then again, I want to ease my anxiety. But what I wish plays no factor in the result. We will find her wherever she is and take it from there.

"Hey, there she is!" I shout and point. Steve maneuvers us close, and we climb out on the rocks near her. She is upright, and everything is intact. She stopped in a little eddy about four miles down from where she began her solo journey. We give Steve our hearty, sincere thanks, and he wishes us luck as I ease his boat out into deeper water so he can be on his way.

While paddling this four-mile stretch again, we happen by a distressed little shorebird chick floating in the water. I scoop it up and look the little guy over. It is mostly brown, with spots of rust and white; the bill is short and slightly curved, and the splayed, long-toed feet are not webbed for paddling. I don't know what kind of bird he is, other than fish bait here in the water. We ease MW's nose into the shore and let the little feller scamper up the bank, where we hope he might fare better. With all the favors and effort perfect strangers showered upon us today, I'm hoping that helping this little guy might, in some way, pay it forward.

Moonlight Paddle

Day 69 (August 21): Today, we portage C. J. Strike Dam without much trouble. Actually, "portage" is synonymous with "trouble." What I mean is that it went without an overabundance of pain, agony, and cursing. Only just the right amount. The half mile in three trips works out to two and a half miles total. This accomplishment earns us a noonday breather in Idaho Power's little oasis here at our put-in. We lie on the lush green grass, beneath shade trees in the hot, dry desert. A comfortable bed could hardly be sweeter.

"This'll be our last still water for a while now," Tom remarks.

"Hmmm—it's going to be luxurious, going so fast with so little effort," I say with a slight smile, relishing the thought.

"Ya know how we've been talking about paddling by moonlight sometime?"

"Yeah . . ." I lean on an elbow, now getting a hint of where he's going.

"The moon's nearly full tonight."

"Well, let's do it." He didn't have to sell me on the idea.

"What do ya say we get going around eight?"

"Good. What do we do in the meantime?"

"Let's stash MW and go for a walk into civilization."

We find our way to a dim and dingy neighborhood bar. A lot of folks are escaping the heat in here. Tom orders a beer, I get pop, and we find a table to sit down. "What is this here?" I point to the markings on the table.

"It's a cribbage board," Tom remarks.

"What's cribbage?"

"It's a game. I'll teach you."

Tom's inadequacies in teaching me soon attract the attention of another bar patron. I think he could hear my voice rising in exasperation. The stranger's explanations are clear and concise and make sense to me. I whoop Tom soundly. I like this game.

By the time we head back for supper, my stomach feels funny, and my head aches. I feel kind of sluggish. Maybe my body is objecting to too much time indoors. I hope supper will remedy the situation.

Tom takes charge tonight since I'm feeling poorly. I guess he figures "Potted Meat Food Product" would be just the thing to put my stomach right. Once Tom fries it up with onion, rice, sweet-and-sour sauce and a can of mixed veggies, you could barely recognize the stuff. I don't feel much better after supper, but we shove off anyway.

Dusk is such a beautiful time of day. The sun has set, but I can make out some color behind the cloud cover. "I don't think we're going to see the moon tonight," I remark.

"I don't think so either. We'll paddle as long as we can." Nothing but placid piddles ripple the water surface. For ten blissful minutes we paddle in silence. Then, in front of us, I see the water rippling. The rippling keeps advancing, closer and closer, until it is upon us— the gust of wind blasts my face.

"Wow—did you feel that?"

"Oh, yeah," Tom replies. The wind is now shaking the shoreline trees that were just a moment ago stock-still. This is the storm's fair warning. "I guess our midnight paddle will have to be put on hold."

"Yeah, let's head for shore." Big raindrops are now plopping on the water and us. As luck would have it, a cove is conveniently apparent. A prominent Russian olive tree behind a tall rock mound has a flat, grassy spot underneath. This is perfect. The embankment provides complete protection from the wind. In the ten minutes it takes to paddle to the spot, unload, and set up, the wind on the other side of our protective barrier is blow-your-hat-off powerful. Whitecaps cover the lake. Fueled from the hustle and not yet ready for sleep, we scurry into the tent.

"How about I whoop you in a game of cribbage?" I suggest. Tom shuffles around, managing to pull his deck of cards out of his pack; he tosses it to me. "They're all in a clump," I observe. Apparently, they dried in a wad after our lock dunking. The game begins by having to pry the plastered cards apart. Yet another storm passes as we huddle in our little green tent, playing boardless cribbage with stiff, crinkly cards. When we finally nod off to sleep, Tom's arm is around me, my head on his chest, queasy stomach long forgotten.

Island Hopping

Day 71 (August 23): After a luxurious thirty-two miles and three days on C. J. Strike flatwater, the river is back to its old tricks. We make acceptable progress—until we hit islands. I'm tired of islands. The benefit of their downriver eddy in no way compensates for the onslaught we have to power through on its upriver side. Islands also channel water into deeper, faster torrents, requiring feverish paddling. Then there are the acrobatic exits when the water gets too shallow to paddle. Clutch the gunnels and leapfrog over the side. I finally understand why this technique is called frogging. Walk MW through the shallows, holding onto her gunnel, until it is deep enough to grab a bite with the paddle. Then, hop in and start paddling straightaway, not to lose momentum. While the stern person gives a final shove, take care to keep MW always pointed into the current. We pump water for a while more until time to hop out again.

This upriver paddling continues to require shouting directions to one another. A regular-conversation voice won't do. We have to contend with the tumult of tumbling water through rapids and the din of ever-present wind.

"Left!" I holler.

"What?" Tom responds.

I turn my head to throw my voice over my shoulder as best I can. "LEFT," I shout louder. We will hit a log on our present course alongside this island. I could, at the last second, draw MW's nose out into the current to avoid it, but then the river would snatch her and turn her downstream. It would be a bear to bring her back. Tom has to ease the whole of MW to the left so her nose is always pointed directly upriver. This way, she sheds water to the sides and slices right through.

"Okay. A little crossbow," Tom instructs. Without changing the position of my hands, I bring my paddle to the other side of the boat. Reaching out as far as I can, I draw the water toward me. This brings MW's nose toward the paddle and keeps us in line with the current. "That's enough!" As we ease on by the offending obstacle, I bring my paddle back to my side of the canoe.

At the end of the island, we get out to stretch our legs. Tom wants to check the map. In a moment, Tom explodes. "Eieeeeee!"

He shrieks a rather unmanly scream and throws the map in the air, grabbing his face. I quickly shove MW to shore and sprint and splash my way downstream to snatch the map from the water where it is swiftly floating away. Tom continues to rant and rave, clawing at his face. "Yellowjackets!" he shouts between curses. "He got me on the nose!" He runs from the point of impact, still emitting wild outbursts, throws himself down on hands and knees, and plants his face squarely in the cold river water.

"I see them. They're all over," I say as I splash my way around him and dash back to the canoe. Our presence indeed displeases these angry flying, stinging, leave-no-prisoners Jedi insects. "Tom, we gotta get out of here," I say as I slip MW back into the water and hop in the bow.

Tom yanks his head out of the river and charges toward MW. "Yeah, let's GO!" He shoves off so hard it nearly gives me whiplash. We power away, motivated like never before.

The angry swarm readily gives chase. Going upriver in a canoe is not an expedient escape plan. Nevertheless, as we stroke and swat, stroke and swat, we somehow put the irate mob behind us without further damage.

The next morning, I crawl out of the tent to find Tom sitting on his Therm-a-Rest chair, holding my washcloth, wet with cold river water, on his face. "Let's see." He removes the washcloth. "Wowww." I step back. "You look like you were in a barroom brawl." His nose and cheek are puffed up like a chubby infant's, and his eye is swollen nearly shut.

"I feel like I got punched."

"Poor baby," I lean over to kiss his unswollen forehead. "I'll take care of breakfast."

Probably the most anticipated event for any expedition, except for meeting one's goal, is the advent of a mail drop. A package with cookies or letters boosts our spirits days on end. In the weekly phone call home, we report to our families the chosen town for a mail stop perhaps two weeks ahead. It has to be a small town right on the river but big enough to have a grocery store and amenities sufficient to meet our needs. It can't be a ghost town.

On the other hand, big cities would not do either. That would involve hiking much too far, and there is less of an opportunity for a safe stash of MW and our gear. Glenns Ferry, Idaho, is our destination. Our pleasure begins the moment we walk into the post office.

"Paddle for Water's here!" the cheery postmaster announces, inclining his head toward unseen postal workers beyond our sight. We are in our PFW shirts that wordlessly proclaim who we are. "Have we got things for you!" he announces, disappearing into the back. I can't help but grin at Tom, partly in Christmas-like anticipation and partly because his chubby little face has that effect on me. The postmaster reappears with an armload of parcels.

We spend some minutes chatting about the nature and condition of the river, about which he seems quite knowledgeable, and about the reason for Tom's fat face. But due to other customers and an anxiousness to open our treasures, we depart. As we turn to go, he remembers an important point: "Don't drink Snake River water! If you do, you'll be forced to return to live in Idaho." We thank him for his warning but think that living in Idaho wouldn't be bad at all.

Sure enough, a box from my mom is here. It contains Dad's Nikon FE camera, a letter from my sister, Anne, and homemade cookies. A package from Mom isn't complete without cookies. We also receive Missouri River maps, a letter from Dwight and from our Texas friend Lydia.

My Nikkormat had failed to produce good pictures lately. The routine is to send the exposed film away in mailers, and the finished slides get sent to my dad. On a recent weekly phone call, Dad reported that the light meter must be off because severe overexposure and underexposure occurred in adjacent frames. Now Dad's camera is here.

As directed by our motorboat friend Steve, we hike on over to the Idaho Power Company to inquire about the river ahead. We still are not sure how far we can go up this thing. The woman there is not nearly as informative as the postman. We leave, having learned that it is impossible to canoe up to this point. Non-canoeists don't understand how crafty a canoe can be.

Blasted Boulders

Day 76 (August 28): Today we find ourselves down in a very narrow canyon—one that the river has been eroding for a very long time. Up above these towering basalt cliffs lies a hot, flat Idaho desert. The river itself is constricted, with a swift current in the middle, but strong shore eddies enable us to sneak up along the edges. Occasionally, we get out and frog. As captain today, I utilize eddies behind the occasional boulder to draw us upward. Then, at just the right time, with MW pointed straight into the onrush, we power our way through the pillow, putting one boulder after another behind us. It amazes me to watch MW defy the forces against her and to think that this is possible purely from the muscle power provided by Tom and me.

Boulders, both above the surface and lurking below, become more frequent and troublesome. When a protruding boulder doesn't allow us to either frog or paddle MW around it, it's a mite problematic. Tom's experience with canoe tricks comes in handy. He instructs me how to line MW around. We tie a throw rope to extend MW's bow painter; then one person, positioned upriver of the boulder, pulls her around the jutting shoreline obstacle while the other holds the stern line for guiding purposes. This technique works fine until . . .

There it is, looming in front of us—a humongous boulder. It emerges out of the cliff on the northern shore and protrudes well into the water, constricting the river into a forceful, exuberant channel. The other side of the river offers no paddling alternative, as the sheer rock cliff drops straight down to disappear underneath the deep, rushing water. This is no good. As we approach the boulder from below, we can see water surging around this menace. We pull out onto the pebbly shore in the calm eddy behind the rock.

We clamber over the twenty-foot-tall river-worn monstrosity near the cliff and find we can stand on top of the boulder and behold a decent class II rapid. "This would be fun to go down," Tom remarks.

"Yeah, but we're going up." I state the obvious. Out of my league here, I have to rely on Tom's expertise.

"We can do it, though"—he responds to the trepidation in my voice. "We can line MW around like we've done before. We'll tie the throw rope to MW's bow line." The bow person has to climb up and over the boulder with MW's painter, and that would require the additional length.

"This is where we'll need our whistles," Tom instructs. The sound of the rushing water drowns out loud voices, even close together. Plus, with the boulder between us, we'll not be able to see each other. Whistles are standard equipment on our PFD zippers, so we each test their effectiveness with a loud TOOT. "One blast means "ready," two blasts means "go," and three blasts means "stop." Got it?"

"Got it," I said, not at all confident.

"Do you want the bow or the stern?" He asks me this only because I am captain today. One look at my face, and he takes charge.

"Why don't I take the bow? I'll go around to the other side of the boulder and let you know when I'm ready. Then you ease her out from behind the rock, set her straight in the current, and I'll pull her through."

"Okay." It seems workable in theory, and it has worked in practice many a time already on a much smaller scale. I am so grateful for Tom's expertise in moments like these.

We climb back down to MW and prep her. Taking the throw rope extension, Tom climbs up and over the rock. I stand ready in the eddy of the boulder with MW parallel to the flow.

A toot indicates that Tom is all set. I toot toot back as I ease MW into faster water out from behind the monstrosity. All of a sudden, MW goes out way too far. I cannot reach her rear end to guide her. I see the bowline taut as Tom pulls, but it only serves to dip her bow down into the oncoming current. We are taking on water. In an instant, she weighs a ton. I watch, flabbergasted, as a heavily laden MW takes off down the river unaccompanied.

I start rock-hopping after her. Tom soon passes me because he is swimming after her. It is indeed a quicker mode of travel, and I am tiring fast, so I hop in too. *Wow, this river moves!* In the foot-first floating position, I bounce off rocks and guide myself into the main flow. *Oh, how could this happen! What went wrong?*

I pray for MW to stop soon. Both Tom and MW are now out of sight. I can't just go with the flow if I am ever to catch up with her. I have to put in some extra effort, so I use my arms to propel me faster downstream. After chasing MW for twenty minutes without success, I see Tom rock-hopping along shore. Bumping and bouncing off rocks, I direct myself over to an eddy and climb out to meet him.

Tom huffs and puffs. "I made some headway rock-hopping, but not enough." He pauses to gulp for air. Between a few more gasps,

"She's floating okay, though," he says. "We'll never gain on her this way." Tom looks up above. I follow his gaze.

"What are you thinking?"

"Our only alternative is to climb out of this canyon and head over to I-84, hitch a ride down to King Hill, and get ahead of her."

I look at the canyon wall. Unlike many spots, this is not exactly sheer. It is, however, one of the tallest we've seen so far in this canyon. I give him one of those, "Are you kidding me?!" kind of looks. He reads it right. "Can you think of anything better?" Put that way, it doesn't seem so outlandish.

"No," I admit. "I'll follow you."

He takes off for the two hundred-foot slope with me in hot pursuit. It is grueling. Every step forward slides back at least half the distance—like trying to go up the down escalator. We have no choice but to keep at it. I try every technique my brain comes up with—dig feet in hard, take big steps, scramble on all fours. Tom must have more adrenalin than I, as he slowly ascends. On two occasions, my legs flatly defy me. They refuse to go. After spending all this time canoeing, they have gotten wimpy, and now when I need them, they fail me.

Exhausted, I finally crest the top, where I see Tom running on the ridge. I have no idea where his strength comes from. He turns to spot me and calls, "I see MW!" as he points excitedly down into the canyon. "Come on! We might catch her."

Stumbling to my feet to try to run after him, I realize I would only slow him down. I wave him on. *Stupid wimpy legs*, I think as I stumble again to my hands and knees, heaving with every breath. Seeing Tom racing off, I run and stumble and run some more on my spaghetti legs for a good fifteen minutes. I finally meet up with Tom, who is ambling back my way.

"I can't catch her from here," he says, defeat and exhaustion in his voice. Let's go over to the highway to get a ride."

I don't know how common it is to see exhausted, arm-waving, soaking-wet, PFD-clad hitchhikers in the desert of Idaho, but I suspect not common. Because of our most desperate, pleading looks, the third car stops for us. (Yes, two cars pass us by!) Even this fellow has to think about it for several seconds as he eases over to the shoulder well beyond us. We run after him as he backs up.

"It's usually my policy to not pick up hitchhikers, but you look like you need some help." This young businessman says he's on his way to Boise. He readily takes us to King Hill. In no less than ten minutes' drive on the highway, we see a sign: Glenns Ferry, 1-mile. Sheesh, we were here two days ago! As he lets us out, we bid our quickest but most grateful thanks.

Immediately, we make our way upriver. My stupid legs are still wobbly, and I stumble and bumble along the ridge. We adopt a search method: I stop at a vantage point to search the river below (and catch my breath) while Tom jogs past me to the next spot with a good view. I trot past him and so on. After two or three miles of hopscotching, Tom shouts . . . points . . . and jumps down the cliff. I look. There she is, sitting quietly in an eddy on the other side of the river.

I giggle with delight and relief, skidding down the steep embankment. At the bottom, we wade into the river and ferry-float across. I fall across MW and kiss her gunwale.

Conducting a quick survey, we find four things missing: a Mitchell paddle, a Norse paddle, the maps, and a seat cushion. We bail her, then float her downriver to the only feasible campsite in view.

Tom strings a huge drying line while I unload MW. If those packs were filled with bowling balls, they would have been lighter. Once MW is empty, we assess her wounds: two sizable cracks amidships on both sides all the way through. She must have breached on a rock with considerable force. We certainly can't travel with a boat practically split in half.

"I can duct-tape her so she'll not take on too much water," Tom declares; "then we can load her up and paddle on down to King Hill and call Dick and Josie." These are our friends in Pocatello.

"But NOT today!" I stipulate. "Tomorrow." There is no way my muscles would allow me to move anymore today.

Drying out after MW's solo run.

Precious little escaped wetness. Our drying line, made up of every bit of rope we possess, is strung between every available tree and held up in between by paddles. Once the line is thusly decorated, I collapse to the ground to survey our work.

With vengeful precision, the very moment I plunk my fanny down, dark, ominous clouds obscure the sun. A sudden wind gust sends our maps flying as the first big raindrops plop, plop, plop noisily about. With slumped shoulders and a soulful look toward Tom, I implore him, as if he had something to do with this turn of events. "In the midst of a drought in the desert, it decides to rain NOW?!"

I think I tripped a trigger. Tom raises his arms to the sky, fists shaking. "Come on!" he shouts to the thunder beings. "Is that all you've got?!" I watch the day's pent-up anxiety erupt from his very core. Dark clouds dribble a few more big drops. "COME ON!" he bellows, body now bent and tense. "WE CAN TAKE IT!" He stumbles back and falls exhausted to the ground, crossing his arms atop his knees to prop up his bowed head. I rise to console him, and as I do, the sky lights up. I gaze upward.

"Wow . . . Tom . . . look up." I gently stroke his bowed head. The clouds continue to roll out, revealing a glorious double rainbow. "You sure impressed those sky demons." Sharing a smile, we sit together to enjoy the show for a few minutes.

Soon, Tom is right with the world. "I'm going upriver to look for the paddles and stuff," he announces.

"Really!? Do you seriously expect to find them?"

"I don't know, but it's worth a try." I let him go, content to sit and peel apart the pages of my drenched wildflower book.

In a minute, I'm startled by his "Woo-hoo," and I look up. There stands Tom, brandishing a Mitchell paddle and seat cushion. Mr. Optimist strikes again. Shortly afterwards I hear whistling. This time he is holding up my Norse and the map bag—everything accounted for. Just the tonic needed to close the book on this unlucky day.

Despite our exhaustion, it is difficult to sleep. The tent is at a terrible slant, and my wound-up nerves take a while to unravel. My mind makes me relive the incident over and over. Tom similarly. We lie contentedly in the tent, Tom's arms wrapped around me, holding me close. This is the most reassured I've felt all day. Things are not so bad. We didn't lose anything. MW is perfectly repairable. And there are friends within driving distance willing to take us in for a breather.

Repair Reprieve

Day 79 (August 30): A week-long stay at Camp Wallabagatchie, as Dick affectionately calls this little abode, is a welcome respite. I share news of my family, whom Dick and Josie have known for years and get caught up on their news. I enjoy strolling around the yard with Josie, discovering how well Idaho suits them. We occasionally run errands with Dick, but generally we try to stay out of the way.

Tom calls Harry Roberts of Sawyer about our mishap. He offers to mail repair materials, but we had already bought some. We do happily accept a new bow seat. Ours has a crack that gives a fearsome butt pinch.

Dick puts us in touch with Ron, who oversees Idaho State University's Outdoor Program. He helps us review the river ahead. Ron asks if the Outdoor Program could sponsor an afternoon or evening presentation about our trip and we happily agree.

Aside from the soft, expansive bed, the best part is the thought-provoking after-dinner discussions, allowing me to know Dick and Josie as more than just my parents' friends.

Josie, a soft-spoken, endearing person, earns her living teaching what used to be called home economics, and she is an exceptional artist, particularly in photography and drawing. Her charcoal portraits of me and my brother and sister have long adorned our stairway at home. She tells me I am one of her favorite people. This flatters me speechless. I never realized I had shown any sign of a personality during our encounters while I was growing up.

On the outside, Dick is a lighthearted man, a virtuoso whistler. I believe no mockingbird or warbler could match his musical talents. Subsurface, Dick is an introspective philosopher. He suggests how ideal the world would be if we stripped people of their many labels:

no Catholics, vegans, engineers, mothers, or anything. If we could relate "human to human," societies would be more understanding and harmonious. Dick suggests truly knowing oneself is key.

After this evening's discussion, I can't help but think of Peter and Michael and the soul-searching opportunities I envisioned having. Was I kidding myself into believing that all life's answers would dawn on me if I undertook a challenging expedition? I still don't have a clue. I go to sleep that night wondering about my purpose and my choices.

Tom finally has all the supplies to patch up MW on our third day, and we are hard at work in the garage. He can get intense when he works, especially with resin that will harden if he doesn't get it where it's supposed to be soon after it's mixed. I am supposed to be helping, holding the patch in place until Tom slobbers it with enough resin.

"C'mon, you've got to be quicker!" Tom snaps. I thought I was used to his barking commands when he gets anxious. I attribute it to his hot-head Italian blood, but this time I lose it. An overwhelming sense of despair overtakes me. Tears gather strength and number that I can't hold back.

"No," I shout, hurling the patch at Tom. I rip off my latex gloves, barge into the house, and bolt down the stairs to dive headfirst onto my soft, cushy bed. The dam bursts. I am helpless to control the flood. Questions fly around my brain like tired birds in desperate need of a perch. *Who am I? What am I supposed to be doing with my life?* Realizing I have no answers fuels my cry again and again and again. *There is nothing positive about me. I am a useless, meaningless un-known.* I try to muffle my wails in my pillow. *What's the matter with me?* I berate, question, and cry until, mercifully, I fall asleep.

I awaken to the announcement of "suppertime." *How much time has passed?* I take account of my behavior as I sit up. I can usually hold my emotions in check. But boy, this time, that didn't happen. I plant my feet on the floor, take a mental check of myself, and nod. I'm feeling better.

Tears and sleep seem to have provided motivation and clarity. It occurs to me now that continuing this paddling expedition is exactly what I need to give my life purpose. I vow to see this endeavor through to the end.

As I head upstairs, an urge to get back on the river takes up residence in my soul. With no amount of uncertainty, I can feel it settling in. This hunger is not satiated by a meal. This pull, this urge, does not stop pestering me until I set my paddle in the water.

Tom completed the repair fine without me. We await the arrival of a new seat, which in two days' time makes its appearance, and Tom promptly installs it.

River Solitude

Day 85 (September 6): We stayed an entire week at Camp Wallabagatchie. It feels much longer. I get the feeling we overstayed our visit but am helpless to do anything about it. Recently, conversations have shortened, and interactions lessened.

Someday, I think, *I'm going to make it up to them. I'm not sure how right now, but I will.* We express our most grateful thanks, and Dick and Josie sign our thank-you paddle.

Dick drives us a long distance to put us back in. He drops us off at Milner Dam, about 84 miles upriver from where we took out in King Hill. This put-in gets us back in the swing of things, paddling a reservoir. Together with Hells Canyon, we have bypassed 189 miles of perilous whitewater on the Snake River.

I feel nothing but relief and joy. Right now, I like the sense of being an isolationist. I always love to hear those stories of hermits living in the woods alone in a shack for years and years before anyone "civilized" finds them—like the guy who lived in a huge (I mean HUGE) stump in the Smokies, complete with bed and all. There, in the wilderness, with only your wit and skill to feed, clothe, and entertain yourself, dependent on no one, in debt to no one—to me, this is truly appealing.

Today, as we wave goodbye to Dick, I am in love with that feeling. No one has to feel obligated to cook us dinner or cancel plans because we are around. I am relieved that they can carry on in their usual fashion. I'm glad we don't have to inflict ourselves on anyone anymore. I don't even want to camp near civilized places. I want to be alone with Tom on the river. I want to sleep in a tent. I want to feel the unencumbered freedom of skinny-dipping. With all its hardships and danger, the river is the only place I can be happy right now. Contentment swarms through me as we paddle Milner Reservoir. My assimilation into a river lifestyle is far and away complete.

CHAPTER 5

Tribulations and Glories

I think a lot of people want to go back to basics sometimes, to get their bearings. For me a good way to do that is to get into nature by canoe—to take myself as far away as possible from everyday life, from its complications and from the artificial wants created by civilization. Canoeing forces you to make a distinction between your needs and your wants.

—Pierre Elliott Trudeau

Pushing Ever Upward

Day 86 (September 7): Today we greet Burley, Idaho. It does not return the favor. The wind tries its best to push us back from whence we came. I bow my head to point the brim of my baseball cap downward so the incessant headwind doesn't flip it off.

I'm now used to doing my job of paddling despite weather conditions. In downpouring rain I plant, pull, feather; plant, pull, feather. I poke my knee up from underneath my spray skirt, forcing the accumulating lap puddle to run off. In scorching heat I plant, pull, feather; plant, pull, feather. I dip my bandanna in the water and tie it around my neck to cool off. In driving wind, I plant, pull, feather; plant, pull, feather. I yank my hat on tighter lest the wind steal it. Each weather condition brings a slight variation in how I do my job. Adds spice to life.

While I paddle mile after mile, the sights and sounds that surround me often fade out of existence. Singing and conversation cease. My thoughts turn inward with every hypnotic stroke of my paddle as the canoe slices through the water. Plant, pull, feather. I lull myself into a contentment that fills my soul. Plant, pull, feather. I am conscious of only myself, alone, a tiny speck in the universe yet wholly complete and even radiant. Plant, pull, feather. Serenity and gratitude fill my soul. It is all I can do to keep from crying.

Before tears burst forth, I shake myself out of my reverie and peer below my hat brim to enjoy viewing some lovely homes on the southern shore. Many have sailboats, and all have private ramps and neatly trimmed lawns. I imagine living in one as I plant, pull, feather. *Which one would suit me? This one with all the windows facing the water?* Plant, pull, feather. *No, that one is more rustic and more my style.*

Plant, pull, feather. *What would I do with all that space?* Plant, pull, feather. *It's a lot to have to maintain.* Plant, pull, feather. *No, none of these would suit me.* The idea of ownership and its accompanying responsibilities is as distasteful to me as a mouthful of dirt. I'm content right now to simply plant, pull, feather.

"We're 950 miles from the ocean," Tom announces as we relax at our campsite outside Burley, Idaho, that night. He is an avid record keeper. He keeps track of how many bridges we pass under, how many power lines we paddle beneath, and how many nights we've spent in the tent instead of under the stars or beneath a roof.

"We've come a long way," I respond.

"Yup, Burley's 4,150 feet above sea level." This bit of trivia, usually just a point of minor interest, takes on new meaning for cross-country canoeists.

I look up from my journal. "Really?"

"Yup." He rattles off the statistics for me. A lot of the elevation gain was through locks. Columbia River locks raised us up 333 feet, and Snake River locks brought us up roughly 404 feet more. Our ride around Hells Canyon brought us up perhaps another 1,000 feet at the most. But no matter how we figure it, we gained significant elevation with paddle power alone. Tom keeps going, "We've gained 1,600 feet just since Glenns Ferry, twelve days ago."

"Wow, so that's why the temps are nearly half." A week ago we were baking in shorts and swimsuits, basting ourselves in the river and conducting crepuscular paddling. Now temperatures dip into the low fifties, and I'm regularly found, as now, in long pants and a wool sweater.

"Well, elevation and time both," Tom said without looking up from his map. I could see he was already concerned about our rate of progress and the obvious passing of summer. We still have a long way to go, and we can fairly well guess that the river will only get more difficult the higher up we go.

Across the river, we see the Cotterel Mountains. Unlike the lush green tree-covered mountains we are used to seeing on the East Coast, these mountains are brown and sparsely vegetated with scraggly yet tenacious trees. Neatly arranged by height, the rounded mountains rise in successive layers, higher and higher until the highest, most distant peak, Mount Harrison, stretches 9,200 feet into the sky. As we speak, dark, ominous cumulonimbus clouds move to obscure it. Time to make haste in erecting the tent. Just before the downpour, we crawl inside.

After the rain, the air is refreshingly crisp. Not yet bedtime, I crawl out of the tent and suck the fresh, invigorating sagebrush-scented air deep into my lungs. Only a minor species until the mid-1800s, sagebrush has taken over the landscape. Cattle have ravaged the prairie grasses, allowing it to flourish. Its sharp, scratchy branches make it unpleasant to encounter and unpalatable for cattle. Now, the aroma of sagebrush almost makes me want to forgive it for its less-desirable qualities.

This evening we are sung to sleep by the strange, eerie cries of coyotes. Doglike yapping and howling ascend to wailing and screaming. The frenzied supernatural sound is hard to envision coming from an animal. As I listen this evening, I think about why Native Americans revered that clever trickster Coyote and imbued him with so many powers.

According to Nez Perce stories, Coyote was chief of all the animals. He named the indigenous peoples who spread out all over the land.

The Flathead tribe tells many a tale of Coyote—an avid traveler who encounters and slays giants and kills man-eating babies. Swimming rocks chase him. As a deity, Coyote is granted anything he wishes but nevertheless dies upon occasion. Upon his death, his friend fox comes to jump over his bones, whereupon he returns to life.

Coyote gets resurrected until he wishes to eat the last of three pig brothers who had built themselves a lovely house. Coyote tries to wile himself inside without success until he comes down the chimney. Sound familiar? Little pig quickly builds a fire in the fireplace where Coyote falls and burns to death. Fox is not there to jump over him, so that's the end of Coyote and the last of the Flathead Coyote tales.

To me, the howl of coyotes is the quintessential sound of wilderness. That night I revel in the feeling that we are truly ensconced in nature's realm. I am a part of the raw and intricate world of wildlife.

I try to perpetuate this intimacy with nature during our daytime paddles too. But my hope that all people can appreciate this connection fades as we paddle along. Never a day goes by that I am not reminded of human meddling. Plastic bags flap among the grasses on the riverbank; beer cans litter the shore; fishing line in tree branches sways in the wind; tires blemish the bottom of the river. Even old car bodies appear along the riverbanks, intentionally placed by farmers in an attempt to prevent their cropland from sloughing into the river.

An attempt at erosion control on the Snake River.

We pull off the river about a mile below the Register Rock picnic area on the south shore. Here is a valley covered with grasses, Russian olives, willows, and junipers. An exceptionally wet spot is home to cattails and rushes. The most notable landmark here, amid a neatly cut grassy field, is a little sheet metal-roofed shack walled on two sides. It is carpeted inside, equipped with a vinyl-covered table, wood stove, trash can, and workbench. On the shelf sits a toy cap machine gun. On a beam, a bumper sticker reads: I'M NOT A DIRTY OLD MAN, JUST A SEXY SENIOR CITIZEN. The old fella's hangout also has a full can of beer and a wine cooler. Tempting—but we leave them alone.

The sexy senior citizen's place is not quite as nifty as our lunch spot of a few days earlier. PEE WEE'S DOGHOUSE was a three-sided, canvas-roofed affair. It was furnished with two bus seats and a queen-sized mattress protected in plastic on a sturdy box frame. The mattress was clean, in excellent shape. Tom was disappointed it wasn't time to stop for the night, but even so, I thought it best not to relive the *Goldilocks* affair.

Register Rock is a sandstone boulder memorializing graffiti scratched into it by Oregon Trail pioneers. The travelers paused here to rest. Scraping their names in the rock, they wanted it known they made it this far. Now the rock has a protective shelter built around it and a picnic area where today's travelers can also pause to rest, but alas, names are no longer accepted on the register.

A few miles further north is a place the Oregon Trail travelers called "Gate of Death" or "Devil's Gate." As if those names were not morbid enough, today it is known by the morose if not accurate name of "Massacre Rock." It is a narrow passage through which the Oregon Trail passed, where travelers feared ambush by hostile natives who were getting tired of intruders tromping through their land. The apprehension was not unfounded as in 1862, Shoshone Indians skirmished with the immigrants not far from this site. Ten pioneers died. Massacre Rock is now a State Park, complete with campgrounds, visitor center, river access, horseshoe pitching area, and dump station, among other amenities. Disturbance by the natives is no longer considered a threat. We take advantage of the ever-precious campground showers before heading into nearby American Falls for another long-awaited mail drop.

How Far Can We Go?

Day 91 (September 12): We get a ride into American Falls from a highway construction worker. There, we fawn over letters from family and a surprise letter and donation from Bill, a high school friend of mine. I LOVE mail drops! His letter is so delightfully unexpected, and his gracious spirit touches me. After the post office, we treat ourselves to the most divine lunch I could ever imagine—a submarine sandwich. All those fresh veggies, meats, and soft squishy bread make my taste buds dance with joy. My tongue frolics in the mayonnaise. My fresh-food-craved body wouldn't let my mind forget this meal for days. We require one more stop at the visitor center to inquire about the river's character from here on up. An experienced-looking woman whose advice we feel we can trust tells us she doesn't think the few ripples around Eagle Rock will be of any consequence. We depart merrily.

Eagle Rock is just four miles upriver from our pull-out at Massacre Rocks. Our understanding is that it is a huge, solitary cliff in the middle of a constricted section of the river. The perfect recipe for fast rapids. But we have the inside scoop from the visitor center lady. We hop in MW, full of confidence at being able to put this thing behind us. Soon after passing the boat launch for Massacre Rocks State Park, we see the monstrosity. It stands bold and defiant mid-river, forcing water around it on either side. We inch up a couple of eddies but then encounter steep walls; no more eddies—only noisy rapids as far as the eye can see.

"This is not going to work," Tom announces. He is in the stern and captain today.

"I'm with ya," I shout over my shoulder as I continue to paddle so that we don't lose ground.

Ever willing to do whatever needs to be done, Tom sees we have to switch tactics. "Let's peel out and go down to the boat launch. We'll have to portage this thing."

"I'm with ya."

Tom paddles forward as I draw MW's nose out into the current, and this "peel out" swings us around facing downstream. "Woohoo—look at us go!" I exclaim in sharp contrast to the slow, laborious progress we made in the opposite direction. Before long, we pull out at the Massacre Rocks State Park boat launch—again.

Lugging personal packs first, we trudge along a narrow path on the river's edge made by sheep or cows or something. After a mile, we dump our load and go back for more. On the way back, we find a dirt road that would be much better for our second trip with the canoe.

"We shouldn't take advice from a non-river person," I comment to Tom to try to block out his bitter diatribe coming from under the upside-down canoe.

"Wouldn't-a-made any difference," Tom mutters. "God! This is heavy."

"Yeah, you would have wanted to try those Class IIs anyway," I observe.

"It would be better than this," and he spewed some expletives before bellowing, "AAHHH," as he rolls MW over his shoulder with a crash onto the trail by his side. "We're going to have to strip 'er down." MW by herself would not be a problem, but tripod, journal boxes, and fuel add considerable weight.

"Good." I like it when he comes to his senses.

"You keep going with the kitchen and water bags, and I'll get the boxes, fuel, and tripod."

"Then we'll come back and do MW together," I add, just to be explicit.

Portaging MW around rapids

A bit of advice here: even if a black-and-white snake crosses your path, keep going and just step over it. A hapless partner gets pretty upset if you stop short without warning while connected by a canoe overhead. The bump on Tom's forehead went away in a few days.

This night's camp is high on the bluff above the canyon, one mile away from our take-out. We hiked that mile five times to get all our stuff here. As soon as I hit the sack, visions of tomorrow's two-mile portage dance in my head.

After a hearty breakfast, I arrange myself like a pack mule. I transfer all the heavy books, binoculars, and lunch from the day pack into my own more supportive pack. Now relatively light, I strap the day pack to my pack. I hang my wet shoes from straps on my pack, put two paddles between the side pockets, and thread the arms of my PFD over the paddles. I carry the camera case and water bottles in front to counter the weight on my back. Tom likewise loads up his backpack with fuel bottles, rope bag, wet shoes, paddles, and PFD and lugs the first-aid kit and the other loose items. Off we trudge like a couple of old-fashioned peddlers bent at the waist, accouterments swaying in rhythm to our sauntering, overburdened, elephant-like gait.

Animal trails and a dirt road ultimately lead to an angler's spot, where we relieve ourselves of our incumbrances and rediscover upright posture and feel fleet-of-foot. From the anglers here, we learn Duck Falls, a small one-to-two-foot drop, is upriver yet. Not to worry. We determine from our conversation that we could probably shove MW up it. Even if we must tug her upriver, I'd rather MW carry all this heavy stuff.

With MW loaded up, we shove off. We haul MW up Duck Falls and a good many other small drops, exhaust ourselves paddling into the onrush of water deflected by boulders, and paddle merely strenuously in the few flatwater sections. Most time is spent outside the boat, making agonizingly slow progress.

American Falls is our next major obstacle to bypass. A city with the same name accompanies this waterfall, and a dam built upriver of the falls creates a nice big reservoir. Boy, am I looking forward to flatwater! The dam is not releasing water upon our arrival, so the falls are a mere trickle.

Arriving at a boat launch, we unload, repackage as before, then set out with our personal packs for the first trip. We hike up stairs, through a grassy spot, up to a fenced-in road, into a village, down Fort Hall Road, through a park, up to the railroad, along the tracks, over the barbed wire fence, across the highway to within sight of American Falls Reservoir. All that's left is to lug everything down the boulders to the water. Ugh.

"No way am I doing that hike again with a canoe on my head!" I say as I unceremoniously drop my load and plop down on my pack.

"I'll bring some ropes so we can solicit a ride with MW," Tom replies as he too, lets his load clunk heavily to the ground.

"That's what I'm talkin' about."

As we plod back for our second load, a kindhearted couple with their motorboat in tow, drive out of the boat launch as we arrive. The motorboater pulls alongside us to ask, "Where are you canoeing?" A curious question since we are not next to our canoe nor carrying paddles or giving any indication that we belong to that lonely canoe lying by the boat ramp.

When I ask how he knew, he replies, "With your tans, it couldn't be otherwise." Tom strikes up a friendly conversation. He does a great job leading up to our present situation. One cannot just come out and beg for a ride. No, this is uncouth. These things have to be approached quite skillfully. To my great delight, Tom—the motorboater—and Ann offer to take our stuff and us anywhere we wish.

"Want to go to Blackfoot?" Ann asks. She is a slight woman with a broad and ready smile. Blackfoot is almost fifty miles away. This is tempting, but we decline. We just need access to the reservoir.

Tom—the canoeist—explains that part of our gear is just above the dam. Tom and Ann gladly take us and our canoe down the dirt road to the spot where our stuff still sits. Then they deliver us to a much nicer put-in. Tom and Ann leave us with two candy bars, two cans of cold Coke, far fewer sore muscles, and a warm spot in our hearts.

Today marks a time for celebration. We have paddled 1,000 miles to reach American Falls. We go to A&W for a celebration feast. Once settled into our booth, I present Tom with a surprise I picked up at the market where we just shopped: one can of Spaghetti-O's, a Snickers bar, and one of those sugar-coated, preservative-laden apple pie things.

"Wow—you shouldn't have." Tom seems genuinely pleased and surprised, despite my having had to confiscate his wallet and kick him out of Ken's Market to make the purchases. "These are traditional river staples," he explains.

"I know. You told me before," I say. It is good to see him smile. "How could you have done without official river food for so long?"

"I don't know," he says, fondling the apple pie. "I'm going to hang on to these," he declares, putting them away in the food bag. I nod in approval. Anticipation is the best way to savor a special thing.

Determined to do something different and memorable to recognize this milestone, we conclude our bone-weary day by going bowling. I trounce Tom. Satisfied, full, and happy (I, the victor, was happier than Tom), we hike back to the river and our campsite. We sleep like woodchucks in winter.

The next day we shove off from American Falls and paddle into the wind until lunchtime when a marina that Tom and Ann told us about comes into view. It is downright civilized to eat lunch at a picnic table while reading a *USA Today* scrounged from a trashcan. While I work on my zillionth PB & J sandwich—our standard lunch item every single blessed day—Tom savors his Spaghetti-O's straight from the can with satisfying "Ummms" and slurpy sounds.

"Want some?" He holds out a spoonful.

Despite the tantalizing offer, I say, "No, I got it for you." Secretly, I lust for some and cast an envious glance in his direction with every yummy sound. I cut an apple and hold out Tom's half to him. We always share an apple at lunch—another habitual practice.

"No, you eat it. I've got my apple pie today."

I withdraw the apple, beginning to realize signs of civilization envy. We would be perfectly satisfied with PB & J if we were unaware of alternatives. Too much town exposure can corrupt a river person. Next thing you know, I'll be longing for a soft bed, potable water at the turn of a faucet, and the ability to travel sixty miles per hour at the turn of a key and mere flex of a foot. It's a dangerous yearning; I must not let myself fall victim to such desires. Then again, what civilized person would find so much happiness in a single can of Spaghetti-O's? Yes, our simple river life is just fine with me.

Windy and wavy American Falls Reservoir is not the easy paddling we were hoping for. Bouncing up and down on tossers is old hat, but I never let my guard down. Weight is low in the boat, life jackets are on, and I read each oncoming wave to make sure we slice through just right. In unison, we each lean over, plant, pull, and feather time and time and time again. It's too windy to converse. We just plant, pull, feather, plant, pull, feather.

The birdlife here is the perfect distraction. With eyes peeled, we notice Avocets, Northern Phalaropes, Forster's Terns, Canada geese, Western Grebes, American Coots, Pelicans, Least Sandpipers, and Ring-Billed Gulls. I see three ibis type birds fly overhead. They have long down-curved bills, narrow pointed wings with necks stretched out in front and feet trailing behind. I take in as many characteristics as possible to look them up when not so occupied. I am getting rather adept at identifying birds by their take-off and landing techniques.

Pelicans ease up out of the water, giving a few pushes with their large, webbed feet in tandem. In landing, with feet out front, they gracefully skate to a halt and settle contentedly on the water, folding wings just so. Mallards shoot almost straight out of the water in a flurry of wingbeats and skate to a landing like pelicans. Gulls depart the water at a more acute angle in a slower, more refined fashion. When ready to land, gulls slowly plunk down nearly helicopter style. Coots are the clowns of waterfowl. At take-off, wings beat furiously as legs seem to go round and round like a pinwheel on a windy day. They run like this on the water for thirty to forty feet to get enough speed for lift. Eventually, their fat little bodies are airborne, and the stubby little wings work hard to keep them that way. Landing is simply a splashdown. Splat splat splat splat splat—a group of them deposit themselves into the water as if dropped. Soon they bob up and down on the waves, paddling along in their cute clown manner. The western grebe, however, seeks food and security below the surface. Their contrasting black-and-white necks make them easily distinguishable from a distance. We only get brief glimpses because, in an instant, they disappear in a curvaceous surface dive. The stunt deserves a perfect "10" Olympic dive for minimal splash.

We continue to hopscotch on this uneven shoreline. Sometimes rock jetties stick out, with sandy beaches in between. I see a potato harvester way up on a clifftop and figure Idaho potatoes must grow here.

Sometimes the wind subsides, but it never goes away. Of the multitude of coves on the lake and only two named on the map, I try to figure out which is Little Hole and which is Big Hole. Our exact whereabouts on American Falls reservoir is never certain. No matter. Eventually, we'll get to the north end where the Snake River suddenly spreads out to become this lake.

American Falls reservoir has rather a strange trait. To look at it on a map, one would be certain a dam was on the northeast end because it ends so abruptly there; but no, the dam is on the southwest (downriver) end. Usually, lakes are gradual enlargements of a river, but not American Falls reservoir. The Snake River travels southwestward from the mountains and then boom—instantly it becomes three miles wide and it is called a reservoir. I mean instantly. Using our map and taking a compass bearing, we try to estimate exactly where the inlet is, but this approach doesn't work. Instead, our plan is to travel along the northern shore until we happen upon the inlet. Not only does the river channel empty into the lake closer to the northwest shore, but the southeast side of the lake is Fort Hall Indian Reservation. We have been adamantly warned—by a U.S. Fish and Wildlife employee—setting foot there would be unwise.

Abortion Point

Day 95 (September 16): We reach the end of the lake and turn southeast to look for the channel. Eventually, we get to a shallow, muddy area. The channel should be south of here. Soon enough, we come upon gushing water pouring into the lake from a constricted channel. The exuberant, tumbling water reminds me of a psyched-up football team smashing through their banner onto the field before a game. Tom aligns MW's nose straight into it. Straining, groaning, and sweating from the first, we inch our way along the vegetated shoreline. Every muscle in my body is involved in this all-consuming effort. Unfortunately, eddies are nonexistent. Infrequent slow spots offer meager respite, but it still takes forward strokes to prevent us from being pushed backward. This exuberant river hurtles onward relentlessly, having no pity for a canoe trying to push against her. After an hour of pouring everything I have into every stroke, I spy a sandy beach on the opposite side of the river.

"Pull over!" *huff puff*, "I need to rest!" *huff puff gasp groan* I holler over my shoulder at Tom. We ferry over, losing ground, but finally reach the site after regaining our lost distance once on the opposite shoreline. On sheer adrenalin, I hop out of the bow and give MW a heave so she is steadfastly ashore.

"This is a bear," Tom says as he stows his paddle and sits hunched over, trying to catch his breath, not even attempting to get out.

"No kiddin'," I huff as I plunk my butt onto the sand. "How much more of this do you think there is?" Tom looks upriver. The bends in the river and brush crowding its shoreline don't permit for a long line of sight.

"I don't know. It's all the same as far as I can see. Let me grab the map." He reaches under the spray skirt for the plastic zip bag containing the map.

"Get the cookies and water too." I flop myself back onto the sand, allowing my rubbery arms to land where they will. "Can you tell where we are?"

Tom plunks down next to me and begins to mull over the map. He glances at his watch. I turn my head to look up at him. "Not really. We've been at this for an hour, though," he says.

"Well, I'm exhausted. How far do you think we've come?"

"Maybe a half mile," he offers.

"Naw, really?" It seems hard to believe that we could cover even that distance at our snail's pace.

"It sure would be nice to know how much longer the river is like this," he says, standing up and straining to look upriver over the riparian vegetation.

It's one thing to encounter a set of rapids with a beginning and an end. But when faced with a constant onslaught with no end in sight and no eddies to help, one cannot help but wonder how realistic it is to be sprinting a marathon.

As we gorge ourselves on cookies and slug down water, we agonize over the maps. It all boils down to a truly disheartening conclusion.

I sit up, pull my knees up under my chin, wrap my arms around them to stay upright, and look Tom straight in the eye. "I guess there's nothing left to do but abort, eh?"

He holds my gaze. "Even if we can keep going at this pace," I raise my eyebrows, "which I'm not saying we can," he continues, "we'd never get there before winter sets in." I don't even ask to have "there" defined. I figure here is "there." I define it as the spot we knew we would encounter someday, the spot at which our paddle power could no longer carry us up the mountains. We sit silently for a bit, digesting our situation and our options. I play with the sand between my toes.

The original idea was not to simply "do" the waterways but to get from the Pacific Ocean to the Atlantic Ocean as best we could by canoe. I can see Tom feels cheated out of the many miles we wouldn't cover because of the swift current. If we skip this section altogether, we will be missing about 190 miles of beautiful mountain-fed river and breathtaking fall scenery.

Tom finally speaks up. "If we can't go up this section of river, that doesn't mean we can't go down." I look at him and he continues. "I'm sure we have time to cover this section going downriver before winter hits." I push out my lower lip and nod.

The river's swiftness and force result from the closing of irrigation canals that usually divert the river's might. Now, reunited and full, the Snake defies our attempt to paddle against it. With this apparent, we decide to do something novel for us—go *with* the flow.

Today we abort the upriver climb to the Rocky Mountains. We are off in a new direction.

Tom seems to accept this decision as the only option. I am secretly relieved to end this folly of killing myself for inches. Deep inside us both, however, rests a gnawing feeling of defeat. It's the feeling of resigning oneself to a compromise instead of achieving the intended goal. We dub September 16, Day 95, "Abortion Day."

The plan is to paddle back down to American Falls, where we somehow get to the town of Springfield, north of the Reservoir, rent a vehicle that we can drive up to Yellowstone National Park, and start our descent.

Recuperated, with a plan, we shove off downriver. With just a slight pull of the paddle, we are zooming along like a bird flying with the wind. The tonic of speed has my head spinning. Before we know it, we get disgorged into the reservoir. There we encounter a grandpa-aged angler and sidle up within speaking distance. After precursory salutations, the angler asks our destination.

"We were tryin' to go upriver," I explain.

"Is that so?" the angler perks up. "How far'd ya get?"

"It took us an hour to paddle up to a big sandbar," I answer, pointing upriver as if that would help him locate the place I spoke of.

"Yeah?" He seemed to know where we meant, anyway. "That's pretty good in a canoe," he compliments.

Before we get out of earshot, I ask, "Is it this fast for a long time?"

"It gets worse the further up ya go."

We nod, share our farewells, and paddle on our way, feeling better about our decision.

I believe anglers. Advice from visitor-center folks or office folks or anyone not actually *on* the river must be taken with a grain of salt. But anglers are on the river, darting here and there in their motorboats, in tune to where the fish are. I'm not talking about your weekend warrior, racing about in a fancy man-toy. No, I mean old codgers like this fella, who have puttered around these coves and bays for years in their plain, paint-starved wooden craft with a little 15-horsepower motor. These are real anglers. They may not tell land-lubbers the truth about fish size, but they know water conditions and are completely honest and congenial with river folk like us. It is reassuring to have our decision confirmed.

Changing Direction

Day 96 (September 17): I feel only partially present over the next couple of hectic days. They involve a lot of citified dealings, such as automobile rental, highway travel, errand running, and hitchhiking. Tom handles logistics. I despair at the loss of our wilderness way of life, not ready for civilization yet. Despite backbreaking paddling, uncomfortable sleeping, outdoor ablutions, and prepackaged food, I am content as a river person. We are in charge only of ourselves and nothing more. Civilization brings expenses, regulations, the need to converse, the need to look somewhat respectable, and other social norms. Ugh. Anticipating these activities depresses me. However, when it comes right down to it, I enjoy my interactions with all the people we meet. They are each generous beyond belief. My hermit's heart is warmed to its core.

Reed, the Bingham County Public Works Director, is our first encounter with civilization. He helps me make the shift from shunning interaction to appreciating contact graciously. He picks us up on the road to Springfield and ends up being our chauffeur for the whole day. He waits while we spend a few minutes on the phone in Springfield to determine we can only rent a vehicle in the larger town of Blackfoot, a few miles further north. Since he was going there anyway, Reed happily takes us back to the river for our stuff, helps us load it up in his truck and carts us to Blackfoot. On the way, we stop in Springfield once again, where he introduces us to Leah, a reporter for the *Blackfoot Morning News*.

Town encounters following a newspaper article usually result in celebrity-like appearances. We get pampered, listened to, flattered, and gawked at, which is a fantastic ego boost; plus, we also get to share our Paddle for Water mission. This time, though, poor Leah got the unlucky assignment of interviewing the vanquished. We didn't feel like celebrities. Neither Tom nor I convey the passion we have for our cause as well as in previous interviews. Defeat does that to a river person.

Leah, however, doesn't see it that way. Her high-energy interview and intense interest help bring us back to life. She feels getting this far is downright impressive. She flatters us so much I am lifted out of my funk. Reed waits during the interview and courteously takes us up to Blackfoot, where he drops MW, our stuff, and us off near a car dealership by the river. We watch Reed sign our thank-you paddle. As he does so, I wonder what kind of person departs from his own schedule to cart two strangers around from town to town all day long. Would I do that if our roles were reversed? Not sure. Touched deeply, I leave Reed with a simple hug. Tom offers a hearty handshake, and with that, we are alone once again.

Our solitude lasts only twenty minutes when Kathy, the *Blackfoot Morning News* photographer arrives. She shoots pictures and even offers us a night at her house. We accept the negatives, which we can pick up tomorrow, but decline the home visit. As hard as it is to do, we need to be right where we are—close to the Ford dealership—

where we can rent a truck first thing tomorrow morning. All in all, it is heartwarming to be around such hospitable people in civilization once again. I go to sleep that night, wondering why I still have this urge to be a recluse.

The following day, a cheery car salesman makes Tom a deal. We have wheels.

Once loaded up, we have places to go. First stop, Kathy's to pick up photo negatives, but she wasn't in. That's a bust. Next stop, post office for a slew of goodies waiting there for us. This is a boon. Then off to the Grand Tetons.

The fall scenery enthralls me. Breathtaking landscapes whizz past like a fast-forward movie. Fall is making a spectacular showing.

Once at the South Entrance of Yellowstone National Park, Nick, a park ranger, assists us in stashing our gear until we return for it later. Then it's back to Blackfoot to return the vehicle. En route, we pay a visit to Dick and Josie, who, I'm thrilled to say, received my sleeping bag. This long-awaited generosity from Jansport will thankfully replace my thin, old, almost-useless current bag. It has arrived just in time to keep me warm in the chilly weeks ahead.

The next morning, we return the vehicle. I'm aghast at the cost. Fifty-three dollars and fifty cents plus twenty-five dollars for gas was more money than we had spent in the last two months.

Now it's time to hitchhike back to Yellowstone. We walk over to the main road, with one stop for doughnuts. I wrote "Tetons" on the doughnut bag once we chowed down the contents. But it doesn't work. Cars zoom by and pay us no heed. I find a cardboard box on the side of the road. I open it up and mark as big as possible: "Conserve Energy, CARPOOL." Surely that would get us a ride. It gets us lots of smiles. After forty-five minutes, chilled to the bone and blown to tatters by passing trucks, Rod stops to pick us up. He is a big man and says he can't pass up a pretty smile. I didn't realize I was smiling out there, but I like him immediately. His car is warm. He takes us to Idaho Falls.

Hitching a ride to Yellowstone

From there, we add x-c canoeists and Jackson to our sign. In a half-hour, a father who just dropped off his son at school takes us as far as a rest stop outside of Ririe.

Our third ride passes us by, slows down, turns around, then comes back. It is a '68 black Ford converted to a pickup. The driver is a guy in his fifties, with unkempt red hair and a tattered coat. I detect a slight twinkle in his eye. When we say we are going to Yellowstone, he retorts, "Why ya going to that thing?"

"To canoe," Tom replies.

"Come on. Get in."

Tom opens the door. The passenger seat is entirely occupied by Babe, whom we are told is a long-haired sheepdog. This is no small pup. Babe looks at us—as best I could tell from underneath all that hair—with an inquiring look. The back seat is filled to the roof with what appears to be all the man's worldly possessions. No one makes a move to help. Tom and I share a glance. I guess the only option is to join Babe. With a bit of jostling on our part and grunting on Babe's, somehow Tom and I squeeze underneath her. With the two of us crammed onto the passenger seat and an eighty-pound dog trying to get comfy on our laps, we head off to Alpine.

A couple more rides after that gets us to Jackson. When Alfie and Miriam from Israel pick us up on their way to Yellowstone, they are amazed about our trip, not quite understanding the need to conserve water. "But you have so much!" Miriam exclaims. Indeed, compared to Israel, we do. They drop us off at the South Entrance, and we feel like calling it a day. Nick, the park ranger, however, says we cannot stay there—requirements of civilization—ugh. He suggests Lewis Lake Campground—the nearest one north. Laden with only overnight essentials, we happen into Rob—another kind soul—who drives us to the hiker/biker campground.

Here, we are greeted by the first snow of the season. Wet and clingy, it enshrouds every bow and twig, creating a gorgeous fairy tale wonderland. Everywhere is a photographer's masterpiece. The craggy, snow-covered Tetons offer a dramatic backdrop for yellow aspens blanketed in white. Thinking how yesterday was the last day of summer, I wonder if we will skip autumn altogether. At long last, we finish gawking and photographing and must now squeeze into the tent for the night. We occupy the last available site in the campground. A couple of snow-burdened spruce boughs graciously provide just enough bare ground for our little tent.

As I don my winter wardrobe, I congratulate myself on lugging my wool sweater, mittens, turtleneck, and tights throughout the blistering-hot summer months. I was tempted many times to send them home. Still, these additional clothes may not be enough.

Come suppertime, the stoves—both low on fuel—don't light. Extra fuel is back at the entrance with the rest of our stuff. Feeling fortunate and curious at the same time to find a motorhome in the hiker/biker campground, we contemplate knocking on the door and asking them to boil us some water. Tom urges me to do it. I dare him. Ultimately, neither of us wants to impose. Instead, we dine on cookies and water while zipped up snuggly into our puffy sleeping bags in our little green tent under snow-laden spruce boughs.

After we hitch our way back to MW, Ranger Nick informs us we are not allowed to paddle in Yellowstone National Park. We must portage a few hundred yards downriver. So, being compliant, we portage, unhappily, some distance, to the location we believe he described. Soon we are gleefully paddling *down* the Snake River. A fleeting feeling of guilt runs through me when we zip by the park boundary marker. Oops.

The river hurries on its way over and past boulders, sweeping around curves, carrying us with it. By bundling up in rain gear and cinching ourselves into MW's spray skirt, we make ourselves impervious to the on-and-off rain. Ordinarily, such weather is annoying, but not today. Today we are paddling *with* the current at the speed of light. We feel no qualms encountering one Class I rapid after another and even shoot a Class II in a steep section. Navigating rock garden rapids is absolutely thrilling.

I don't know if I can appropriately convey the delight an upriver paddler feels when starting to go downriver. Despite the soggy day, I giggle, I laugh, I hoot with delight. With minimal effort—sometimes none at all—we make fantastic progress. Going down doesn't suck your spirit dry, then spit it out exhausted and spent. Descending this river energizes my soul.

A family of seven curious otters passes by. Each otter pops up, eyes us momentarily, then disappears under the surface with a splash, only to reappear and reassess our progress. They send me into joyous giggling fits.

You Call This a Lake?

Day 98 (September 19): By the end of our first downriver day, we enter Jackson Lake in Grand Teton National Park. Jackson Lake is a natural lake, but a dam at its southern end greatly enlarges its capacity, allowing for irrigation downriver.

The original log and crib dam, constructed in 1906 across the outlet of Jackson Lake, lasted only four years. A more permanent concrete and earthen dam replaced it. Begun in 1911, completed in 1916, that dam still exists today—mostly. At the time of our arrival, the U.S. Bureau of Reclamation is reinforcing the dam to withstand earthquakes the nearby Teton fault may trigger. This means the lake is practically drained, leaving the upper reaches a snaky, shallow, sandy, braided, stump-scattered maze. The flow is hardly discernable. Choosing between the main channel and any number of long, windy dead ends proves problematic. The widest option isn't necessarily the correct choice, nor is the channel most directly ahead. It takes a discerning eye to read which option has the most vigorous flow. I think I am getting it down until the fifty-fifty fork.

"Which way?" Tom asks.

"Well . . ." I hesitate. I evaluate the critical juncture where the water has to make a choice, and it gives me no clue. Water seems to be flowing equally into each channel. I have to take a guess. "Right," I say definitively. Within five minutes, we find ourselves paddling in increasingly shallow waters. Within ten minutes MW scrapes the bottom, and like imbeciles we brace our paddles against the sand to haul ourselves onward. "This is just a shallow spot." I actually have no idea. "The water keeps flowing this way pretty steadily. It'll open up." It doesn't. We're grounded.

"Where'd the water go?" Tom asks drolly. When we have come to a complete halt, I turn around to look at him.

"I guess we should have taken the left fork." Here, a "should-of" is in order. We sit for a moment, neither of us wanting to step into the icy mountain water from under our cozy spray skirt on this chilly, rainy day. The spray skirt completely envelops the canoe opening. We have it cinched around our bodies.

"We've got to get out," Tom concedes. "Let's push her backward." He unfastens himself from MW and steps out into the water that was snow just a couple of days ago. "Brrrrrrr" precedes some choice expletives. This is by no means motivating me.

"But I'm so warm in here," I whine.

"Fine, stay there," he says to my surprise as he persists. "Use your paddle, and I'll pull MW back." I plant my paddle in the sand to push us backward as he gives one good heave. MW moves maybe an inch. Well, this won't do. I reluctantly un-velcro and un-cinch and step out, knee-deep in ice water. With unison grunting, we heave her backward and push her two, maybe three feet in squishy, cold sand. Then using MW for support, we yank our feet out, take a couple of steps forward, and heave her again.

"How can we paddle this far but can't paddle back?" I inquire at one of our short rest breaks.

"Water level must be dropping."

"But it's raining. Why isn't it rising?"

"I don't know, Nance," he says, obviously irritated. "Ready, HEAVE." MW moves a foot and a half. "God, this boat is heavy." Tom's exasperation is building.

"Why don't we lighten her up?" I suggest, trying to be chipper.

"Yeah, sure, why not." I'm afraid he's super annoyed with me for getting us stuck.

We start at our respective ends, unsnapping one side of MW's spray skirt. With a grunt, Tom heaves a personal pack onto his back. I do the same but without as much grunting. Floundering and slogging through knee-deep water, I follow Tom to deposit the packs at the nearest dry spot. Then we trudge back for MW. At least the hard work is keeping me warm. We tug and schlep and grunt. I'm not feeling chipper anymore. On the bright side, MW comes along more willingly as we pull her until she's afloat again. Slogging back to fetch the packs, we wrestle them into the boat, clip them in, snap up the spray skirt, settle ourselves in, and paddle onward with little conversation.

This arduous routine, we carry out two more insufferable times. I feel like a wet lab rat flunking the maze.

Pooped, wet, miserable, cold, Tom declares it time to stop for the night. I'm relieved to oblige. The campsite, a little grassy knoll, looks to be the only possible spot for a tent anywhere around, though it's not the site we registered for. We camp illegally, but neither of us is in a mood to care.

Supper hastily made and eaten, campsite tidy, we climb into our little green tent for the night. I flop down on my sleeping bag, exhausted. Tom is already zipped into his.

"Hey, I'm sorry I was such a jerk today." Tom turns to me.

I return the gaze. "You've done worse. At least you didn't yell at me."

"I am trying to be better."

"I can tell." I smile at him. "Don't worry about it. We're good." I get out of my cold, wet clothes, put on my dry, long underwear and a dry T-shirt, zip myself into my bag, and curl up into a ball to warm up. "Man, am I cold."

"We could zip the bags together to share body heat," he says in a hopeful tone.

"Yeah, right," I reply and roll over, still curled in a ball. After a half-hour, "This isn't working," I say. "I'm still frozen."

"My offer still stands."

I'm tempted. Very tempted. "No funny business," I instruct.

"No funny business." He sounds sincere.

"Okay." We jostle around, opening both bags up, putting his at the bottom and zipping them together into one big bag with us sandwiched in between. He pulls me toward him, and I spoon next to his warm body. "Closer," I urge.

"I can't get any closer." We jostle a bit more, and he puts his arms around me. "AAAH!" he shudders with a sudden intake of air.

"Oh, sorry."

"What the . . . ?"

"My toes. They're really cold."

"Don't let them touch me."

"Oh, all right." I curl up into a ball again and hold my toes with my hands. Tom shares his spare heat, and I am warming up by the minute, including my heart. We fall asleep together.

The next day, the continuous meandering is increasingly frustrating. Back and forth, back and forth, this is indeed a snaky river. After an hour of paddling, we can still make out every blade of grass at our previous night's campsite.

Magnificent Tetons

I distract myself with the gorgeous scenery. To the east, Pilgrim Mountain displays a splotch of golden aspens shining amid a background of evergreen. To the southeast, I see beautifully dusted in the season's first snow, Crystal Mountain, Pyramid Peak, and other parts of the chain of peaks. Behind us, Grand Teton looms at 13,766 feet, and Mt. Moran, the second-highest Teton, reaches 12,594 feet. The treeless summits remain shrouded in clouds, but an occasional visible summit confirms they are white with snow.

Arriving at an actual lake—with lots of water that can float our boat—I see steam rising along the right-hand shore in the distance. It can be nothing but a hot spring. How enticing! To congratulate ourselves on completing the maze, we decide to indulge in a hot-tub style soak. We park MW on a gravel beach a short hike from the source of the steam. Crouching at the edge, Tom determines, with a tentative touch, that the water is indeed very, *very* hot. Bathing is not an option. Orange and green algae decorate the edges and bottom. By the abundance of large animal bones, it is evident that deer or elk fell victim to deceptively thin ice here. What a way to go—cooked to death in a hot spring.

On the majestically beautiful but perplexing Jackson Lake

Once reunited with MW, we set off to cross the glassy calm lake toward Elk Island and our official campsite in an attempt to do something legal for once. We paddle and paddle and paddle and paddle, but the destination does not seem to get any nearer. Being away from the shore, it is often hard to gauge progress, but usually landmarks provide assurance.

"Are we moving?" I ask Tom.

"Yeah, I don't see why not," he replies. "But I know what you're saying. We don't seem to be getting any closer."

I look behind us. "We seem to be putting distance behind us. We just don't seem to be subtracting it from the front."

"Want to pump water?" Tom asks. This is our term for fast water-heaving to get MW flying. We mostly do it for sheer exercise. It's an excellent cardiovascular workout and a great way to warm up cold bodies—plus it shifts MW into high gear.

"Yeah." Even before I join in, I can feel MW lurch forward from Tom's surge. After about fifteen high-powered strokes I count down: "Three . . . two . . . one . . . switch," and we trade sides simultaneously. Paddling fast and hard on one side causes muscle fatigue pretty quickly, so when it starts to come on, I call for a switch.

After about a minute and a half of that exhausting exercise, I call for a stop and survey our situation. Looking at the water, it seems we are slicing through at an excellent clip. Looking at our destination is different. "Well, maybe it's closer," I say, befuddled.

"I don't think so," Tom replies, perplexed. "This lake has something against canoeists."

I reflect on how the braided river had us stymied for two days. Now the open water has us downright bewildered.

"It's got to have something to do with the mountains making the lake look smaller than it is," Tom proposes.

"Whatever it is, it's freaky—like an optical illusion."

To add insult to injury, a breeze begins to blow. In about ten minutes, we are fighting three-foot white-capped bowlickers. It's hard not to feel like this lake has something against us. Now anxiety tops off my vexation. We are out in the middle of this sinister lake that, moments before, was tranquil and smooth. The shore behind is now distant, and the shore in front doesn't seem to be getting closer. There is nothing to do but keep pushing onward, hard and steady, guiding MW to ride the waves in her usual dependable fashion. After nearly an hour, we reach the nearest shore. What I figured to be a twenty-minute zip across the lake took an hour and a half. Nerves frazzled and muscles fatigued, we look for a spot to camp. Again, we'll have to camp illegally. Forget the stupid regulations.

Determined to get off this freaky lake pronto, we skip breakfast the next morning. The dam is tucked into one of these coves, but which one? We forge onward, hoping the darn dam is around the next bend. It never is. As soon as I accept that this beautiful lake will imprison us for days, I spot Jackson Dam.

We *never* gladly portage—but today we do. Tom whistles and I hum as we lug our cargo a quarter mile twice. No one is working at the dam today—it's Sunday—so we go about our business without hearing, "You can't go there" or "You need a permit." Before long, we are cheerfully dipping our paddles in the wild and scenic Snake River, continuing our voyage in Grand Teton National Park.

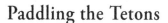

Paddling the Tetons

Day 100 (September 21): A riverside information center is just the place for a potty stop. That part of civilization, I like. Here at Pacific Creek Landing, the ranger registers our boat while providing a detailed map of the river with all its significant landmarks, channels, and landings from here to Moose Landing—the length of the park. Here is what we have to look forward to: channels leading off from the main flow that get blocked by strainers (downed trees whose branches allow water through but not canoes), logjams, sharp curves, tantalizingly deceptive wrong turns, and strong current. By the time we get to Moose, we'll have negotiated colorful areas by the names of Disney Channel, Anthills, Cougar Cut-off, Deadman's Bar, Bump Stump, Frustration Ponds, Dustbowl, Peek-a-boo Point, Smilie's Slip, Deadend Right, Deadend Left, Many Moose Island, Last Chance Left, and Last Chance Right and The Maze (not again!). To top it off, we hear of a history of fatalities and get fair warning to be careful on the river. Sounds fun. Off we go.

This is nature at its most inviting. Aspens sport their brilliant yellow. Pristine snow covers the rugged terrain and dusts every tree. A stately bald eagle watches us pass. A beautiful cow moose snaps her head out of the water as we glide around a bend. Eyes and ears fix upon us as water streams from her head. She pees in the river—maybe to express her disgust —then turns to lope up the bank, leading her calf to safety.

This wilderness is my favorite section of river yet. Both Tom and I add Wyoming to our skinny-dipped states—an exhilarating thrill on a fall morning. It is hard to believe one little dam can separate a nightmare lake from a dreamy river.

Grand Teton National Park is due south of the famed Yellowstone National Park. Whereas Yellowstone, America's first national park, was established in a mere two years, Grand Teton faced a much more difficult road. As early as 1897, various proposals to the government to protect these majestic mountains, lakes, and valleys fell on deaf ears. In 1917 the more influential voices of Stephen Mather, first director of the newly formed National Park Service (NPS), and Horace Albright, superintendent of Yellowstone National Park, added their impetus, promoting the expansion of Yellowstone into the Tetons. But locals were passionately divisive. Government intervention was unwelcomed, as sheep ranchers, Jackson Hole businessmen, farmers, and even U.S. Forest Service (USFS) personnel opposed losing acreage from more "useful" purposes. The loss of tax revenue and grazing lands, as well as the freedom to do what one wants on private property, were compelling arguments.

On the other hand, many feared the loss of the grandiose wilderness as, even then, rampant commercialization was beginning to citify the mountains and lakes. Mather and Albright felt protection under the NPS was necessary to prevent over-exploitation. Such bills were forged and brought to Congress, debated and defeated. Eventually, when the prospect of dams loomed, consensus for protecting the lakes and peaks prevailed, allowing President Calvin Coolidge to sign a bill into law establishing 96,000 acres of parkland in 1929. This did not include the valley of Jackson Hole. Seeking private investors, Albright got John D. Rockefeller Jr. involved. He purchased 35,000 acres, intending to turn the land over to the NPS. These acquisitions became fodder for more polemical engagements in courts and Congress. After waiting fifteen years for his gift to be accepted, Rockefeller felt compelled to address President Franklin Delano Roosevelt. His ultimatum: *either preserve this as parkland, or I will sell it off to the highest bidders.* FDR established 221,000 acres as Jackson Hole National Monument in 1943.[7]

Again, controversy flared. Ultimately, objections waned when the beautiful vistas, regal mountains, verdant valleys, and pristine lakes brought in tourism dollars. President Harry S. Truman signed legislation to make one all-inclusive 310,000-acre Grand Teton National Park in 1950. Grand Teton National Park, born of over fifty years of debate and controversy, lay juxtaposed to Yellowstone, America's sweetheart park—both magnificent and worthy of protection.

We see the Grand Tetons in a way most visitors cannot—by river. Twisting and turning, the Snake's meltwater bounces along, tumbling over rocks, rushing back and forth, carrying us forward in its grand adventure. Even on my day to captain, I christen myself "navigator" and choose the bow so I can more easily maneuver MW around obstacles, of which there are many. Mostly, I aim to avoid the big waves in the main flow on the outside of curves and skirt by the shallow spots on the inside of bends. I keep MW's nose right in the middle, and Tom makes the rest of the boat follow.

"More right," I bark to Tom as I crossbow draw to avoid a logjam.

"Is that a canoe in there?" Tom asks.

I look as we whiz by. "Ohhhh, I think so." I'm instantly sober. A yellow canoe is firmly entrenched in the logjam, half in, half out, gunwales facing upriver. The river is not letting go of that boat anytime soon.

"We should probably report that," Tom says.

"Yeah, good idea." We paddle along with a little less frivolity, grounded in the fact that even a small miscalculation could spell disaster.

Stopping at Moose Landing, we report the canoe to an NPS ranger stationed there. They had already received word about it. We are now leaving the national park and entering Bridger-Teton National Forest.

Captain or not, I continue, ensconced in the bow. Though having the utmost confidence in Tom's paddling abilities, I feel much more comfortable being the one to spot pillows and other obstacles and deftly maneuvering MW's bow to avoid them. I concentrate on my art, bark orders to Tom when needed, and feel secure that, after a hundred days of paddling, my skills are honed, my confidence strong.

"Imagine what this would have been like coming up." I prod Tom to conjecture as we zip along.

"There's no eddies, and it's fast. We wouldn't be in the boat," he replies, meaning that we'd be lining or frogging or portaging the whole time. It would be disheartening to find out that we had turned around too early on a perfectly paddle-able river. We take comfort in having made a solid decision to change course. I'm pleased we canoed this beautiful section—going with the flow.

Grand Canyon of the Snake

Day 104 (September 25): Running south in western Wyoming from Jackson Hole to Alpine, the Snake River Canyon, otherwise known as the Grand Canyon of the Snake, lies within the Bridger-Teton National Forest. Known for its excellent fishing, it hosts some of the best white-water rafting in the U.S. The question is: can we paddle this?

Everything we see and hear about the canyon talks about rafting and kayaking. Nobody canoes it. Now, at the end of September, every single rafting outfitter in Jackson is closed for the season, including the three outfitters at Hoback Junction. So, information is hard to come by. We finally run into two fellas at the Hoback General Store.

"Oh, just go for it," one fella says. "There's only two spots with big waves, and they can be skirted."

"I floated it in August," the other fella adds, "and the raft guide had to look for the few big waves to make any excitement out of it."

With that, our maps, and the information from the Grand Teton Park Ranger, we determine that at this water level, *we can do this*. Paddling onward until we put in twenty-six miles for the day, we pull out at Elbow Campground, a U.S. Forest Service site just north of the canyon—likewise closed for the season. I guess we have it to ourselves. This campground is designated "primitive," but with a picnic table, fire ring and pit toilet, it's downright luxurious.

Waiting for better weather before running Grand Canyon of the Snake

I have been paddling in my long underwear, pants, and rain pants on my bottom half, four layers on my top half under my PFD, and mittens. It sometimes snows, rains frequently, and the temperature never rises above 50 degrees Fahrenheit. We pitch our little green tent under the boughs of another generous spruce tree. It is a beautiful place to overnight. Luckily, we are in no hurry to do this canyon. If we are going to dump, we'd best have some sunshine to dry our clothes and warmer weather so as not to get hypothermic.

The next day we unzip the tent door to find an inch of very wet, heavy snow. It's covering the ground and still coming down. We hitchhike to Jackson to kill time.

We unzip the tent door the next day to find deeper snow, still coming down in big, clumpy flakes. We take hikes, read, journal, photograph, and mend mittens.

The next day, we unzip the tent to find even more snow still coming down. After digging out, we hitchhike to Jackson to kill time.

The next day, we unzip the tent to find rain falling. It rains without stopping all day long. We write letters, listen to the radio, share stories of our family Christmas traditions, and nap.

This continues for a week. A whole week!

Finally, our day comes. The sun shows itself, and we jump at the opportunity. My stomach is tense, and I accidentally knock the scalding hot chocolate water off the stove, but despite my trepidation, even I don't want to wait any longer. When we are all loaded up, we don our wits and paddling jackets to tackle the Class II and Class III and maybe IV whitewater ahead.

We stand on the bank. Tom looks me in the eye. "You'll do fine. Just shout directions to me real loud."

"Right," I respond in my anxious brevity. After he hugs me, we go to our respective seats.

"It'll be fun. We can do this, no problem." Is he bolstering himself or me?

This is the most gnarly whitewater I've ever run. Raft companies make thousands of dollars each year, scaring the wits out of paying customers by crashing through giant standing waves, twirling off boulders, and sliding down drops in this stretch. All their flyers attest to this, despite what the guys in Hoback testified to. We strap ourselves into the spray skirt, kneel down—me in the bow and Tom in the stern—and launch ourselves into mayhem.

"Right there! Between these rocks! Head for the V! Good line!" Tom shouts. I anticipate and follow his line of thinking, instructing him with my shouts of "Right," accompanied by a draw, or "Left" with a crossbow draw to avoid the pillows and visible rocks. In beautiful synchronicity, we dance between rocks, follow downstream "V's" and maneuver MW into water going where we want to go.

"Let's check out what's coming," Tom says. It could be a Class IV rapid. We pull ashore in an eddy behind a rock, unstrap ourselves, and walk downriver to a boulder—atop of which is a good vantage point. Tom points out a route.

"See those anglers? We'll eddy out behind that boulder downriver of them."

"Right."

"Then we'll ferry across to the eddy behind that boulder midriver."

"Right."

"Then we'll peel out to our right and run river left of that boulder there."

"Right."

"And remember to LEAN DOWNSTREAM."

"Right."

"That will put us in that chute, leading to that big standing wave. You'll get wet, but it's the place we have to go."

"Right."

Cinched in once more, we attempt the plan, which doesn't go

exactly as expected. Somehow, we end up at the standing wave that was our destination, anyway.

"Slow! Back-paddle!" I shout from the bow, and we each shove water forward, so we don't launch ourselves too deeply into the wave. I peer down momentarily from the precipice of the drop before me. I fall into the trough with a firm low brace, and MW's bow then slices through the rolling menace. The curl smashes me in the face and deposits gallons of recently thawed snow on my lap, most of which my spray skirt deflects. Blinking to squeeze the water out, I now dig forward, hard, to pull Tom through the hole.

MW pops up on the other side of the standing wave as I feel her stern dipping down in the trough. As on a teeter-totter, he goes down, and I go up. Momentarily up in the air, I have nothing but air for my paddle to grip. Luckily, we have enough momentum to free ourselves from this roiling grip but no time to congratulate ourselves. Here comes yet another standing wave. And so it goes. After this, staying dry is no longer a goal. Wave crashing is necessary and frequent.

The six-inch gap in my spray skirt allows lapfuls of water into MW. This water shifts around, making maneuvering dangerous. "Pull over!" I shout, spying a small sandbar. In a few powerful strokes, we shove MW's nose to shore. We un-tether ourselves from MW and hop out. The first of many times to bail.

The routes that we scout seldom work as planned. A couple of times, we run rapids backward. But according to Tom, just as long as you don't enter a rapid broadside, you're good. The bare-bones necessity is to avoid boulders and hydraulics. Hydraulics are nasty suck-you-under, spin-you-around, and maybe-someday-spit-you-out washing-machine type water currents found below clean-cut drops. Even small ones kill. We skirt around one ledge but line MW around another particularly steep one.

In the end, I am soaked, euphoric, relieved, exhausted. We shove MW's nose firmly ashore, downriver of the huge asphalt rafting company take-out. This completes ten miles of whitewater exhilaration.

"Wow, we did it!" I beam and scream out a laugh.

"Yup, and you did good!" Tom says as I yank MW further ashore.

"Wow, we did it!" I can't help but say it again. I let out another unabashed laugh.

"We did!" Tom is beaming too as he emerges. "And MW did great!"

"She is awesome. I don't know what could tip her." I feel like a proud mom, and I cannot stop laughing. "But I'm glad it's over." My brief life until now had not yet known death-defying exhilaration. My soul feels like celebrating. A whole weeks-worth of pent-up nervousness comes out in fits of shameless laughter.

"Me too." Tom gives me a big hug, and I hug him back. "You did a great job," he says.

I'm pleased with the compliment. Giddy with happiness, I plant a big kiss on his smiling mouth. I hold onto his PFD with both hands, shake him back and forth a couple of times, causing his head to bob limply, and shout, "We ran the Grand Canyon of the Snake!"

"It was a bit more than what the guys in Hoback described."

"A bit?! I'll say." I let Tom go with a playful shove.

"I think I've turned you into a white-water junkie," he says as he regains his footing.

"I don't know about that, but *man* it was exciting!"

Only well after our run through the canyon did I find out that many of these rapids have names. Three Oar Deal is a ledge rapid, apparently very dangerous (up to class V) in high flow. Big Kahuna is to avoid. Lunch Counter is said to be the biggest rapid in the Snake River Canyon, capable of making ten-foot waves in high water. Other rapids throughout our run had names, but we didn't know or care. All that matters is that we successfully ran the Grand Canyon of the Snake in an open canoe.

"Well, let's unload," I say. "If we don't, we'll turn into popsicles." We are both soaked to the skin. We quickly unload MW, bail her out yet again, set up camp, and change into dry clothes, still euphoric with relief and delight.

Most reasonable people who run whitewater do it knowing that there are dry clothes in a warm place they can go to afterward. A large part of my overall anxiety about this run is that all our possessions go with us. Thanks to plastic zip bags and plastic garbage bags, we each have dry clothes and a dry sleeping bag. We are chatty and exuberant. The rest of that day, we spend reliving rapids, extolling the virtues of MW, reveling in the beauty of the canyon, and drying clothes around the fire. What more could one want on a sunny fall day in the mountains?

Hitchhiking and Mail Drops

Day 111 (October 2): After the mountain meltwater frolics around in the canyon for a while, it tumbles down into Palisades Reservoir. This lake is an impoundment of the Snake River, mostly in southeastern Idaho, with the upper reaches extending into Wyoming. The scenery embodies mountain majesty, and fall beauty feeds my soul. In the distance, snow blankets craggy tops of Powder Peak, Indian Peak, and Sheep Creek Peak. Evergreens march up the valleys and spill over the summits of the smaller mountains. Sun sets the aspen ablaze in fiery yellows while mountain maple and hawthorn sprinkle the surrounding hills with splashes of red and orange. I am intrigued by a common plant underfoot bearing succulent white marshmallow-like berries. Each morning, a delicate frost decorates grasses and flowering plants. We have less than twenty miles to paddle on this breathtaking reservoir, so we take our time to enjoy the scenery and birdlife. Bald eagles, common mergansers, belted kingfishers, common loons, and Western grebes get logged into my journal.

We are eager to hitchhike to Roberts, Idaho, but it is an eighty-mile road trip. No matter that it takes all day. We need groceries and a mail drop awaits. This excursion calls for an early start on a beautiful frost-covered day. With empty backpacks, we head past the forked burnt tree, beyond the old road, along the cow path, through the draw, and over the fence to Route 26. We must hitch to Ririe, then to Rigby, then to Roberts. Tom must come across as an ax murderer because he is getting no takers in the first two hours. I take over the thumbing, and within five minutes, I score. That day we enjoy the company of interesting generous folks who don't mind offering us a ride:

- A young man who informs us that bull elk season will start in two days and suggests we wear bright clothes to prevent getting shot.

- A Hispanic father who spoke almost no English, saying nothing while his son chatted away happily entertaining us.

- A sheepman from Rigby. He is making arrangements with farmers to lay his sheep over when he brings them down from the mountain pastures a week from now. He says he only lost thirty-five sheep this year— all to coyotes. That wasn't bad, considering that a bear could take twenty in one night. We wait while he stops at a farm to request permission.

- A man who told us his cousin drowned on the Snake when he and some fishing companions didn't want to row at a critical time, and their boat got caught in a strainer. Many folks share river horror stories with us. It's a kindness, I suppose.

- Craig, an avid photographer, traveler, and free spirit who let me ride on the couch in his camper, whereupon I promptly fell asleep.

After today I know this about hitchhiking: forget young single women, elderly drivers of either gender, campers, families, and truckers (truckers probably have rules against picking up hitchhikers), but smile at the single men, especially if in pickups. Ultimately, we are dropped off right at the post office in Roberts.

"What's it say? What's it say?" I cajole Tom as he reads a letter from Grand Targhee Ski Resort in response to our applications.

"We're employed!" he announces without lifting his eyes from the acceptance letter.

"Most excellent!"

"Yeah, I'll have to shave my beard off, though."

"Well, that's okay. You can do that, right?"

"Oh, yeah. That's no problem."

"What are we going to do?"

"I'm a line cook, and you're in the cafeteria." Tom looks up from the letter to smile at me.

I meet his eyes and nod my approval. "We can do that."

Our fate for frozen-river season is finalized. Our timing reaching the Rockies is such that overwintering is necessary. Employment gets checked off the "to do" list. Now to find a place to live and figure out transportation before reporting to work in a few weeks.

This stop at the Roberts post office produces our winter clothing, pre-boxed in anticipation of this season. Like a giddy girl on Christmas morning, I put everything on and clap my mittened hands, happy to be reunited with snuggly things. With my pocketknife, I gingerly slice open another box from Tom's mom—stuffed with letters from friends. Tom and my surroundings fade away, as one by one, I read words of support and encouragement. My eyes well with tears, and I don't even try to repress my smile.

We could make good time descending the upper reaches of the Snake, but we don't want to. Paddling clear fish-laden waters fringed with peach-leaf willows is glorious. An occasional strainer prevents too much wistful daydreaming though. I have that yellow canoe in Grand Tetons National Park imprinted in my head. Getting out and heaving MW over a gravel bar to avoid strainers prevents us from joining all the trapped debris. We get a weightlifter's workout and MW gets belly scratches.

In a week we reach Roberts again, this time by canoe. Time for laundry and shopping. Town is only two miles away this time, so we don't need to hitchhike. This fine Saturday, we expect more mail at the post office, but a sign on the locked door informs us it's closed all weekend, not to open again until the Tuesday after Columbus Day. My shoulders slump. One day is much like the rest on the river. As we shuffle back to MW, arms full of groceries but no mail, a car stops beside us. It's the postmaster. She recognizes us from our previous visit.

"Did you get your mail?" she asks out of her car window. I wonder how she thought we could, being closed and all.

"No, do we have some more?" I ask.

"Oh yes, come on with me." We hop in her car. She opens the post office just for us, and we eagerly accept a box of cookies, our Grand Targhee contracts, a couple of money orders, and a package of letters from our Texas friends. As she drives us back to the river, the kind motherly postmaster in her fifties admits that she nags her children not to pick up hitchhikers. We promise not to tell her family.

While cooking breakfast ten days later, I hear baa-ing of sheep and tinkling of a bell. I look up from my work to ask Tom, "What is that?"

"Don't know. Let's see." We run to the highway to see what the commotion is. There, a huge flock of sheep is taking up the entire road, kept together by a dog and a man on horseback. The sheep are following a goat sporting a bell on its collar. The goat is tied to the bumper of a truck that leads the whole procession. The man driving the truck is our shepherd friend who gave us a ride last week.

"How are the canoers?" he asks through his open window. We exchange pleasantries like old friends as we walk beside his truck. When, finally, our conversation lags and I fear we are getting too far from our breakfast, we step aside and watch the parade continue down the highway. A driver brings up the rear. I see he is frowning and craning to see how he can get by this inconvenience. Soon, the shepherd on horseback gives the dog a word, and masterfully, in thirty seconds, that dog had a lane of highway cleared of sheep—allowing the driver to pass.

Irrigation Dams

Crops would never get a foothold here were it not for irrigation by the Snake River. The river is sliced by a staircase of diversion dams that feed water into irrigation canals. From two to five feet high, these dams are a canoeist's vexation. We have to get out, unload, haul stuff for maybe sixty feet, take two more stuff-hauling trips, repack everything, and launch again—only to encounter another dam. Three or four tiny portages each day grow tiresome and are beginning to get on our nerves. Just running the blasted things looks very tempting. If there is a small breach in the dam, we run it with a hoot and a holler. If no breach—mostly the case—a thrill ride is replaced by a toilsome task met with grumbling, grunting, and ever-worsening moods.

Ever since settlers first put down stakes in the arid Western states, water rights have been a contentious issue. When we speak to the media, Tom and I share ways individuals can shrink their water consumption. Thoughtful practices—such as turning off faucets when not in use; choosing water-saving toilets; and landscaping with water-efficient plants—soon become second nature that contribute to shrinking our water footprint. Planting only native plants or hardscaping the yard prevents the wasteful practice of lawn watering. However, we are keenly aware that we are water-rich Easterners talking to water-deprived Westerners. I don't want to be an outsider, shaking my finger. Everybody here probably practices water conservation already, either by choice, necessity, or decree.

According to the 2015 report by the United States Geologic Survey (USGS), about 14 percent of all the freshwater pulled from surface and groundwater sources is used for washing, toilet flushing, lawn watering, and other ways water is used in the home. On the other hand, irrigation accounts for 42 percent of all freshwater usage.[8] Out West, in terms of volume, agricultural requirements for water outweigh all other uses.

Of the entire world's food, 40 percent is grown on irrigated land (according to GRID-Arendal data). Approximately 70 percent of the fresh water used in the world goes to this purpose.[9] Of the United States' roughly 396 million acres of cropland, 54 million acres were irrigated in 2017.[10] Among the fifty states, Idaho ranks second in the amount of water used for irrigation in 2018. California was number one, using four times as much water as Idaho.[11] Wow!

Sprinklers water 67 percent of the irrigated land in Idaho.[12] We have seen plenty of these spidery two-armed contraptions that look like a monstrous mutation of your little lawn sprinkler. It is a big rain tree that looms over the crops. All along its length, pressurized water sprays out ports. Two center supporting wheels allow it to travel the length of a field. Research has shown this to deliver only about 65 percent of the water to crop roots.[13] Most of Idaho's remaining irrigated land is watered by flood irrigation—the most common method throughout the world. Here, water is diverted into ditches traveling in furrows between the crops. Much of that water evades crop roots either by evaporation, seeping down deep, or runoff.

Technology exists that allows for much more efficient, less-destructive use of water. Drip irrigation systems deliver water directly to the roots through tubes with holes either just above or even below the ground. Negligible amounts of water are lost. Its use is on the rise worldwide, but as of the year 2000, according to the USGS, less than 10 percent of irrigated land in the United States is drip irrigated. In Idaho, less than 1 percent of irrigated land is watered this way. Idaho farmers are not unlike many others who opt for less expensive, albeit more wasteful technology.

Public policies still need to make strides to encourage efficient water use. Incentives can be given to farmers to install drip systems. Even in our own diets, we can do more with less water by eating lower on the food chain. Raising beef takes multitudes more water than growing a grain crop. The cow requires water, as does the grain that the cow ate. If we skip the cow stage, that cuts the water consumption way down.

As suspected, many of the gates on these irrigation canals are shut. The growing season has come to a close, and the water runs rambunctiously down the river without diversion. We are happy to be joining it.

American Falls Reservoir Again

Day 126 (October 17): We eat lunch at Abortion Point. This is the spot where we abandoned our upstream battle a month earlier. Now we know it was a prudent decision. We spill out onto American Falls Reservoir yet again, find a campsite, have supper, and decide to take advantage of the calm night and full moon for a moonlit paddle. Maybe this time will be the charm.

A gentle glow from the rising moon replaces the fading sunlight. We slice through the calm waters, each in our thoughts. I can't help but smile, taking in the serenity and grandeur of our surroundings illuminated only by moonglow. Clouds gradually accumulate overhead, like a ghost convention, snuffing out our moonlight. The gentle evening breeze turns into bluster, and placid piddles become tossers. The distant lights of Pocatello that gave us a firm reference point before are now shrouded in clouds. We can't see a thing. I concentrate on maintaining this heading while propelling us toward the unseen shoreline with powerful strokes. I can feel each of Tom's strokes in the bow doing the same. Heart-pounding, muscle-engaging tenseness replaces serenity. Our moonlight paddles never go as planned.

To ease our anxiety, I come up with an idea. "Hey, let's sing moon songs," I shout to Tom.

"What? Did you say moon songs?" The wind demands loud shouts.

"Yeah. Any song referencing the moon is game. You start."

Soon I can make out "By the Light of the Silvery Moon" wafting back to me. We sing loud enough to pierce the night. I next come up with "Moon River," and we croon like howling wolves. No doubt pure lunacy overtakes us, and we belt out "Blue Moon," "Mr. Moon Mr. Moon," and every other moon song we can think of. There's quite a lot, really. Bellowing songs in the darkness to the beat of our strokes is just the mental distraction we need to keep our angst in check. At last, a dark looming landmass becomes visible. Anticipation replaces uneasiness, but it still takes a lifetime to reach it. Eight miles seems like twenty when crossing an open lake in the dark. To my great relief, MW's nose crunches solid ground. Jumping out, Tom pulls us ashore.

Overwintering in the Rockies

Day 136 (October 27): Hitting the Rockies just in time for winter deflates my preconceived idea of an uninterrupted journey. I hold my canoeist heroes, Verlan Kruger and Steve Landig, on pedestals. They crossed the snowy Rockies on foot, pulling their boats like sleds behind them. Wintertime in the Rockies was just another challenge for them.

Winters here are severe and interminable. We probably won't hit the river again until at least March, maybe April. This is only October. Then again, my other expedition heroes, Lewis and Clark, waited out the winter months twice. I shouldn't feel defeated. It was as prudent and necessary for them as I know it is for us. Our over-wintering camp is a little rental house in Driggs, Idaho, a sleepy town nestled in Teton Valley at the foot of the Teton Mountains.

For the first months, we are as happy as the Corp of Discovery at Fort Mandan, their first winter layover. Like them, we dance with the natives and make new friends. But the similarities stop there. There is no sleeping with Mandan women, hunting for bison, chasing after the Sioux, or extricating our "pirogue" from the ice. Instead, on my lunch breaks, I learn how to telemark ski. I get to live under a roof, cook in my own kitchen, and sleep in a real bed. We sometimes visit Jackson Hole, Wyoming, on the other side of the Tetons. In my quieter moments, I marvel at the wintertime beauty of the majestic, jagged mountains.

Driggs, Idaho, is a small town in the middle of Teton Basin. To the east are the Tetons, to the west, the Big Hole Mountains. In this town of roughly eight hundred people, there are motels for tourists, mountaineering shops for climbers, real estate firms for investors, and supply shops for ranchers. People from all over the world come to ski these beautiful mountains with their abundant snow, incredible vistas, and rugged peaks. No, winter here is not bad at all. It's just long. And when I get that wanderlust longing, I feel stuck. If it weren't for my new friendships, I would be sorely depressed.

It was the first day of work, and the shuttle bus carrying workers from Driggs up the mountain to Grand Targhee was nearly full. Tom and I had to sit separately.

"Hi, I'm Nancy," I said as I sat down next to a slight, dark-haired woman.

"Vancie," she responded with a handshake.

Thinking I didn't articulate well enough, I tried again. "Nancy."

"Yes, nice to meet you, Nancy. And my name is Vancie," she said, enunciating very clearly. This little miscommunication turned out to be the beginning of a warm and special relationship. Tom and I celebrated Thanksgiving, Christmas, and birthdays with Vancie. She waited tables downstairs in the bar at the ski resort. Vancie was new in town, like us, but she ended up falling in love with the area and settled there.

Jerry, Tom's kitchen boss, often bought Tom a beer for "a job well done." Whenever my spirits needed bolstering, jokester Jerry was my go-to man. Chris, Virginia, and my other newfound Targhee friends turned a cold, snowy winter into a warm embrace.

Our winter here in the Tetons has been astonishing, but I begin to get extremely antsy as four months turn into five. With each new snowstorm, I take solace in that we don't have it as bad as the Corps at Fort Clatsop—their second winter stayover. Fifteen miles from the Pacific Ocean, Lewis and Clark's crew battled constant lousy weather, venereal disease, influenza, tedium, monotony of diet, and food shortage. We don't have it quite that bad. Meriwether busied himself with journal entries. I buy a sewing machine and design and sew a three-piece spray skirt for MW, fleece pullovers, mittens, and hats for each of us. William Clark occupied himself with map-making. We research Yellowstone River access sites, conditions, and character. By the time April rolls around, we are pumped and ready to hit Yankee Jim Canyon on the Yellowstone River.

CHAPTER 6

The Yellowstone

*The way of a canoe is the way
of the wilderness, and of a freedom
almost forgotten.*

—Sigurd Olson

Yearning for the River Life

"A puppy," I say.

"A puppy?" he replies.

"Yeah, I want to get a puppy."

Tom scrunches his eyebrows together, pouts his lower lip a bit, and scratches his burger-smelling hair as he searches for what question to ask first. He finally comes up with it. "Where did you get this idea?"

"Well, Andrea, the cashier's dog, had puppies. They're going to need to get rid of them, and it struck me, I would LUUUUUUVE to have a cute little river companion."

"I'm cute. I'm a good river companion." Tom adds with a wink, hoping for a gushing compliment.

I don't bite. "Even Lewis got a dog, Seaman, a Newfy, to accompany them on their expedition." I knew this would convince him. Merriwether Lewis purchased a Newfoundland dog for $20. Not sure why, but it made sense to me. We exchange overemphasized smiles.

"And you think, with all our stuff, we'd be able to fit a dog too?"

The cutest member of the expedition.

"Yeah, sure, not a Newfy, but there's room for a smaller dog. It'll be great! We'll have a little river dog. We need some zip, some zing put back into this trip." I don't know how to put it exactly, but for some reason, I feel a puppy will fill that emptiness that I haven't been able to escape these last few months holed up in Driggs. Oh, it's beautiful here, but I ache to be back on the river. My yearning for river life is becoming overwhelming.

In this way, Sirius becomes our third expedition member. I don't buy one of Andrea's puppies; I don't have twenty-five dollars to fork over. I looked in the paper for free or cheap puppies, and a couple of people came to show me their cuties. I bought the remaining female of a litter of half-husky, half-border-collie pups for five dollars. I choose her over the part German shepherd and part something-else-rather-big-sounding pup because I figured, for canoeing purposes, she would be the smallest of the options. As it turned out, my ninety-five-pound sweetie proved over and over that I made the right choice, but my reasoning fell flat.

I was more than ready to unencumber myself from house, job, money, and all the trappings of modern society and once again embrace the river life. The river is uncomplicated. We are in charge of only ourselves. The challenge lies in pitting our wits against whatever Mother Nature throws our way. On the river is where I can feel the hand of God, strengthening me, guiding me, protecting me. I need to nourish my spirit once again. The river's pull is strong and enticing, and I know that's where I need to be.

Tumbling Down with the Yellowstone

Day 1 (April 24, 1987): Reports of ice-free waterways on the other side of the mountain range give us the green light. Today is the chosen day. Vancie gladly offers to drive us and all our stuff the four hours up to Gardiner, Montana, to put into the Yellowstone River. We arrive the night before and camp among the elk at Mammoth Hot Springs Campground. Sirius is unsure about these huge creatures, but she soon ignores them and happily occupies herself scampering down hills and playing with sticks and pinecones. She never wanders far. Little does she know what's in store for her tomorrow.

Peeling out to run Yankee Jim Canyon. Photo courtesy of Vancie Turner.

Ten miles below the put-in is Yankee Jim Canyon, the stomping ground of Yellowstone Raft Company and their clientele who want a

thrilling river trip. Whether we should paddle all our worldly possessions through this exciting whitewater is debatable. But after we inquire
with the rafting company and do a bit of scouting, a sense of adventure
and a certain lure prevails over precaution. Remembering the thrill of
Snake River Canyon, even I concede. We take it on, fully loaded.

Not wanting to give Sirius a terrifying first impression of canoeing or risk her safety, we let her ride in Vancie's truck for the nine-
mile length of the canyon. Vancie also serves as our photographer and
safety line in case we need her. She drives her vehicle along the river,
stopping at accesses to snap us running the rapids. I don't have to
worry about Sirius, and we also have support in case we dump.

What a thrilling way to begin this second leg of our journey.
Donning paddling jackets and full spray skirt, we attack the canyon,
full of jitters. At least I'm jittery. Tom admits he too gets butterflies
every time he runs whitewater. But it's very simple, really: avoid the
rocks, avoid the eddies, and avoid the huge waves; stay in the water
that is going where you want to go; and don't get broadside. Simple.

"Ready?" Tom calls up to me as we approach the first rapid,
Yankee Jim's Revenge.

"Yeah, I guess so," I reply. He can hear the anxiety in my voice. "We
can do this," he yells. I am in the bow position and Tom in the stern.

I know we can do it. I have confidence in MW and Tom and even
my own paddling ability. These facts in no way serve to calm my fears.

"Good line," I shout as we shove off. "Follow the main flow."
Revenge is a reasonably straightforward chute full of standing waves,
so we just follow the flow. Down we go into the first drop. Here we
gooooooo! My paddle bites the water and grabs when I need it to. I
draw, I brace, I finesse. I keep MW's nose pointed where I want her
to go. MW bounces up and down from trough to peak like a bucking
bronco. I get drenched as each wave surges over the bow.

"Whoo-hooooooo," I holler as we emerge from the tumult, still upright. My jitters have metamorphosed into ecstasy.

"Yahoo," Tom shouts, "what a ride!"

"Yeah, what a ride." I am definitely feeling the effects of adrenalin. The river is welcoming us back to the fold. I am fully baptized.

Running a rapid in Yankee Jim Canyon. Photo courtesy of Vancie Turner.

"Boy, this water is cooooooold," I remark, thrusting a knee up into the spray skirt from below to push the accumulated pool of water off. Spring runoff is biting. Thank goodness we have paddling jackets that velcro tightly around neck and wrists. They cinch up around the waist and overlap the spray skirt that is snapped over the whole opening of MW. My new homemade nylon spray skirt is water-resistant but not waterproof. It deflects waves sure enough, but water drips through lap puddles. Our hands, encased in paddling gloves, are likewise tightly cinched. Nothing, though, insulates us completely from this frigid snowmelt. We avoid rapids when we can, but sometimes we have no choice but to run them. Big House is a tough one, boasting a giant standing wave down the middle. We gallop our noble steed down river left—reaching, drawing, bracing, maneuvering. Now one with the river, dancing its dance, feeling its rhythm. Tom and I have lost none of our paddling chemistry over the winter. MW responds to our every whim and request, seemingly to revel in the fun and adventure.

Skirting rapids when we can. Photo courtesy of Vancie Turner.

We bounce through Boxcar, the last of the big rapids. Vancie is below this drop, waiting with Sirius.

We shove MW onto shore, and I sit in the boat, stilling my heart and dissipating my adrenalin. Sirius runs over to greet me, so I extricate myself from the boat, hop out and hug my fluffy little pup. Running this canyon would have been tumultuous for her, if not disastrous. Above deck, she'd be tossed overboard. Below deck she'd be sloshed around like in a washing machine. I'm grateful not to have put her through that. She'd never have gotten in a canoe again.

"Wow—you guys are drenched!" Vancie remarks after sizing us up. Over lunch, still bubbly with excitement, we relive exciting rapids for Vancie's benefit. Eventually, we bid our wonderful friend a bittersweet farewell, sealing a lifelong bond with hugs and kisses.

This first night's camp is in a cottonwood grove in a pasture. Getting out to scout, I have to circumnavigate unusually large cow patties. "Look at the rubbings on these trees," I point out to Tom. We've camped in many a pasture before where the inhabitants pay us no mind. In retrospect, the steering-wheel sized patties, the pawed-up ground, and hair ingrained in the bark of nearly every tree should have given us a hint of something unnerving.

One of the roughly two-thousand-pound bulls comes over to investigate us once we're settled. I immediately snatch up Sirius and put a good-sized tree between Mr. Hamburger-on-the-hoof and us. I holler to Tom, who is fishing, but he doesn't hear. So Sirius and I watch the bull. He watches us, frequently looking over toward the tent, where my bright red sleeping bag is draped. *Doesn't red stimulate bulls? Is he thinking of charging that? I could swear I heard these fellas are actually color-blind and not stimulated by red. In a bullfight, the movement of the matador's cape gets them all riled up. Right? Should I put my sleeping bag away? No, that would move it and provoke him. Why oh, why does he keep staring?* Finally, I quit hammering myself, as it seems the stocky fellow just wants to figure out what sort of intrusion this is. After fifteen minutes, he tires of this boring game, ambles over to a tree twenty feet from us, and proceeds to scratch. In time, he leaves. Okay, not a bad fellow, but I hope he doesn't return with his buddies.

He returns with his buddies. By then, all three of us are snug in bed. I peek out of the tent door. It seems his friends are all larger than the scout. The tent gets curious stares, but then they pay it no mind. Snorting appears to be the main order of business till head butting comes into vogue. A flimsy nylon tent affords no protection against a herd of clashing Goliaths pushing each other around. What a way to go—squashed under the head-butt loser who trips on our little nylon tent cords. This must stop.

"What do we have to scare them away with?" I ask Tom.

"I say we throw sticks and rocks at them."

"Do you think clanging pots and pans would help?"

"Couldn't hurt, but they're buried in the kitchen under the trash bag."

"Do you think they'll get mad and charge?"

"I don't think so."

"Are you sure we should do this?"

"Not at all. Do you have any other ideas?"

I don't have any. Like getting psyched before a football game, Tom and I storm out on the count of three. We pelt those fellas with anything we could find. "Get outta here," "Let us sleep," "Go play someplace else." They stop and stare. That's all, just stare. They don't budge. Getting up our nerve, we try false charges at them. We make them skitter a few feet away. They obviously don't think we are of any danger, but we sure make ourselves annoying. After being entertained by our crazy antics, the bulls amble a safer distance away. We climb back into the tent to calm an extremely nervous pup.

I go in first and scoop Sirius up. "Okay, next time we consider the size of the patty before choosing a campsite," I say, just so we are both clear on that point.

"Poop size. Got it."

None of us get much sleep that night. The heavy breathing of bedded-down bulls is not exactly a lullaby.

Poor Sirius has no idea that canoes, tents, animals, and all sorts of surprises will become her fated way of life. Sirius turns out to be an excellent river dog and avid camper. At campsites and during lunch, she never wanders far. Sticks, bugs, grasses, and pinecones are all entertaining toys. Recognizing her need for exercise, we figure

Tom might take her for a walk while I fix supper. Sirius will have none of it. If we don't all go, she won't be a part of it. So, we all take walks together. Sirius is not inclined to get in the water, which is a good thing. Paddling with a water breed, who would be jumping overboard to swim all the time, wouldn't work. She is merely a wading dog, inclined to go up to her belly. In the canoe, she often sleeps between the feet of the person in the stern. Or she will station herself on the upper deck, on top of all the gear. I feel like her minion, transporting her to the far reaches of the earth. And she, my queen, relaxing on her boat, watching the world go by.

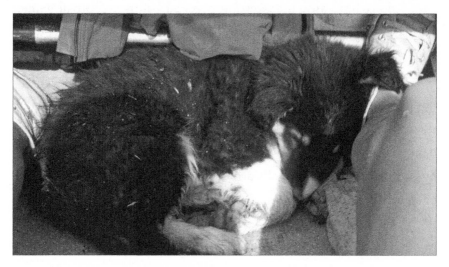

Snoozing pup between my feet

Outdoor Living

Day 3 (April 26): Now, it's back to the basics. Living outdoors 24/7 has its challenges. Today begins like many others. I awake to Tom's rustling. He partially unzips his sleeping bag. I'm vaguely aware of

Tom grabbing some pants, and I hear zzzzzip for the bottom of the tent door and zzzzzip for the vertical. He pauses, body inside the tent and feet outside, while he puts on his sandals from the vestibule. A third zzzzzip for the vestibule allows him to emerge into the day. I hear the zzzzzip of the horizontal zipper, zzzzzip of the vertical door zipper, and know I am alone for a while. I smile and pull the bag over my head to see if I can get back to sleep.

"C'mon, sleepyhead," I hear from without. My eyes pop open at the intrusive sound. He shakes the ridgepole of our tent. "Time to get up."

"Noooo," I whine.

"C'mon. I've been up forty-five minutes already."

Gee, I guess I did fall back to sleep. "Okayyyy. I'm workin' on it." I squirm over from lying on my side to flat on my back and fold down the sleeping bag hood covering my face. The roof's yellow brightness penetrates my eyelids and tells me it is indeed daylight. "What time is it?"

"It's 7:30."

I muffle a "hmmph." Fluttering my sleepy eyes, I give them a good wake-up rub. I shouldn't be sleeping so late. While they are practicing staying open, my eyes study the interior of our little tent between blinks. The yellow roof and green fly overtopping it create an orangey glow inside. My towel hanging from the clothesline along the ridgeline forms a suggestion of a partition. My bra hangs there too. I sit up, reach my hand over to the mesh pocket beside me, and fumble around for my glasses. I distinguish them from my lip balm and tissues, unfold them, and put them on. The sleeping bags are atop our Therm-a-Rests, which, as I roll over, I find that Tom has removed his. Special covers for these inflatable mattresses allow them to double as chairs, and I suspect Tom is now sitting on his outside. They make sleeping on the ground bearable—not comfortable by any stretch, but that inch-and-a-half of air and foam provides insulation from the cold and relief from the hard ground. I extract today's clothes from my fleece pillowcase and note that the annoying object poking my head last night was the jackknife I forgot to take out of my pocket before stuffing my pants in there.

I dress in whatever emerges from the sleeping bag first, squirming around as needed. Once clothed, I stuff my sleeping bag into its stuff sack lined with a plastic garbage bag to stave off wetness. I do this again for Tom's bag.

I emerge as Tom did—feet first—into the vestibule. I put my sandals on, then tote my towel into the morning air. For the first time in about ten hours, I stand erect.

"Mornin', cutie."

"Hmmph." I know he is joshing me, as my hair is wild and I'm a horrible sight. Some folks can't talk before coffee. For me, the turning point is washing my face. He lets me go about my business.

When Valerie Fons Krueger gave me advice about taking time for myself, I took it to heart. I know she experienced clinical exhaustion on her expedition, so her advice was hard learned. Every morning I take the time I need to prepare for the day. This does not mean a shower and application of makeup, by any means, but I do have a routine. After going off into the woods to pee, I grab my washcloth off the clothesline and toiletries from my pack and head to the water's edge.

I squat on a suitable rock, douse my cloth in the cold water, add a little soap and surprise my face with it. Ahhhhhh—instantly refreshed. I am jolted awake with its coldness. I feel alive and awake.

Each morning I baptize myself in the water of our journey. This water is going where I am going. It has been where I have been. I have performed this ritual nearly every day from the very first moment of paddling. It is my wake-up and my anointing. The water and I make a pact: the river becomes a part of me in cleansing, and I become a part of the river as we travel companionably together. Only where the water is too adulterated do I abstain. Today I look out over the river and decide this will be a good day.

Just because we are river people doesn't mean we aren't clean. "Showering" river-style can take two forms:

- Our ritual is to skinny-dip in each state we pass through. Early one morning on the Yellowstone, I "do" Montana. Before either Tom or Sirius noticed, I stripped down and jumped in. Jarred by the profound cold, I screeched bloody murder and soon had them running to my rescue.

- When a river submersion is not possible or even when it is, I am invigorated with another, often more agreeable bathing custom: bare myself to nature under the handy solar outdoor shower hung from a tree branch. Feeling the breeze caress my body where breezes seldom blow is liberating and sensual.

The Yellowstone in the Springtime

Day 4 (April 27): Birds abound here on the Yellowstone. Most are in pairs at this time of year, establishing nests, sitting on eggs, or already leading a clutch of chicks. Mergansers, mallards, cinnamon teals, red-tailed hawks, Canada geese, whistling swans, and great blue herons are daily companions.

"What is that?" I blurt as I maneuver the boat through a rapid around one of the countless bends in the river. Something splashing around in the water catches my eye.

"Whoa, I think it's a bald eagle." Tom sees it too.

"Is it snagging a fish?" I ask as I give the bird a wide berth. I turn into an eddy and slide MW up onto a gravel bar downriver of the bird. By now, the eagle, also standing on the gravel bar, is glaring at us. I have never been so close to an eagle before. It's magnificent. Its right wing is drooping down at an awkward angle, and it just hops away from us without trying to fly.

"Looks like it's injured. We should get this to a game warden," Tom suggests.

"Yeah, or wildlife rehabber," I add. Thoughts of capturing this bird are quickly dismissed as soon as we voice them. Even seemingly injured, this bird is by no means inept. First, she is huge. I'm guessing she's a she because female bald eagles are about a third larger than males. Her head would probably come up to my thigh if we were to stand together. Her talons are like needle-tipped scythes, and her fierce golden eyes are as intimidating as a guard dog snarling and straining on a chain. This is out of our league.

"We should just report it," I say. To me, this is just one of the hundreds of unnamed twists and turns on the Yellowstone River, but we make note of our location as best we can.

In about two miles, we land in Springdale, where we find the postmaster's house. She helps us ring up the Big Timber game warden, who promises to try to find the eagle this afternoon.

The pale green of the surrounding hills and the newly opened cottonwood buds remind me it is still early spring. Yet the sun speaks of summer. I paddle in shorts and T-shirt day after day here in late April in the mountains. I am thankful for a steady breeze to keep me cool.

"Why does the wind only blow on the river?" Tom asks as he would a student. We sit now on a pebbly shore, eating PB & J in the hot, baking sun.

"Yeah, you're right. It's hot and calm onshore here, and on the river it's cool and breezy." All morning, we have been fighting a stiff headwind. "Maybe the wind just now stopped?"

"I don't think so. I noticed this difference yesterday too," Tom said.

I nod, taking another bite of my sandwich and thinking how right he is. I watch Sirius sniffing around the beach. "It has to do with the temperature gradient," Tom continues. I recall the bank sign in town yesterday flashed 78 degrees. It's the same if not warmer today. The science teacher is ready to explain. "The sun heats up the land, causing the warm air to rise upslope. The cooler air from the valley and all along this cold river flows upriver to fill the void."

"Makes sense." I nod. "But maybe it's because we go so fast!" I look his way with a corny smile and raised eyebrows.

Tom laughs. "Yeah, that must be it. Are you done?"

"Yup, let's go. Here, take a last swig of water." He does as he's told, and I stuff the leftovers back in the daypack as we get up to leave. Sirius lifts her head from her game of ant pouncing to notice we are heading for the boat. "C'mon pup" is all the incentive she needs to bound after us. "Sit down and wait, please," I instruct her, and she does just that. She anxiously awaits the magic words while maintaining a seemingly torturous sitting position and never taking her eyes off me. "Okay, hop in." These are the words she was waiting for, and she bounds for the boat, making a valiant effort to jump aboard. Her front legs succeed, but her rear end doesn't make it. Her back legs spin while she tries to pull herself up on top of the gear. I give her bottom a boost, and our queen resumes her throne on the top deck. We shove off. Right away, the cooling wind greets us.

The Yellowstone is a continuum of twists and turns. Outside curves create curly waves; inside curves are too shallow to paddle. Any lower, and MW would scrape her belly on the pebbly bottom. Any higher, and the waves would splash water into the boat. Once again, we navigate that fine line between eddylines and boisterous waves at this perfect water level.

If we don't, and the bow gets caught in the eddy, a dumping could be in store. The trick is to anticipate the change of water direction at the eddy line and lean and brace accordingly, allowing MW to do a lovely pirouette. Balance is key.

Once facing upstream in the eddy, we nose MW out into the current again and power through the eddy line, leaning downstream. We are once again on our way. Hey, doing a 360 like this—an eddy turn—is all in good fun and puts a little excitement into the day.

The river is clear, clean, and only mildly silty. Sand and pebbles, churned up by the frisky current, sometimes tickle MW's hull. The result—quite alarming at first—is a sound as if she is dissolving right out from underneath us. Maybe that's what a boat sounds like when she giggles.

We travel along, passing towns such as Livingston and Big Timber, Montana, enjoying forested hills and beautiful bluffs. Eventually, the Yellowstone widens and straightens as it accepts contributions from other rivers. Past Reed Point, the Boulder River joins the Yellowstone. In Columbus, Montana, the Itch-Kep-Pe (Rose) Ak-Ja (river) enters. Lewis and Clark adopted this descriptive native name because wild roses covered the river shoreline. Now, it is known as the Stillwater River. I guess Itch-Kep-Pe is probably too hard to pronounce or too difficult to write on maps. The growing Yellowstone still meanders, seeking its easiest path, but there is not nearly as much braiding around sand bars and islands. With each incoming river, the Yellowstone gets murkier.

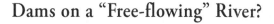

Dams on a "Free-flowing" River?

Day 9 (May 1): Today brings a new sort of outdoor challenge. Just west of Custer, we portaged a dam. I didn't expect this. Tom kept calling the Yellowstone "America's last free-flowing river." I recount the event in my journal: "A warning sign spanning the river foretold of a diversion dam. It was about one mile before the dam itself, and yup, it was necessary to portage. We paddled right up to it, made three trips of about five hundred feet, and left the five-foot drop behind. I hope there are no more."

There's more. This is one of seven diversion dams across the Yellowstone that we encounter.

The problem with these dams is severalfold. They are not very high, which makes running them tempting. This, we do twice. These two dams had—either on purpose or naturally—crumbled away in a spot that created a chute we could ride right through. Running the dam is not only fun but fast and painless. The bow person gets a little wet as we smash through standing waves, but it is unquestionably better than portaging.

The hydraulic at the bottom of these dams is the real danger. We have to unload, carry, and reload the three hundred pounds of gear just a few feet for three of these dams.

Another problem with these dams is that they are impossible to see from upriver until you are practically on top of them. This seems hard to believe, I know. The crest of the dam—the top edge—is undifferentiable from the rest of the river beyond the small waterfall. The densely vegetated shoreline gives no clue of an impending drop either. Only the sound of roaring water is our clue that we are sneaking up on a dam.

We are approaching an island, and I, in the bow, have to choose which side to take. I choose right.

Soon after the fork, I shout, "Get left" to Tom in the stern, as I hear the sound of a low-head dam waterfall ahead. He soon has us hugging the island's shore.

"What do you say we turn around and try the left fork?" Tom suggests, in hopes that the other side doesn't have a dam. I agree. Our bodies are not used to this going upriver stuff anymore. Pulling with my back, grunting, using every muscle, we gradually make our way back to the head of the island against this relentless current.

"Hit the eddy!" I holler in my weak, high-pitched girly voice, which is all I can muster. There is a good-sized boulder just upstream of the head of the island, forming a decent eddy. I realize that if we push just a bit beyond the island to the eddy, we can pause there, then peel out into water going left of the island. If we turn immediately, the current will push us right against the island and pin us there. Tom doesn't hear me. Nor does he see the rock and eddy from the stern.

We start to turn. The river grabs MW's nose.

"No," I cry and try to correct it but cannot.

The river pushes us broadside, and *bang*, we end up pinned alongside a logjam at the head of the island. One slight tip upriver allowing the water over the gunwales would pin MW like that yellow canoe on the Snake. I sit there momentarily my heart thumping hard and fast, partly from the physical exertion, partly from the precarious position I don't want to worsen.

"Get out!" Tom yells in his taking-charge voice, jarring me into action. He is already standing on the logjam. "Don't tip the boat," he instructs. I clamber out, and we each grab thwarts and heave the canoe forward. It budges a bit. Sirius is frantic and wants to get out too. Tom shoves her down off the gear and into the bottom of the boat.

"Heave!" he says, and we make a little more progress. A dozen heaves later, half the boat is in the current flowing past the island and almost ready to go. "Hop in," Tom instructs, and I crawl over the gear and Sirius to take my bow position. I push with my paddle for the next of Tom's heaves. A final heave sends us racing down the other side of the island. He must have jumped aboard at the last second.

Although I secretly fume at Tom for turning the corner too soon—thinking he should have known better—I don't bring it up. I know I failed to communicate when it was necessary, and I am also to blame. He doesn't concern himself with the day's events either, except to grumble about low-head dams. But when it comes to getting us out of a jam, I can always count on Tom. He knows what to do, and he doesn't waste time. I am very glad he is a part of my life.

Six days later, Tom turns twenty-seven. We celebrate by taking a day off. We hang out at our campsite and cook a delicious birthday meal of steak and sautéed vegetables topped off with black forest brownies baked on our campfire. His old age turns him somewhat melancholy. Unbeknownst to me at the time, he writes in his journal, "My trip with Nancy has taught me a lot about people and love . . . I learned what real love now means. I find that Nancy's mere presence makes my day better. We've been together twenty-four hours a day for almost a year now, and I could go on forever this way. We'll see if I can convince her."

The consummate outdoor baker shows off his birthday brownies

CHAPTER 7

The Miserable Missouri

You gain strength, courage and confidence by
every experience in which you really stop to
look fear in the face. You are able to say to
yourself, "I lived through this horror. I can
take the next thing that comes along." You
must do the thing you think you cannot do.

—Eleanor Roosevelt

An Ugly Transition

Day 24 (May 17): Leaving the frolicking mountain-born Yellowstone for the boat-ridden Missouri pains me. The dreary, windy rain manifests my feelings. On this day, we abandon the wilderness where I can envision a band of mounted warriors on a butte above the Yellowstone River. Not one of the 23 days and 510 miles went by without sighting a new bird.

Where the Yellowstone speaks of wildlife, the Missouri speaks of commerce. The Yellowstone's bed is pebbly; the Missouri's bed is viscous clay. Yellowstone water is clear; the Missouri's is muddy brown. The Yellowstone flows naturally in sweeping curves and over rocks; the Missouri belches muddy eruptions from unseen forces below. Maybe it is a self-fulfilling prophesy, but I don't like the Missouri from the start, and it doesn't like us either.

The Missouri River starts in the Rocky Mountains of Montana. It drains parts of ten states and two Canadian provinces before joining the Mississippi just north of St. Louis, Missouri. The USGS considers it the longest river in the United States,[14] the Mississippi its nearest rival. We will be on it for quite some time.

From Sioux City, Iowa, northward, the U.S. Army Corps of Engineers have harnessed the Missouri River for irrigation, hydropower, recreation, and flood control. We need to bypass five of the Corps' dams and paddle their impounded lakes. The dams don't have locks, as the river is not navigable for large boats north of Sioux City, so we will have to portage around each one. Again, I'm not looking forward to this leg of our trip.

Granted, the Missouri is an important waterway. It has helped build our country—facilitating travel, commerce, and industry. Today we can add recreation and hydropower to that list.

We take out at a boat launch where the Yellowstone dumps us into the Missouri. All three of us step out into the mucky clay. Anglers line the shore. Each wields a very long rod fitted with a great big reel. Tom wanders off to relieve himself. I lumber over to an angler.

"What are ya fishin' for?"

"Paddlefish," he replies without a glace my way.

"They're big fish?" I ask, nodding at his gear.

"Yup." He turns his head away from me to spit, but not taking his eyes off where his line enters the water. "The biggest one from this 'ere spot weighed in at eighty-one pounds." He never looks at me, utterly intent on fishing. As I gaze around, everyone seems fixated on the task at hand.

I figure these fish must only run for a short time, or else, all these people wouldn't be out in such miserable weather. The tents and trailers in the nearby field indicate that this is more than a one-day affair. One tent has blown over—still flapping in the rough wind. I take my photo and plod back to the canoe, Frankenstein-like, with a globby buildup of mud on my shoes. Tom is already there, scraping clods off his shoes after having washed Sirius's paws and placing her in the boat.

As a sturgeon relative, paddlefish are one of the largest freshwater fish in North America. They can grow to over five feet long and commonly weigh 60 pounds but have been found to reach over 150 pounds. The body looks sharklike, with similar fins and rough skin instead of scales. The snout is paddle-shaped. Where a swordfish has a sword, a paddlefish has a paddle that can be about one-third its body length.

Researchers believe this paddle, covered with sensory organs, helps it to locate its primary food: zooplankton. During the spring spawning runs—which coincide with our visit—paddlefish head upstream. According to the North Dakota Game and Fish Department, this confluence, and the last thirteen miles of the Yellowstone River we just paddled, are the best habitats left for these large fish. So, anglers gather in large numbers behind dams, deep waterways, and at this very junction in hopes of snagging a paddlefish.

Being filter feeders, paddlefish are not attracted to bait. Instead, they must be snagged on a big hook. I take it from my informant's attentiveness to this task, it requires concentration to detect a fish's presence and act quickly to snag it. Due to severe river alterations and past overharvesting, paddlefish numbers have dwindled drastically since 1900. In North Dakota, Montana, and at least eight other states, they are listed as endangered or threatened. State authorities highly regulate harvesting, but siltation, dams, channelization, and desire for meat and caviar have forever impacted many of our nation's big river inhabitants like paddlefish and sturgeon.

We paddle along in the choppy water. After a while, we come upon something odd in the water.

"Do you see that?" Tom says, pointing with his paddle.

I look and see a small blue object. "Yeah. What is it?"

"A float of some sort."

"It's bobbing strangely." It disappears underwater for a second as we watch, then comes back up, paying no heed to where the wind would push it or the current carry it.

"Head over there. Let's check it out." This is a mystery we have to solve.

I deliver Tom, in the bow, to the left of the object so he can reach for it with his right hand. He reaches down and picks it up. It's a plastic oil bottle with a fishing line attached. Tom pulls on the line. The line yanks back. Hand over hand, Tom reels it in. At the end is a carp. A rather big carp, with a line attached to its dorsal fin. As Tom tries to lift it out to free it, the carp gives a final desperate flip, landing in the back of the boat with Sirius and me. Both of us, in our own unique ways, emit startled yips. I nearly drop my paddle. Sirius, both curious and cautious, advances to sniff the fish, whereupon the fish convulses again, sending the pup skyrocketing out of my reach, yipping and yipping.

"Come here, Puparoo." I reach out for her as the fish gives another big squirmy flip. "Come here, Sirius!" I can't have her hopping about, rocking the boat.

"Toss it overboard. Scoop it up. Toss it out!" Tom hollers.

The boat is pitching; the dog is yipping; I am calling; Tom is yelling; the fish is flopping. A slapstick comedy could not come close to reenacting the ridiculous commotion. Somehow Sirius does a flip of her own, right over the fish, landing close to me. I quickly scoop her up. By this time, Tom has crawled over the equipment and is there to set things straight. He cuts the line with his Swiss army knife, scooping up the carp and tossing it overboard. We all go back to our respective places.

"Well, that was exciting," I conclude, relieved we got through that without tipping over or losing the pup overboard.

Tom gives me a look over the rim of his glasses and shakes his head, none too happy with the ruckus. "Yup. Real exciting." Then he changes his tune. "Why would you do that to a fish? Maybe it's someone's sick idea of a joke."

One method of carp fishing involves the use of a float. A monofilament line is rigged with weights, bait, hook, and float, but it is designed to have the carp go after the bait, which is near, or a part of the hook, to catch the fish in the mouth. Here, the hook firmly pierced the dorsal fin. Tom and I discuss and conjecture as we paddle along. We conclude this is not traditional fishing gone awry. This was a setup. Animal cruelty. It baffles and saddens me. Meanwhile, Sirius keeps her gaze on the water from her perch atop the gear, perhaps wondering when our next uninvited guest will suddenly drop in.

Lake SaYUCKawea

Day 27 (May 20): Our first days on the Missouri are miserable. When it is not raining, it is overcast. When it is not blustery with tall waves, it is slightly windy with less intense waves. Our campsites are well-used angler access spots, littered with bottles, cans, monofilament lines, wrappers, and other trash. We need to clean up before pitching the tent to make the sites amenable. This proves necessary after Sirius's newfound joy becomes chewing on and rolling in stinky fish heads.

After three days of dreary weather, we finally get a beautiful sunny day. Fluffy white cumulus clouds hang in the distance, and a calm breeze keeps us cool—perfect paddling weather. On this day, we enter Lake Sakakawea. This enormous lake starts just past Williston, North Dakota, and extends one hundred fifty miles to its enforcer, Garrison Dam, near Riverdale. The lake is over two miles wide, even at this narrow riverlike beginning. Not knowing where to go, the slowed river meanders out toward marshy areas. Then it spreads over a forest of drowned trees, emerging from the water like toothpicks. These dark, nearly branchless tree trunks appear to wear hats, as each sport a heron or cormorant nest. The stalled river creeps up every draw, making the shoreline ragged with deep coves separated by protruding points. We are forced to begin a huge "connect the dots" game by paddling to the tip of one point, then adjusting our direction for a beeline to the next point. Paddling time between points is anywhere from thirty minutes to an hour. This is a lovely lake, and it is such a beautiful day. It must be a good omen.

"What do ya say about doing a twenty-four-hour paddle on this lake?" Tom asks.

"That'll be a challenge," I reply. "We haven't had much luck with nighttime paddles, though."

"We're now in the Central Time Zone," my ever-vigilant keeper of data remarks. "The sky stays light until about 9:30. How 'bout we get a good night's sleep and start in the morning?"

"Sure. Sounds good to me." We paddle along merrily, singing when the spirit moves us, happy to have a lovely day for once.

That night we find an excellent campsite on a small stone beach nestled between two towering bluffs, a wall of shrubs and trees up the bank behind us. Scattered driftwood provides convenient backrests. Tomorrow we'll get an early start to enjoy this beautiful lake.

Perhaps it has a menacing reputation to maintain, but for whatever reason, the lake has other ideas. Like a heavyweight prizefighter insulted by being called a pussycat, Lake Sakakawea seems compelled to correct our benevolent misconception of her.

I pop awake in the pitch dark to the sound of a violent slap, slap, slap of the tent's nylon fly. When wind starts howling at night, I figure a storm is approaching. I lie there wide-eyed, praying ripstop nylon is accurately named. Soon I hear the tinkle of stakes hurled on the rocks as the wind yanks them out. Instantly the tent wall heaves in, tossing me over onto Tom.

"Sorry," I say as I try to counter the move, "but it's pushing me."

"Not a problem for me." I think I detect a little mirth in his alert tone.

"You're awake too." I state the obvious as I struggle and squirm in the confines of my sleeping bag to push the tent wall back with much vigor but little luck.

"Why is the wind starting to blow now?" I ask. Usually, winds die down after sunset.

"I don't know, but I don't like it," Tom responds. The wind is now howling. Every gust sounds angry.

"Shouldn't we do something?" I finally blurt out.

"Let's try to get everything up to that meadow closer to the trees." Tom now has to shout. He has obviously been lying there, formulating a plan, while I wriggled around like a caterpillar in a cocoon. "We can each hold onto two corners and drag the tent up the rise."

"Carry it erected?"

"If we can. Like we did at Hood River. Now, get your shoes on and come out right after me." I find my shoes by feel and think about all the ways this could go wrong. Namely about becoming a human kite.

"Do you see Puparoo?" I shout, but he doesn't hear. Sirius is not in the vestibule, where she sleeps. I give her a holler but realize my voice is too wimpy to be of much use in this wind. She'll have to fend for herself because I sure can't do anything about her now.

I crawl out on the heels of Tom and am immediately met with an insulting slap of high-powered wind mixed with a dash of stinging sand. I squint to keep it out of my eyes but soon find there is no advantage to keeping my eyes open anyway. It's pitch-dark.

"I've got this side," he hollers above the gale. "Go to the other side." I grope around the tent and grasp the bottom of two leeward corners of the tent where they attach to the poles.

"Ready?" Tom hollers above the wind's roar.

"Ready," I yell. With that, we lift, and immediately I'm knocked onto my butt by billowing nylon.

"Hey!" I hear Tom yell. "Come on!"

I scramble to my feet, digging into the pebbles to prevent take-off. Using a headlamp, Tom can get an idea of where to go in the dark. I stumble over every driftwood log. It doesn't make any difference that the tent engulfs me, obscuring my view. There is no view to be had in this darkness. As the front of the tent gets higher, I know we are going up. I crawl, scramble, and climb up the bank, pushing that nylon blob wherever he tugs it.

"Here's the spot. Put 'er down," Tom yells. "Put the stakes in."

"Yeah, right," I reply sarcastically, too low for him to hear. "I've got one. How many do you have?" Tom has none.

The wind is not quite so ferocious up here. But it still howls. The nearby trees strain, moan, creak, and screech.

"Then let's get rocks or logs to weigh it down." I rummage

around and come up with a few suitable stake sticks and put them to good use. While groping, I am accosted by my frightened, whining pup. Overjoyed, I give her a hearty hug and smooch, then shove her inside the tent for safekeeping.

"Let's get the canoe," Tom yells.

"Okay," I answer, grabbing his belt and following him blindly back down the bank. Straining to go with the wind, she has skittered a few feet, but because of our habit of clipping personal packs to the thwarts of the overturned canoe at night, she is still earthbound. We yank, drag, and hoist the canoe up the bank to the more sheltered area and tie her to a tree. Lastly, we wrangle the kitchen and personal packs up the bank with no shortage of grunting, groaning, and scrambling on hands and knees.

Tom and I clamber inside the tent and try to put some order to its contents. We climb into our sleeping bags. I situate Sirius on my sleeping bag and wrap my arms around her. Tom scoots close to me and wraps his arms around the two of us.

No sooner do we settle down than the deluge of rain, which so politely waited until we were snug in our new location, begins to torture us. Why not? Bring it on. In this way, the three of us spend a fearful, sleepless night amid crashing waves, creaking trees, slapping nylon, and a wind-provoked tent that keeps pushing and prodding me like a restless, obnoxious bedfellow.

We stay here three restless days, cooking in the vestibule, reading and writing in the tent, taking periodic walks if the rain lets up intermittently. By the fourth day, we are beyond restless. The wind isn't calm, but enough is enough. We have to get out of here. Bowlicker waves force us to wear the spray skirt. The sky is overcast, the air is cold, but we are content to be on the water again despite the rain that continues to fall.

The lake never let her nasty reputation come under question

again. It is hard not to take her treatment toward us personally. The spirit of this lake didn't seem to fit its namesake, Sacagawea (also spelled Sacajawea or Sakakawea), the indispensable member of the Lewis and Clark Expedition.

In 1800, a Hidatsa hunting party abducted a group of Shoshone women and children. Sacagawea, then twelve years old, and the other captives were taken to live in their Hidatsa-Mandan settlement in what is now central North Dakota. Three to four years later, Toussaint Charbonneau, a French-Canadian fur trapper who lived at the settlement, took Sacagawea as his wife. Lewis and Clark arrived in the settlement in the fall of 1804 and built Fort Mandan nearby, where they overwintered. The captains hired Charbonneau as an interpreter and welcomed Sacagawea to join the expedition. Charbonneau, Sacagawea, and their two-month-old baby headed west with the Corps of Discovery in the spring.

Sacagawea turned out to be more of an asset than her husband. She facilitated communication between her Shoshone people and the captains; eased relations with other tribes; identified landmarks and provided guidance; secured wild food and medicines; and even saved valuable cargo when the boat she was in nearly capsized, all while caring for an infant. In his journal, Meriwether Lewis described Charbonneau as, "perhaps the most timid waterman in the world," but he ascribed "fortitude and resolution" to Sacagawea.

This lake is not the Sacagawea I've read about. This lake is possessed with a malicious spirit. I nickname her Sa-YUCK-awea.

The spirit Sa-yuck-awea blasts us with persistent winds. There is no escaping her. Mornings, evenings, nighttime, she sends her winds to torture us. Four or five times a day we bail out the waves that smash between the snaps on the spray skirt or soak through the top. The tossing makes Sirius seasick. Sa-yuck-awea turns us into spaghetti-armed, frozen-fingered, short-tempered grouches. She even manifested herself as that cunning coyote of Native American lore.

"Shhhh," Tom whispers. "Look to your right." We are on our lunch break, seated against driftwood that the waves had pushed to the back of the beach. Sirius is engrossed, squashing bugs by the water's edge. She pounces, slaps her paw down, even smashes them with her snout.

I look to my right. "Ohhhhh, wow," I whisper. A beautiful silver-haired coyote is walking our way. It seems intent on finding the best path to the beach without getting too close to us. It doesn't so much as glance at us. While it's obscured by the undergrowth lining the beach, we strain to track its progress. Then, carefully, it steps out into the open and slowly, crouching, inches toward Sirius.

"It's stalking Sirius," I say, half concerned, half fascinated. Tom puts a hand on my lap to curb my instincts to foil the coyote's plan. It is still many yards away. He wants to see if Sirius notices. Our Puparoo, however, continues her game, blissfully unaware. Before it was close enough to charge, we both feel compelled to put an end to this *National Geographic* moment.

"Don't eat my pup!" I shout, ejecting myself from the log, waving my arms, and running toward Sirius. "Scram. Get out of here!" I hear Tom hoot and clap, right behind me.

Sirius immediately perks up in time to see a bushy tail of something scamper off into the undergrowth, then looks at us running toward her like maniacs. In her face and body language, I can see that she is thinking: *What was that? What just happened? What are you doing?* I scoop her into my arms, reassuring her that what she missed was well worth missing.

That night, we make camp in a pleasant little hollow under the protection of a huge cottonwood tree. The wind is still blowing relentlessly, but not on us. We hear the waves crashing, but not on us.

"I let that coyote get far too close," I reflect as I stir the New England clam chowder soup in one pot and the noodles in the pot on the second stove. Happily chewing a stick, Sirius is lying close by.

"But nothing happened. We wouldn't have let it get that far," Tom said.

I give Puparoo a loving pat. She looks at me, gives two wags of her tail in thanks, and goes back to annihilating her stick.

"I'm going to take a walk," Tom announces—outdoor-speak for "I have to pee."

By the time he gets back, I have the noodles in a bowl and am pouring the soup over them for a hearty supper. From behind his back, Tom presents me with a bouquet of wildflowers.

"Wow—how beautiful!" I put down my pots and bowls to accept his gift.

"There's seven different species here."

My heart is instantly warmed. "That's so romantic. It's so unlike you."

"I know, huh? Smell the pale-yellow paintbrush one." I do and find it quite sweet-smelling. "This, I think, is a purple lupine of some sort, and this white trumpetlike flower I don't have a clue, but it grows in small spiky clusters." He tells me about each of the seven flowers. Usually, I'm the flower expert, but I let him be the botanist this time. I reach up to pull his head down so I can plant a big kiss on his lips. I put some water in a cup, plunk the flowers into it, and set it between us as we share a hearty meal. That evening we all go to bed, feeling a little more loving and a little more loved.

Get Us Off This Lake!

Day 34 (May 27): Inevitably, another day dawns, and we must get back to work battling Sa-yuck-awea. Abused for six days by wind, waves, and rain, I'm ready to be rid of this lake. The map we have is not nearly as detailed as we would like. It is four in the afternoon, and I'm feeling grumpy and tired.

"As close as I can figure, Garrison Dam should be around one of the next few points," Tom reassures me, trying to be optimistic. He is captain today.

The hills and buttes and rugged cliffs surrounding this reservoir create an incredibly ragged and confusing shoreline. Water, having filled all the low places, makes deep coves—each of which has coves of its own. From above, I bet it looks like millions of millipedes spreading out from the center. Higher elevations stick out into the lake as peninsulas. We cross each cove from one peninsula point to another making as efficient a course as possible.

"Good," I say, "Let's paddle until we get there. I don't care how long we have to go tonight; I want off this lake!"

"Yup, let's just go and camp at the boat launch by the dam tonight," Tom says.

We proceed from point to point. We watch the sun set. We watch the stars come out.

"Now, it's got to be around this point," Tom says.

"Isn't that what you said about the last seven or eight?" I remark.

"Yes, but it has got to be this one."

Well, it isn't. And it isn't the next one or the next one either. Like false peaks to a mountain climber, each peninsula is followed by yet another. In between every point is another killer cove crossing. The wind never goes to bed with the sun. But we keep pushing, believing that the dam's lights will lead us off this cursed lake around the very next bend. But it is never there. Another cruel joke by Sa-yuck-awea. Will it never end?!!

"We're not going to get there tonight," I relent.

"I guess I don't have a clue where it could be or how close we are." It is hard for Tom to admit defeat.

"My hands are raw, my muscles are screaming, and my eyes are going to shut down. I want to stop."

"How about that dark spot at the next point?"

"Sure. I don't care what it's like."

We unload enough to find our flashlights. There is one grassy spot big enough for a tent. It is severely slanted. I don't care. The distant flashes of lightning negate the idea of just throwing our bags on the ground and sleeping tentless. After misplacing the stakes and putting the fly on upside down while Tom squares away the canoe, I finally get things in order, and we climb in. I put Sirius's sleeping mat in the vestibule, and she plunks down on it at the same second. She is as tuckered as we are. Several times we wake up to find ourselves in a heap at the low end of the tent. We squirm to the top to sleep for a while during the trip back down. Of course, did I mention that it rained?

Almost teary-eyed with relief after three more hours of false points the next day, we arrive at Garrison Dam. Canoeists, by nature, detest portages. If they liked carrying stuff, they'd be backpackers. I feel like the only survivor at the end of the horror flick, doing anything in her means to escape the haunted house where blood, terror, and carnage rule.

I don't care how many miles I have to portage to get rid of Lake Sa-yuck-awea. Fortunately, it takes only two trips. I hear Tom whistle while he portages. So unlike him. Smiling, I lug my loads, full of gratitude to be rid of this 152-mile-long malevolent lake.

We saunter into Park City, a little town by the dam. A warning sign by the boat launch reads: 71 people have died on this lake. The store clerk tells us a kayaker going from Oregon to New Orleans wrote to her, saying this was the worst lake he'd encountered. None of this surprises me. It helps me realize the lake spirit isn't out to get us personally. She's evil to everyone.

To confirm our belief in the lake spirit Sa-yuck-awea, the next day, the next, and the next are lovely. The sun shines, the sky is blue, the clouds are amiable, the breeze is slight, and the river is pleasantly smooth. It reminds me of when evil Sa-yuck-awea invited us into her evil clutches nine days ago.

I suppose when the weather is nice, Lake Sa-yuck-awea might be beautiful. I can see green vegetation sprinkled with wildflowers atop the buttes. Tree-filled draws stretch down to meet the lake at stony beaches. Cliffs streaked with black and yellow tower above us as we round each point. The water is nicely clear but cold—colder than even the Yellowstone. A lapful from a big wave takes your breath away, and you have to get rid of it fast. An occasional angler can be seen on the lake. As we paddle by, I wonder why they are out in such horrid weather. I'm sure they're thinking the same about us.

River Life on the Missouri

Day 39 (June 1): We relax at our campsite among some tall cottonwoods offering protection from the wind and oncoming rain. Tom is just coming back from the tree where our solar shower hangs, having used it to wash his hair. Our nifty solar shower has been heating up water all day, sitting atop our gear as we paddled along.

"Oh gross!" I wince and shudder. I'm sitting on my PFD, petting and inspecting Sirius. Daily tick checks are necessary, and she is the prized tick collector.

"It's like a huge, bloated raisin. Looks like it's about to burst!" I nab its head between my nails next to Sirius's skin and yank. It comes out but leaves Sirius bleeding. "Oh gross, gross GROSS!" I cringe and drop the nasty varmint on Tom's box for him to kill. We never let these critters get away with their dirty deeds. Tom takes his knife, cuts it in half. It leaves a big brown bloody smudge on his box. Tom checks me. He gets one off my scalp, my underarm, and my lower back. One angler told us it's a bad year for ticks. Looks like for ticks, it's a good year.

I use the rest of the solar-shower water for my hair and an upper body half-bath. With river dunkings, five gallons is adequate for full showers and hair washes for us both. We plan to call the newspaper in Bismarck and need to look decent for a brush with civilization.

Clean of ticks and dirt, Tom tells me the result of the project he's been working on. "Looks like our total expenses for May were two hundred seventy-four dollars and twelve cents." He keeps all our receipts in an envelope taped in his journal.

"We eat a lot of food, I guess."

"Well, we sent some packages once, and we went out to eat a few times too."

"I guess that's not bad though, eh?"

"No, remember we budgeted five hundred a month. We're doing well. We're usually around three hundred." Our record of not paying for a single night's stay continues unbroken. After all, who would charge us to sleep in a cow pasture with patties as dense as the flies who frequent them?

In North Dakota, we are interviewed and photographed for the

Bismarck Tribune. We know the story came out the following day because all the anglers we run into over the next few days say things like, "Are you the canoeists in the paper?" "Hey, I read about you two!" and conclude with well-wishes. I like this. It gives me a sense of celebrity. It goes a little differently if there has been no recent publicity or if we run into anglers who only use a newspaper to wrap fish. As we approach an angler in his boat (only because he's on our heading), social etiquette calls for someone to speak. Usually, the angler gives in first.

"Mornin'," he says today. Some of my favorite openers are, "Looks like work to me." This one is more typical. Or better yet, "How far you boys from home?" I guess I'm pretty masculine-looking at this point.

"G'morning," Tom replies. "Any luck?"

"Naw, just nibbles." By this time, we're even with his boat.

"How far have you rowed?" Anglers don't understand the difference between paddling and rowing. This doesn't offend us anymore. (Okay, I feel compelled to point out some basic differences. Oars are used for rowing boats like skulls and rowboats. They attach to the boat by oarlocks, and—except in a dory—the rower faces backward. Paddles are used in canoes and kayaks and standup paddleboards. They are handheld and much lighter, and the paddler can face the direction of travel.)

"Twenty-one hundred miles," Tom says. By this time, we're pretty well out of earshot, and the conversation must end. I wonder if anglers think we are sassy jerks. Or if they believe us. Either way, we envision the struggle they must have to process this bit of information. If we're lucky, they reel in, start their motors, catch up to us, and learn we're telling the truth. Then they might give us a fish—that is if we're really lucky.

Sirius is attentive and smart. She knows all the usual commands and some unusual ones. "Hop in" means time to jump in the canoe, and "over" means to move off the sidewalk or road. She also is more comfortable waiting outside stores when we shop—she usually goes to sleep. Each morning as we begin loading MW, she sits expectantly onshore for her cue—a bit paranoid about being left behind. When she hears, "Okay, hop in," she does so, now without any help. She usually lies queenlike on the upper deck, enjoying the passing scenery. She still takes snoozes below deck. This day, on Lake Oahe, she sleepily crawls up on deck. From the stern, I am there to enjoy the comedy as she sits down precariously on the edge. She stretches with a big puppy yawn, loses her balance, and tumbles into the water.

Our queen above deck on a rare calm and sunny day.
Photo courtesy of Diane Tunney.

"Pup overboard," I shout to Tom, half laughing, half concerned. I start to back-paddle. Sirius immediately pops up, looking alarmed, and swims quite adeptly straight for the boat. I'm glad she doesn't get disoriented. I scoop up my poor frightened little pup and place her in the middle of the upper deck.

"What a way to wake up, eh, pup?" I say as she sits there, getting her bearings. I recount the preceding events to Tom, and we both have a good laugh at poor Sirius's expense. She promptly gets me back by standing up and shaking off, showering me with more water than I thought a single fur coat could hold.

The wind is a daily companion. No, I wouldn't call it a companion. One travels willingly with a companion. The wind is more like a pebble in your shoe. Sometimes the pebble shifts to a spot where it's not so bad, and you forget it's there. Sometimes it's smack dab under your heel, and you cannot think of anything else. We just become inured to that relentless, fickle Missouri River wind that chastises us daily. It often picks up in the evening or night or calms down during midday, as apparently the wind and sun have no relationship on the Missouri. We adapt as best we can by paddling on the most protected side of the river, crossing to the opposite side when it seems to have subsided a little, and switching paddling sides often.

Most of each day's wind-weariness is slept away at night. The next day, I feel ready to hit the waves again. Some fatigue remains, and our weekly day of rest replenishes us a bit in both body and spirit. There is, however, a cumulative effect that gets tucked away, deep inside, each day building up without much notice, gaining force to eat away at my insides.

Wind and Wave Weariness

Day 45 (June 7): Mobridge is today's destination—a tiny town but perfect for a day off. We don't have to go far. The bridge is in sight. We hardly pay attention to the persistent wind until we pack up and load MW by the crashing waves on the pebbly beach.

"Now, we'll just have to get out there past the breakers as fast as we can," Tom instructs as I look at the approaching waves crashing ashore.

"Right."

"Just paddle hard and keep us from turning while I shove off," Tom said. He is the captain today.

"I got it," I say, making sure Sirius is below deck. I climb in, push off with my heavy-duty Norse paddle as Tom shoves off, and we paddle straight into the oncoming waves as quickly as we can. We take on about three buckets of water. Once past the breakers, Tom pivots us on the crest of a wave, and we head in the correct direction. The waves and wind are going our general direction but at an angle. Tom has a terrible time trying to bail and maintain our heading at the same time. All he actually has to do is rudder; the wind and waves alone propel us at an unnerving clip. I glance at the shoreline to see trees and rocks whiz by.

Of course, it's us doing the whizzing. Each wave scoops us up from behind, lifting the stern, propelling us forward as we surf the face of each wave. These are the biggest waves I've ever paddled. But the waves travel faster than us. Each lets us down into the trough until the next wave picks us up and pushes us onward. I can only paddle when the water is below me. My paddle doesn't reach the water when I'm above the trough. It is a roller-coaster ride on four- and five-foot waves, and I don't like it one bit. I keep thinking of Verlen Kruger's mishap in the Pacific Ocean, where he "caught a wave wrong," flipped, and couldn't roll up. Besides, all this up and down bucking bronco bit is making me seasick.

Tom doesn't seem to be sharing my petrified feelings at all. Occasionally, he breaks out into the Hawaii-Five-O theme song or lets out a "Whoo-hooooo." MW is riding fine. She always rides the waves like a champ. But I can't get the possibility of a slight miscalculation out of my head.

That threatening feeling back by my tonsils grows more urgent. I'm torn between trying to suppress it or just tossing my cookies overboard to be done with it.

Now our nervous pooch decides to stand up on the top deck. She's probably queasy too and certainly wet from the water we've taken on. "Sit down, Sirius," Tom yells. "Lay down!" A pup overboard would not be so easy to rescue this time. I turn around and take out my anxiety on our drenched and bedraggled pooch.

"LAY DOWN, SIRIUS!" I demand and force her into lying down. "STAY THERE!" She is frightened enough to do as she's told, thank goodness.

We pass under the US-12 Bridge in Mobridge and spy a cove where the breakers will not be so severe. Coming into the beach, just as we hit stones I jump out and pull MW up as far and as fast as I can, trying to beat the next wave. Tom jumps out to help with the last heave and we are ashore. I give Sirius the word, and she immediately hops out and walks off her sea legs.

"Wow, those are some waves, huh?" Tom says with excitement. "They must be four, five feet, I'd say." He's pumped.

"Are you nuts? That scared me to death!" I glare at him. He now looks at me and sees that I'm shaking with nerves.

"Ohhh, I didn't know." He comes over to me, but he doesn't know what to do.

"Any one of those waves broadside could easily have swamped us." My pent-up fears are escaping.

"Yeah, I know," he says, "but I didn't let that happen. I wouldn't let that happen."

"We are NOT going back out until that lake settles down," I insist.

He nods, acquiescing to my sudden authoritative rage. "Well, we've got lots to do in town, and I'm sure it will calm down soon enough." We both know he has no way of knowing this, but he has to say something reassuring. He finally hugs me. It isn't a very comforting hug, but it helps some.

After securing MW, all three of us hitch a ride into Mobridge with an angler. We shop, get a sandwich for lunch and eat in the park. When the rain comes, we seek shelter in the filthy bathroom. The dark clouds come and go, but the one over me lingers. When we arrive back at the boat, the wind, sentinel of the rain, has ceased, and we depart in calm conditions to Indian Creek Recreation Area for our camp. We pull into a modern camping facility with trailer pads, electric outlets, fire pits, and showers across the street. En route, in our silence, my dark cloud thickens and threatens to deluge. I slump down on the sand as soon as we arrive.

Tom finally broaches the subject. "What's the matter, Nance?"

All I need is some warm affection, to feel enveloped in some strong manly arms, and to know there is someone to support me. All I get is a cold interrogation. I try to express my thoughts, but the sobbing and tears are the best explanation. Tom is confused. Doesn't know what to do with me. He busies himself unloading and settling into an inconspicuous spot.

That evening in the tent, I can't get past the half-awake, half-asleep stage. I'm exhausted but too emotionally charged. Tom reads and writes in his journal. I feel so separate, so alone. Why am I doing this anymore? It doesn't make any sense. Everything seems to turn me into a nervous wreck. My inner strength is depleted, and I'm getting bolstered by no one—not even Tom. Again, I can't hold back the tears. Finally, at long last, Tom puts his arm around me and sincerely says that he cares. I hold him tight and cry in relief.

Another trip into Mobridge does wonders to recharge my batteries. Even though I'm sure our out-of-the-way spot is still on a campsite that probably has a fee, no one approaches us. An angler gives us—all three of us—a ride into town right to the post office, where a mail drop is waiting for "Paddle for Water." We take our packages out to a nearby bench and revel in our good fortune. The anticipation is almost unbearable. One package is from Sue, my supervisor at Camp Cullen, where I worked before beginning this trip. I open it enthusiastically, and the first thing I see is a silly little toy—a pneumatic green jumping frog.

"What did ya get?" Tom leans over.

"It's another Frogbert," I say, taking it out and jiggling it in his face. "Remember this guy?"

"How could I forget?" This plastic frog has a hose attached to its butt. The other end of the hose is a bulb that, when squeezed, inflates the frog's rubbery legs so it kicks and jumps. I had one at Camp Cullen (for some reason I can't recall), and I brought it along when a bunch of us went out to a bar one evening. I made Frogbert hop across the table, cause a napkin to jump, and swim in a water glass. It was hilarious. Our laughter captured an audience. Eventually, a cowboy came over and offered me twenty-five dollars for Frogbert. Of course, I accepted. I think it only cost me a buck, and I knew where to get more. I sit here, reminiscing over this little toy, only to be interrupted by Tom, "What else did she send?"

"Oh, right, look, it's a sachet." I read Sue's note. "For my underwear and stuff." I dig around a bit more and find a beautiful white crystal hung on a thread. "And this"—I hold it up for Tom to see— "is a crystal for strength." I marvel at it shimmering in the sunlight. Tom puts it on me. It never leaves me from that time afterward.

Sue has no idea how timely this package is for me. Mom sent cookies and granola bars and the local paper. We go to the library, where Sirius entertains herself by snapping at the sprinklers outside. Everyone we meet in Mobridge is friendly and gracious. Bob, an angler and real estate agent, drives us back to our camp and tries to get the *Mobridge Tribune* to write an article about us. The guy never comes, but Bob stops by later in the day to give us a *Tribune* and chat awhile. All of Mobridge's hospitality does wonders to boost my confidence, self-esteem, and motivation. Thanks, Mobridge!

Tom and I mend our chasm too. He lets me read his journal entry of the previous day, in which he chastised himself for not embracing me when I told him I felt "so alone." He said he sensed the distance between us and knew the paddle had been hard on me and cursed himself for not being more sensitive. We determine we need to be more attentive to each other. Tom too, is feeling wind weariness, and we express our mutual hope that our lows don't hit at the same time.

Journaling has become much more than just documenting our journey for both Tom and me. Recognizing right from the start that recording events of the day, towns we pass, mileage we make, people we meet, and adventures we have would be important, we devote time each day to journaling. Poems, diagrams, and brochures embellish the pages of handwritten text.

Soon we come to recognize the value of a journal in handling emotional upheaval. I use my journal to vent fear, pain, anger, and love. Later, when I can look back at my entry in a new light, I may share it with Tom. In this way, we discuss, learn, empathize, and take a step forward in understanding each other. I share with him a poem I wrote five days ago:

I'd like not to wish you
My dearest friend,
May the wind and the current
Forever travel your way.

They will carry you along.

You will go unimpeded.

It will be nice.

It will be easy.

But improvement does not come with ease.

Growth comes through hardship

Fortitude through trials

For when you fight,

You cry.

You wonder, Why?

Then strength grows

Character builds

Perspectives widen

No, I do not wish

For all to go smoothly

But may your trials make you strong.

May your efforts bring fulfillment.

And may there <u>always</u> be

At least one force

One support

That goes along

To help and encourage you

As far as you may go.

We paddle when the wind is tolerable and stop when it's a menace. One windy afternoon turns into a pleasant visit with a family. Sirius runs around with eleven-year-old Molly and seven-year-old Megan, having a wonderful time. Tom and I chat with the adults who, while lounging in their beach chairs, keep alert for the tinkling of a little brass bell, indicating a nibble on one of their many fishing lines. The best part is the blissfully cold root beer Jill offers. For river people who drink warm Kool-Aid˚ daily, ice-cold drinks are an underappreciated luxury of civilization. We shove off with a pocketful of butterscotch candies and their good wishes.

According to our Army Corps of Engineers map of Lake Oahe, Little Bend Recreation Area is equipped with cold drinking water, picnic tables, and vault toilets. Sweet! I couldn't be happier if it were a Marriott. Located on the narrow neck of a loop in the river, we could walk perhaps five hundred yards and cut off seven miles of windy lake paddling. When you're wind-worn by blustery lakes, portages don't seem so awful. A shortcut is enticing.

Well, the Army Corps must have camouflaged this one. Before long, the lake sweeps back southeast again, and we are rounding the point of the peninsula.

"What happened to the park?" I demand.

"I don't know. I never saw it," Tom says with a voice of resignation and a hint of bewilderment. Then, "And what are you yelling at me for?"

"I don't know." I turn off my brusque demeanor. "I was just hoping for a few amenities." My bottom lip juts out inadvertently. Why do I let my expectations get so high? I watch motorboats whiz by and wish I could be in one. A speedboat would get us to where we're going in no time flat and without effort. I just long for a cold refreshing drink.

We pull into shore to reconnoiter. All three of us disembark to stretch our legs. Tom scours the map to see where we could have gone wrong. He points out coves and possibilities. I refuse to look, taking my anger out on the map.

"If it weren't for this stupid blasted map, I'd never know what we were missing!" I rage. Tom is taken aback by my outburst. "We should just throw it out!" I grab the map from his hands and throw it to the ground. The wind immediately hustles it away. Tom scampers after it and catches it before it blows into the water.

"This spot's nice," he says upon his return. "It probably wasn't much of anything, anyway," referring to the park.

"Ach," I guffaw as I stomp away and squat down on the stony beach. I feel defeated, weary, cheated, and just plain grumpy.

"C'mon, let's go for a dip. It's hot," Tom says, trying to bolster my spirits.

Temperatures these days are well into the 90s. If something good can be said about it, the wind on the water is often cooling. But sometimes even the wind is hot. By paddling in our swimsuits, we are ready to jump in at a moment's notice. We do. The swim cools me off in more ways than one. When I come out of the water, Tom is sitting on the beach.

"Do you want to pull out at Pierre?" he proposes.

"Pull out?" I am aghast at the suggestion and stop short. Despite my feelings of despair, I never thought that quitting was the answer. "Goll no," I say without hesitancy. Hearing myself say this, I realize I must have some motivation left. My initial reaction kind of surprises me. I don't doubt the sincerity of his question, but I think he is relieved at my answer. I sit down beside him and start processing.

"Two more days will make a full year," Tom says. He doesn't have to explain it to me. He allotted one year for this trip. June 14 is the day we set out on this journey. "We're just not making the mileage in this wind." He is finding it hard to keep motivated too.

Now it is my turn to reassure. We sit, consoling one another until Sirius runs up, playfully yipping, saying it's walk time. "What we need is to get away from the river for a while," Tom concludes, getting up at Sirius's urging.

"Yeah, that sounds good." I stand up too.

"Wendy lives in South Dakota, doesn't she?"

"Yeah, let's call her." Things were looking up.

"I could have a cold beer." Tom smiles.

"I could have a bowl of cereal with milk."

"It can rain and blow all it wants 'cause we'll be under a roof."

"We can hop in Wendy's car to cover miles and miles and miles without moving a muscle." The joys of civilization are endless. We have a refreshing walk, cleansing our souls with anticipation of a leisurely respite and seeing our dear friend. We waste no time in finding a phone to make arrangements to meet her at the Downstream Recreation Area Campground below Oahe Dam. I can't wait.

The Benevolence of Friends and Strangers

Day 53 (June 15): Wendy lives in Britton, tucked up in the northeast corner of South Dakota. She didn't let on that it would take her four and a half hours of driving to fetch us. This didn't daunt Wendy. Tall, soft-spoken, gracious, and sensitive, she requests a couple of days off from her job as District Park Naturalist at Roy Lake State Park, Fort Sisseton, and Sika Hollow to spend with us.

The temperatures are in the high nineties to low one hundreds. This summer already had nine record highs. While Wendy goes back to work, we sit in Wendy's house, drink cold pop from the fridge, bask in the air conditioning, watch the TV, and discuss how people don't even recognize these modern conveniences as luxuries.

Wendy takes us back to Oahe Dam four days later. I feel relaxed. Recuperated. Basking in her hospitality was just the tonic my body and soul required. We part with a ceremonial paddle signing, hugs, and well-wishes.

We retrieve our canoe and gear from Mr. and Mrs. Schultz, the campground hosts, who let us stash MW under their trailer. Neither is very cordial. While hauling gear to the river, I feel their judgmental gaze boring into me. Upholding our "free camping" policy doesn't fit with their "pay for camping" policy, so Tom is motivated to move along.

Our old nemesis, the wind, greets us heartily. A storm is brewing to the south. An angler just coming in shakes his head and says, "You're braver than me." I do not let this get to me. I will not let my happy mood get spoiled.

Paddling out of Oahe Dam stilling basin, we encounter whitecaps. Steep banks line the river and defy retreat, so we keep paddling. After a half-hour, we find a viable spot above a five-foot bank we can clamber up. Having scouted the campsite and found it suitable, Tom stays atop while I unhook, unload, and piece by piece, heave the gear up into his outstretched hand. In ten minutes, all our stuff, including MW and Sirius, is atop the cliff in a secluded wind-protected spot. It starts to rain. I am happy. I am happy. I am happy. If I repeat it often enough, it may begin to ring true.

This section of the Missouri River is a series of lakes. Lake Sakakawea is in the upper reaches, followed by Lake Oahe, Lake Sharpe, Lake Frances Case, and Lewis and Clark Lake before we hit Sioux City. South of Sioux City, the river is unimpeded to allow for navigation. On these big lakes, the wind is relentless. I would sometimes think back to our shakedown trip with Steve and Diane on Keuka Lake in New York. That wind caused the strong-armed farmer and my cross-country skiing girlfriend to abandon ship. They provide me a point of reference, as they are determined people who would not give up easily. We regularly paddle in wind and waves considerably more severe than that. We use the spray skirt when needed and frequently bail accumulated puddles out of the boat. Stopping midday allows Aeolus—the Greek wind god—to howl and roar and stir up waves as much as he wants. We put in miles late at night or early morning to avoid the worst of his rages.

This schedule provides ample opportunity to meet folks. If not for the manifold benevolence of strangers, my teetering motivation would falter. Take, for instance:

- Byron, the ten-year-old Sioux boy from Fort Yates who interrupted his swimming to talk to the canoe-ing strangers.

- Leo Koerner and family, who quenched our thirst with ice-cold Cokes while portaging around Oahe Dam.

- the father and son anglers who motored up beside us to give us three walleyes, and the angler who helped Tom clean and fillet them.

- the woman in the camper who came to deliver "the rest" of the chicken parts to Sirius. Sirius had stopped earlier and stolen a piece right off the plate by her door. Oh yeah, the woman also gave Tom and me some homemade rolls.

- Elmer, Delmar, and three other grandpa-type anglers who camped near us. They allowed us to use their table and enjoyed talking to us about our trip from an angle we hadn't approached before, asking, "When are you going to settle down to have your family?" They fed us a fantastic breakfast of pancakes and ham.

- two Bureau of Indian Affairs police officers at Big Bend Dam, who warned us of the danger of leaving our canoe unattended while we sought to go to town.

They watched MW until we returned.

- the husband, wife, and two daughter boaters who motored up to us with the usual set of "How far are you going?" type questions, leading into a long and pleasant conversation. They motored back from whence they came. They came out specifically to talk with us.

- Ray and Edna Hennings, living on Lake Francis Case. They spotted canoeists and motored out to meet us. We had a friendly conversation, and they left us with two cold Cokes.

These folks gave us the energy, drive, and inspiration needed to carry us between Mobridge and Fort Randall Dam. Unintentionally, they encouraged us to brave wind, waves, thunderstorms, ticks, scorching heat, and difficult portages.

Having completed the length of Lake Francis Case, we arrive at Fort Randall Dam. That Army Corp of Engineers doesn't think about canoeists when building these suckers. A recipe for the portage goes something like this:

- Begin by unloading everything onto riprap above the spillway.

- Haul all gear over the rocks, careful not to twist an ankle while carrying fifty-pound packs and a sixty-pound canoe.

- Go up steps to deposit gear near a chain-link fence that extends in both directions ad infinitum. Gate is padlocked.

- One person climbs the six-foot fence to the other side.

- Remaining person shoves each piece of gear up over fence to the other person, including canoe and squirming puppy, concluding with oneself.

- Because fencing around spillway and cement walls prevents reaching the water, don packs and trudge along the fence, down a gully, over a beaver dam, up through waist-high grass to a level spot.

- Continue across the level spot to a road, which leads to a boat launch.

- Drop load on nearest picnic table.

- Sit. Drink hot Kool-Aid˚ in 100-degree heat.

- Scheme how not to do that again with kitchen and canoe.

- Begin return trip, looking unequivocally bedraggled. (Not at all difficult.)

- Engage with Mr. and Mrs. Gary Taylor, who happen to drive alongside in their truck camper, pulling a motorboat.

- Cleverly craft a conversation not to let the Taylors get away.

- Graciously accept the Taylors' offer to drive us to our remaining gear and transport it to the boat launch.

- Part ways with hearts full of gratitude.

Testing my Hardiness of Spirit

Day 67 (June 29): Our reward after bagging Fort Randall Dam is a boost from the frisky river. Once released from its prison behind the dam, clear green water washes us downriver. I smile to see the sandy bottom speed by with little effort on my part. It slows and widens out to become Lewis and Clark Lake in a few miles. Now, as the river swings east, Nebraska borders the river to the south while South Dakota rims the northern shore.

For the first time, trees are somewhat common between Lake Francis Case and Lewis and Clark Lake. We've seen a few here and there—but now, you can rightly call the collective an honest-to-goodness woods. Red cedar, ash, and cottonwood dominate. Cattail marshes separate eroded bluffs of golden sandstone.

Everyone who owns a motorboat is out on Lewis and Clark Lake: some pulling water skiers; some pulling kids on inflatables; some ferrying anglers; and some racing around for pure joy. All produce bouncy wakes, making the three of us bobblehead dolls. Sirius, lying on her perch atop the gear, finds the action entertaining. Trailers and cottages pack the shorelines, each with a corresponding boat dock. With a storm in hot pursuit, we finally settle on a downright horrible spot beside a soggy cattail marsh. Tall grass prevents safe stove operation here, and mosquitoes buzz and prick mercilessly. We leave before breakfast the following day.

No longer an adventure, this is a difficult task I must convince myself every morning to get up and face. Each day now feels like a very hard job. Fighting wind, waves, heat, and rain drains my inner strength. Physically, the elements are manageable. The waves are never more severe than what we've paddled in before—which isn't saying much. We must be vigilant not to allow the wind and waves to take command of MW. Rain comes frequently. Temperatures are regularly above one hundred degrees. Canoeing is our job, and we do it adeptly, with strong-honed muscles, efficient paddle strokes, an intimate knowledge of our craft, and a practiced eye on the elements. And yet, a mental war is waging between motivation and exhaustion. Each morning I dig deep within myself to look for the stuff I'm made of. *I'm not done yet. I can still do this.* My mantra.

Tom is here for me. He bounces back from hard portages, exhausting paddles, or rainy nights surprisingly well. He complains a lot when it's happening but seems to put it behind him in short order. I envy that.

We both look for ways to distract ourselves from our work. We play games like "I'll sing a line, and you name the song" or "You name a character, and I'll guess the TV show." Or maybe we pick a theme such as "sunshine" (an especially good topic for a gloomy day) and take turns singing as much as we know of a song containing the word. These singing games are rather torturous for me. Tom is what you'd call musically challenged. He has no sense of rhythm, seldom uses the correct words, and can't carry a tune. But he is loud. Today we plod along mostly in silence.

"Guess what that is down there." Tom interrupts our long silent paddle on Lewis and Clark Lake to indicate the end of the lake ahead on the horizon.

"Gavins Point Dam," I reply with a frown. He knows I know this.

"Not only that, but our last dam on the Missouri."

"Ahhh." I let him continue.

"Want to take a tour of it?"

"Sure, why not? I reply. "After the portage?"

"Yeah. Have you figured out how to portage it yet?"

"Well, I think so. To avoid the powerhouse and spillway, which we need to do, I don't see any way to portage it without doing it twice."

The powerhouse is tucked against a tall cliff on the Nebraska side. Extending 8,700 feet toward South Dakota is the adjoining spillway and earthen dam. Behind the powerhouse and spillway is the Missouri River. Behind the earthen dam is Lake Yankton, with its accompanying campground, picnic areas, and other recreational amenities.

My plan is this: land mid-dam; empty MW on the rocks and carry gear up over the grassy dike; carry gear down to Cottonwood campground directly behind the dam; rest and eat lunch; load up and set out in Lake Yankton; paddle over to the beach; unload again; carry gear over the training dike; load up and put in the river once again; paddle away.

We carry out my plan to a T except for the "paddle away" part. Instead, we paddle over to a boat ramp to catch a tour.

Another pleasant addendum to my plan is meeting a guy named Steve Fish while eating lunch. Sirius attracted him, or maybe it was the canoe and all our gear. "You guys canoeing the river?"

"Yumph," Tom answers him with a rude mouthful of sandwich. Steve tells us that he and another fella are taking three days to raft one hundred miles from Sioux City to Omaha this upcoming Fourth of July weekend. He is giddy with excitement. Steve pulls out his Coast Guard map and booklet, lays it out on the picnic table, and jabs it periodically while he shares his plan enthusiastically. We part, expecting to see each other on the river.

"Remember when we were that excited about our expedition?" I ask Tom.

"Yeah."

"What happened to that?"

"We started the expedition."

We camp five miles downriver that night in Riverside Park in Yankton, South Dakota. Like little trolls, we seek out a hidden corner under a weeping willow where no one will notice our canoe or tent. To celebrate our last dam for a long time, Tom suggests we hike into Yankton for a feast and take tomorrow off. I like celebrating things, even if we observe the same thing repeatedly. We find Bonanza, and indeed it is. I stuff myself. It is worth the three-mile round-trip hike. Upon return to our campsite, we see the road filled with cars.

"They've found us!" Tom remarks sarcastically. It's a summer band concert. What a delightful surprise. We grab our pufdas and plunk down just in time to hear the last number. Bummer.

In no time, the park is ours again. This is fine as two portages, eighteen paddling miles, and at least three miles of walking have pretty well tuckered me out. Despite weariness, neither of us can get to sleep. When we are secluded, I always feel so much more relaxed. Tom tells me a bedtime story. I am nearly asleep, listening to the story of Zork.

Celebrating Independence Day River Style

Day 71 (July 3): Fireworks, apple pie, family picnics—this is the stuff of Independence Day. But the motorboaters around Sioux City get a little jump on the holiday. They launch their speed boats and careen up and down the river, eventually staking claim to a nice little sandy beach where they set up camp. They play volleyball, sunbathe, have a cookout, erect sandcastles, shoot off bottle rockets, and generally have a blast. It's nice to see folks enjoying their river— mostly. At least, this is what I keep telling myself every time a speedboat zips by, leaving us to bobble up and down in its wake. Not one slows down for us. Not a one. But there is a bright side.

"Hey, canoers, want a brew?" a bare-chested fella in a swimsuit, holding a beer can, calls out to us as we paddle by his sandbar. Tom doesn't need to be asked twice. We pull in and chat while Tom slugs a brew, and I relish a cold, sparkling pop. After twenty minutes, we shove off downriver.

Earlier, the U.S. Fish and Wildlife Agency had posted signs warning visitors to avoid areas used by least terns and piping plovers. In seeming contradiction, the National Wild and Scenic River system listed this fifty-eight-mile section of river—between Gavins Point Dam and Ponca State Park—as a National Recreation River. Tom got his hands on a canoeing information guide. It cites twelve access points, such as parks and boat ramps, advising that the "wooded sandbars and islands make great stopping places." I wonder what the least tern and piping plover know of this.

On the endangered species list since 1985, the interior least tern (*Sternula antillarum athalassos*), the small cousin to a gull, has been struggling due to loss of nesting habitat in the Missouri, Mississippi, Ohio, and a few other inland river systems. It nests on sparsely vegetated sandy or pebbly beaches. With the construction of these dams, nesting areas disappeared under impounded lakes. Now that the dams are upriver of us and the river runs unimpeded, we paddle by sandy beaches, sandbars, and islands that least terns and weekend warriors like so much.

The Northern Great Plains piping plover (*Charadrius melodus*) population is classified as "threatened" under the Endangered Species Act. These shorebirds have the same nesting requirements and therefore face the same troubles. Although both species arrive here to mate, nest and rear their young as early as April, they may finish raising a brood by the beginning of July. But nesting can last into September or October. When it comes time for us to claim a sandbar for the night, we scour it for signs of the birds or their nests in the sand and find none. Hopefully, the area is populated with "early birds," and they have completed their life-cycle duties before weekend warriors invade their space.

Waking up to nature's fireworks and enduring drizzle the next day, I peer out of our tent to find Ponca State Park filled with campers. Sioux City residents flock here as it's only a twenty-five-mile drive northwest of the city. I treat myself instead to a real toilet. When I return, Tom has Sirius tied to our picnic table.

"What's Puparoo tied up for?"

"She is sooo in the doghouse," Tom replies, frowning at my cute little puppy, who greets me with an eager wag. "She saw a dog over there"—he indicates a group of campers in the distance—"and went to visit. She wouldn't come back when I called. She kept running away. I went after her, and she went bonkers. I ran around, trying to catch her, and she jumped up on the picnic table and grabbed a polish sausage right off a man's plate!" I'm wide-eyed, listening intently, trying to envision a grown man chasing a puppy around the campground. And yet I'm horrified at my pup, who usually behaves so well. Tom continues, "She took the sausage down under the table and ate it right under the man's legs. I couldn't get to her."

"What did the people do?"

"Nothing. They didn't help at all!" Tom's voice takes on an even higher pitch in his exasperation. "They just laughed and laughed."

I'm sort of sorry to have missed the chaos, but I would have been more horrified and embarrassed than Tom. Fourth of July mania must affect us all.

From here on, the U.S. Army Corps of Engineers has altered the river to facilitate commercial traffic. Rocks line outside embankments to prevent erosion and underwater wing dikes jut in from the inside bends, making the river channel self-scouring. Water ushered along these dikes shoot off the end, making great boosters. We can easily rack up twenty-five to thirty miles a day with the increased flow.

The alterations also include blue and white signs along the riverbank counting down the miles to Cairo, Illinois. As of July 5, when we first started noticing the markers, we are 739 miles from the Ohio–Mississippi confluence. We no longer have to take a string to the river channel on the map and measure it against the map's scale to estimate our mileage. Wild, natural river has given way to a veritable river highway.

Winnebago Friends

Day 73 (July 5): Once again, we break our vow not to camp on an Indian reservation. Funny how lofty attitudes change when one is tired, cranky, crampy, dirty, and hungry, *and* the sky is again threatening to dump gallons of rain.

"Hey, let's check out this beach." I point my paddle river right, on the Nebraska side for Tom, in the stern, to see. Iowa is now on river left as the Missouri now forms the border between these states. "There's a path leading up the bank. Maybe there's a site up there."

Tom shoves MW's nose onto the beach. I hop out, heaving the canoe forward to perch it squarely onshore in one fluid motion. I head up the bank. Tom and Sirius hop out and follow. My heart sinks as I crest the rise and regard Styrofoam cups, beer cans, candy wrappers, dirty bundles of discarded clothing, cigarette butts, cheese puffs, cheese doodles, and snack wrappers strewn about. Shoulders slumped, I scrunch my nose in disgust when Tom steps up beside me. Neither of us speaks, but in unison lift our eyes to the sound of voices. Three guys, about thirty feet away, are leaning against the hood of a truck, laughing, chattering, and slurping brews.

One of them spots us standing motionless amongst the trash. "Hey, how ya doin'?" Rats. Escape is now out of the question.

Tom, feeling more neighborly than I, strolls over to the truck and strikes up a friendly conversation. To my relief, the guys are welcoming rather than annoyed at our intrusion.

Then the clouds let us have it. I run down the bank to cover MW with her spray skirt, Tom in hot pursuit. Abandoning beer cans on the hood, all three guys skitter down to lend a helping hand.

There is something genuine about these three. I forget the trash.

"Is it okay if we pitch our tent here for the night?" I ask.

"Sure, go right ahead," Tyler says. "No one will bother you."

Single file, we trudge up the bank. The guys saunter over to the truck to reclaim their beers. We tag along. No use putting up a tent in the rain. Best we wait it out, garbed in our rain gear. With a perfectly good vehicle in which to escape the rain, the guys stay outside with us under the trees, unmoved by the soaking.

Tyler, John, and the quiet one are Native Americans living on the Winnebago Reservation that borders the river here. John claims to be an ex-cornhusker—*whatever that means*. He proudly shoves his fist my direction, adorned with a substantial piece of jewelry. I examine his Big Eight championship ring with sincere interest and now realize he was on the University of Nebraska football team. Invigorated by us—a fresh, new audience—he regales us with football stories, animatedly reenacting plays, made even more incredible with each telling. A continuous flow of jokes has me laughing hysterically.

The rain stops. The guys depart. We set up camp in the farthest-away corner of the party site, alone at last. After cooking supper in the vestibule during the next rainstorm—yes, there's always another rainstorm—I feel a bit crampy and just want to sleep.

No such luck. A car pulls up. Tom conducts a brief conversation through the tent window. I know it's rude, but I am cranky—lying down—so I let Tom handle it.

Within a half-hour, the rain has stopped and feeling a bit better, I'm up and out, feeding Sirius while Tom is bundling away the kitchen for the night. Another car drives up. *Public parks are not this busy.*

A woman and two Native American men step out of the vehicle. The woman, Janet Rice, introduces herself as "the granddaughter of the white man who dumped the Winnebagos here." She holds a beautiful basket filled with U.S. government-surplus food.

"This is a gift for you. We want you to have this," she says. "In return, we ask only that you pray for the Winnebagos. When *we* pray, He closes his ears. When others pray, He listens." Tom and I are speechless. I think my jaw dropped for a moment, trying to fathom the meaning of this extravagant gesture toward us river bums. I am reluctant to accept it but realize that not accepting is refusing to help. Suddenly, I feel significant. It makes me regret that I'm not closer to God. Feeling unworthy, I start to get a little choked up.

Janet goes on. "Last year, three in our Winnebago council went to Washington to ask for food. They were each big and fat." The others laugh. "What food we have is not nutritious." Tom puts out a hand to take hold of the basket handles. He has to quickly brace it, with his other hand underneath to support the basket's surprising weight.

"I'm not sure how much pull we have"—I finally find some words—"but we will keep you in our prayers." Tom reiterates a sincere thank-you. We watch as they drive off, our last visitors for the night.

Prior to the 1830s, Winnebagos occupied what is now central Wisconsin and northern Illinois. After a series of treaties, with their population decimated by smallpox, the remaining members sought refuge in Nebraska. In 1865, the government established a reservation for them, and it is here that we now meet. From Janet, Tyler and John, we learned the Winnebagos are people with troubles, whose identity and lands have been usurped; they are trying to rebuild with what little has been left to them. As Tom and I sit and sort through the contents of the basket, we are reminded of the shameless story of one race decimating another, which continues to repeat itself throughout history. We talk about this as we snack over U.S. government peanuts, cheese, and orange juice. How at a loss we feel to help these fun, generous, hopeful people. But mainly, we contemplate our own thoughts in silence. Will prayer be enough?

As we pack up the next morning, the kitchen weighs a ton! It has all that canned surplus food in it. Peanut butter, fruit cocktail, canned beef, canned pork, canned beans, veggies of all sorts, spaghetti noodles, rice, powdered eggs, and more—crammed in with the rest of our foodstuffs. But it's the basket that is the most difficult to transport. Once underway, I struggle to manage Sirius and a beautiful basket between my feet in the stern. Tom finally comes up with the solution of tying it on top of the stern deck. The Wicked Witch of the West bicycling song from *Wizard of Oz* immediately comes to mind, and we occupy ourselves for all of ten minutes singing that. Two days later, we mail it away to my folks in New York for safekeeping.

The Last Straw

Day 77 (July 9): The days continue to be drudgery. When not raining, it is threatening to rain. The routine of breaking camp, looking for a new camp—day after day, setting up and taking down—is getting tiresome. One campsite is infested with houseflies. The noise never ceases at the next camp between a railroad bridge and an automobile bridge. Nothing is ever right. Our foul moods augment every little thing. We try to boost our spirits with a fast-food breakfast but are aghast at how much packaging they use. It is not a happy meal.

Tom is hitting bottom. Maybe I leave him too much of the work. I always feel guilty in the morning when I have to do "me" stuff: wash my face, brush my hair and rebraid it, go to the bathroom, pack my clothes; while he does "us" stuff: fills the stoves and cooks breakfast. In the endless wind on the lakes up north, I had hit my low. Tom is hitting his now. We are both doubting our purpose. Tom writes:

> The day accurately reflected my mood, shitty. Today I've felt that I've had enough. I'm sick of the continual loading, knowing the day will end with just more unloading. I'm sick of camping out each night after paddling by nice weekend homes. I'm sick of the same stupid comments day in and day out by people we meet. I'm sick of battling the bugs and the weather. I'm also sick of searching for water and longing for cold water. I'm sick of living on the fringe of society, yet I have no desire to rejoin American society.

Tom tells me he could almost call it quits in Omaha.

I can't say why this shores me up. I feel better now than on Lake Sa-yuck-awea. Not great, but not bad enough to stop. If I quit now, I won't have any sense of accomplishment. And I don't know what I'd do once back in society. I'm almost afraid of going back. I try to be supportive of Tom. It is difficult for him to keep up the facade, mechanically loading and unloading each day.

We need something new. A morale boost. I write to our friend Nancy Waters in Columbia, Missouri, to ask if we can visit.

We stop for lunch in Haworth Park in Bellevue, Nebraska. A nearby picnic table looks enticing. As I spread the peanut butter, Sirius gives a yip in the direction of MW. I don't think anything of it and ask her to be quiet. Upon our return to MW, we notice that a small Styrofoam cooler we rescued from the water has been smashed, and the spray skirt is unsnapped. I shudder as I get in.

"No, it can't be." I use my feet and hands and eyes to look under the bow seat, only to find it empty.

"What?" Tom said.

"The camera box. Did we bring it up with us?" I know full well I left it tucked under the bow seat. "It's gone."

"Are you sure?!"

"Tom, it's gone." I poke around again as if that will make it reappear. Tom grows furious.

"The fishing pole, it's gone too," he notices. "And my binoculars."

I'm trying hard to believe this isn't happening. The pelican case holds not only our cameras and lenses but all our valuables—postal money orders and traveler's checks and whatever cash we have on hand. We felt comfortable leaving it there, as we could see anyone approaching the boat—from land. It takes a minute for us to realize thieves approached it from the water. The thieves must have quietly floated down to MW, hugging the nearby shore. Sirius knew and I told her to be quiet. What a fool I was not to heed Sirius.

"We've got to call the police," Tom says. There is a payphone in the park within sight. I follow behind, head bowed, silently chastising myself for not taking the box with us. We always do, except when within view of MW. I thought we were this time. I never thought of a river approach. I dread a call I must make to Mom and Dad to ask for the serial numbers of the camera equipment. One camera belongs to Dad. I have to break the news to him.

The police arrive quickly. While Tom talks with them, I break the news to Mom and Dad. Whenever I call, they both get on the line.

"Oh, I am so sorry, Dad." I try to hold it together. "Our camera box got stolen, right out from under our noses. I lost your camera. We have the police here and maybe if you can find the serial numbers they can find it. Oh Dad, I'm so sorry." If I kept talking, I figured I could keep from crying.

"Don't worry about the camera," Dad says. "Are you okay?"

"Oh yeah, yeah, they just took our fishing pole, and Tom's binoculars and our money and traveler's checks were in the box," I blabber on and on.

"That's all replaceable," he interrupts. "I can send your Nikkormat out to you if you want."

"Oh, I don't know." By now, the dam holding back the tears is about to break.

"I'll try to find the serial numbers. Don't you worry about the camera."

I can see through my tear-filled eyes that another storm is

about to drench us, and that was enough for my own storm to erupt. Blubbering and tear-streaked, I try to say how difficult it has been lately. I don't know what to do in this latest string of bad omens. I don't know what I said, but my words meant little; my tears said it all. "We may be home soon, anyway."

"We can come get you," Mom says. Their willingness to do anything for me makes me cry even harder. Gratefulness, guilt, love, exhaustion—it all comes out in tears. "You go and stay in a motel tonight," Mom instructs. "Call us when you get in." It's as good an idea as any. With another storm about to descend, I feel it is high time I get off the phone and get moving.

Tom has no trouble doing a motel tonight. We pack up, arrange to lock MW at the concession stand for *The Belle of Brownville*, a tourist riverboat, and head off to the nearest motel. Luckily, I keep my Mastercard in the wallet with us.

I let Tom take a shower first—he's always quick about it. Then it's my turn, and I forget about water conservation and luxuriate in it for a good ten minutes. Mom and Dad call back a couple of times to give me serial numbers and tell me that a Mrs. Ripski had called them. She found our traveler's checks and money orders in the park. She turned them over to the police. How about that? The kindness makes my tears well up again.

Tom is inconsolable. Sunk into himself. Even the good Samaritan turning in our traveler's checks and money orders isn't good news for him. He made calls to cancel our money orders and traveler's checks today, so we'll have to see if we can reinstate them tomorrow. What a pain!

Sirius has no trouble falling asleep on the rug in the motel room. Johnny Carson puts me to sleep. In my dream, I clobber those thieves with my brawny arms and sturdy paddle.

In the morning, it is easy to decide to stay one more night under a roof.

The following morning, we need to hit the river without a camera or lenses, binoculars, fishing pole, or pelican case. With a ninety-five dollar motel bill, we have to get going. Tom is despondent. Even the cinnamon rolls I bought yesterday don't stir him. As we stroll towards Hayworth Park, Tom falls behind. Bad sign. I put my gear down on a picnic table, and when Tom comes along, he is in tears.

"I just can't do it," he sobs. "I can't bring myself to load up or sit in that canoe anymore." I've never seen him this frail and defeated.

"Come, sit down here." I gesture to the table. He drops himself onto the bench, hunches forward, and buries his head in his hands.

"Let me hold you." I console, wrapping my arms around him as I settle down next to him. Not overly enthusiastic either, I'm not very convincing. Nevertheless, I hold him and we rock back and forth.

"Walking here is like walking off to prison," he says, wiping his snuffling face with his sleeve. We talk, cry, comfort, and try to reason out what to do for the next hour. There is such a long way to go, and Tom can't go even an inch further.

As for me, somewhere deep inside is a glimmer of perseverance. I don't know what nourishes it, but I'm not ready to give up just yet. Then again, Tom's well-being is more important. I agree to call it quits here and now.

Now I'm the blubbery one. The decision is made, and I have to go along with it. I already ruled out my folks coming to fetch us. It's too far. Tom works the pay phone to find a drive-away company or car-rental agency. I wouldn't be understood through my sobbing. He comes up empty. It would be over a thousand dollars to rent, and there are no drive-aways available. Finally, Tom grunts, "Let's load up and get out of here before I change my mind."

I jump. Any second he could change his mind. We pack MW in silence. He is slow, lethargic, robotic. Now, it's my turn to step up.

When my spirits hit bottom on the windblown lakes, Tom's perseverance saw me through. I've got to help Tom overcome his low. The thing is, I'm not sure I can pull that off.

Once loaded, I take the stern and push us, joining logs, branches, and trash dislodged from the recent storms in a rain-swollen river. In my dispirited mood, I feel like just another piece of flotsam in a whole parade of flotsam, aimlessly and wordlessly flowing toward the sea.

The tension and despair are palpable. Sirius gives me a curious look when I let out a whimper. Occasionally, Tom's anguish bubbles to the surface with sobs he can't hold back. I see he is struggling with inner demons. Instead of steady evenhanded strokes, some are powerful and jerky with anger, while others are wimpy with defeat. I can't think of anything uplifting to say, so neither of us speaks. My innards feel tied up in a knot, stressing over Tom's uncharacteristic sullenness. I'm at a loss what to do.

Around lunchtime, after about two hours of this torture, Tom announces, "Let's stop here"—indicating a green grassy spot with nearby concealing trees.

My stomach is complaining of hunger. "Good. That will make us feel better." I shove MW's nose into shore, and we slide to a halt.

"I'm done."

I sit in the stern to let this sink in. There is no use bucking it. I can't talk Tom into continuing because I don't have any motivation either.

We plunk down on the grass. I sit next to Tom, whose bowed head rests on his knees. We've got to find our lost spirits. Something else has to be done, and I don't know what it is. We pour over our maps and discuss our plan of action. It doesn't involve paddling. It involves friends.

"Nancy and Bill are in Columbia, Missouri," I offer. "How far away is that?"

Tom pokes around the map. We have just passed where the Platte River joins the Missouri and find ourselves in Plattsmouth, Nebraska. Tom measures and calculates. "Looks to be about three hundred miles."

"Wow. Well, if we can get there, I bet they'll take us in and let us rest while we figure out what's next."

"Yeah, well, Nancy told us to call her when we came by. It's just a long way to hitchhike, that's all." As the prospect of getting off the river becomes more doable, Tom's demeanor brightens.

"Well, what do we do with our stuff?" We seem to be in part of the yard of a house up yonder.

"We'll lock MW up to these trees. She'll be well hidden, and it's high enough. Let's put everything we don't need underneath." Now Tom is in a hurry. I scramble to keep up.

With only our personal packs and food for Sirius, we take off for the highway to hitchhike our way to Columbia, Missouri. There we'll rest, recuperate and reconsider our situation at the home of our friends, Nancy and Bill.

Friends to the Rescue

Day 79 (July 11): Mike picks us up on I-29 for a short twelve-mile-mile ride in his white pickup truck. Not only does he give us the rest of his chocolate milk (my very favorite drink), but we stop at his friend's house for some water for Sirius. I forgot to bring water. Sirius cowers near me at the sight of the two Chinese fighting dogs. I don't particularly like the looks of them myself. Mike is extremely kind and takes us up the ramp to I-29 and backs his car down again.

Tom is in a good mood. I haven't seen him this happy in weeks. Hitching in the hot and humid weather would usually have him in a foul mood. He is set on the idea of stopping. Gene, the trucker, once he saw us, is also set on stopping. It takes a good half mile and some screeching noises to bring his big 18-wheeler to a halt alongside the highway.

Then, he starts to back up his big rig along the shoulder as we run up to meet him, backpacks bouncing and puppy flopping about in my arms. The passenger door opens. Tom climbs up, and a conversation ensues. Tom motions to me. I climb up a step, hand the pup to his outstretched arms, and continue the climb, ending up on the passenger seat across from a man whose bearded, amiable face smiles at me. I smile back. His name is Gene.

Gene starts the slow process of picking up speed, shifting through gear after gear until we once again travel with surprising speed—compared to what we are used to—down the lightly traveled highway. Now I haven't been in too many 18-wheeler truck cabs. This one is remarkably noisy. The rumble of tires on the roadway, the hum of exploding cylinders in the engine, and now and then grinding gears make conversation a challenge. We have to shout across the expansive cab, plus Gene's thick Southern accent takes repetition and translation to understand. I get reasonably adept at picking up keywords. And shaking my head and smiling after my "What?" "What?" get too tedious. But I do pick up essential facts. Gene's cargo is frozen turkeys suspended on racks in the semitrailer he hauls. This is one of his many trips from Nebraska to Florida.

Tom and Sirius are situated behind Gene and me in the sleeper section. Lucky guns; they get to sleep. Gene says only one passenger is allowed in these rigs, so I, as the woman in the group, am the chosen passenger. Tom and Sirius hide behind the curtain when we pull through a weigh station. I can't help but wonder why someone would go through such trouble to give us bedraggled river folks a ride. It was a pain to stop and pick us up along the shoulder of the highway and travel through the weigh station, even when he's already overweight, but this kindhearted soul doesn't think anything of it.

I wish I could talk more with him without so much effort, but after the first half-hour or so, we seldom chat. Six hours later, we part fast friends. My heart glows by yet another selfless act of generosity by a perfect stranger.

Potty, food, phone—my priority list. I let Sirius do her thing before we go inside the truck stop where we say goodbye to Gene. I guess Sirius is allowed in the cafeteria since a girl who works there thinks she is cuteness itself (of course she is) and gives Sirius a part of her sandwich. Like us, Sirius hasn't eaten since breakfast. Bill arrives. We share some pie with him before he takes us home to surprise Nancy with two river bums.

So what are river people supposed to do with themselves for five days in civilization? We sleep soundly on the foldout bed in the baby's room (luxurious beyond belief). Water of any temperature you choose comes out of the sink faucet with the turn of a handle. We revel in modern amenities.

Sirius is happy to find a canine friend in Bowser. Happily chasing and barking at one another, they run around the backyard. They curl up together when playtime and mealtime are over. I accompany Nancy to the Aquacise class she teaches. Both Tom and I have a lot of catching up to do regarding TV watching. We try to earn our keep by cooking dinners and mowing and raking the lawn. We even babysit eight-week-old Forrest, giving Nancy and Bill a night out. During our suburban bliss, we formulate a plan.

Our plan is to pull in some new blood for a one-week paddle to get us on our feet again. Tricky doing since most of our friends have actual jobs with finite vacation time. How about my spontaneous friends—Steve and Diane? Would they be crazy enough to come paddle with us again after what we did to them on the shakedown trip? Yup, they would.

Steve and Diane show up at 9:30 Friday night with Mom and Dad's canoe, lots of food, hugs, laughs, and a hankerin' for adventure. They caught me poised with liquid embroidery stuff over a couple of T-shirts I intended to surprise them with, but their surprise busts my surprise.

"So you guys need a morale boost, huh?" Diane inquires. We share the foldout couch that night.

"Boy, do we ever. Up on the lakes further north . . . I've never been so depressed," I reminisce. "The wind . . . the waves . . . we never got a break. And the rain . . ." I trail off, look down, poke a bit at the pillow. "Remember our shakedown trip?"

"How can I forget?"

"Worse than that, day after day. It really got to me." Diane is propped up on her elbow, slightly nodding—her head supported by her hand—giving me that penetrating look that used to make me so uncomfortable but now I know is attentiveness. I continue: "Then we got our camera stuff stolen, and that was a blow." I pause, remembering. "When Tom asked if I wanted to call it quits, something inside of me kicked in." I frown and try to explain something I don't understand myself. "I didn't want to quit at all. Even though it was hard and I was miserable sometimes, I still had some drive. Can't understand it, but I still do."

"You wanna keep going?"

"Yeah . . . well, no . . . not really." This is a harder question than it should be. "I just don't want to quit before it's done." To "keep going" and "not quit," in my mind, are quite different. "I'll feel miserable if we stop. I don't want to fail." I pluck away at my bedding again with downturned eyes. "Physically, there's no reason why we can't keep going. This mental exhaustion bit has me stymied, though." I glance around and sigh. Diane says nothing, just lets me carry on. "Tom's turn has come. He's totally out of motivation, and I don't know what to do."

"Well, if need be, we can all try to squeeze in my Escort when we get to Atchison," Diane offers.

"Well, we're not there yet." I smile a thank-you. "We should get some sleep. Busy day tomorrow."

Funny how just talking things out with a friend helps ease a burden. We roll away from one another and try to sleep. My mind can't turn off, though. I'm trying to figure out this transformation in Tom. He has always been confident, strong, decisive, competent. All these qualities I admire in him have been overtaken by despair. Why? What can I do to change that?

It is not the trials and tribulations of the trip and the weather that has put Tom in the dumps. He says that on the surface.

A couple of weeks ago, he asked me to marry him—for the second time.

The first time Tom proposed was when we overwintered in Driggs. One quiet evening he just popped the question. No fanfare. No starry eyes. No kneeling. No "I love you" prelude. No romance. He thought we were at "that place." I didn't.

The second time was—come to think of it—just before he gave up on the trip.

Heartbreak can do that to a person.

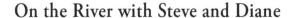

On the River with Steve and Diane

Day 86 (July 18): With Bill's help and a lot of logistical finagling, we take off in two cars the following day. We stop at Bill's friend's house in Atchison, where we get everything and everyone in Diane's car, drive up to MW, unload the second canoe and our gear, say goodbye and thanks to Bill, who drives Diane's car back to his friend's house, then drives his car home, leaving her car there for Diane and Steve to pick up in a week. Phew. Logistics complete. We retrieve our gear, which is right where we left it.

"Wow, I guess you guys were in a hurry to get off the river," Diane comments. She is looking on as I find the source of the stench in our kitchen pack. The remains of canned meat had spoiled and leaked out. Maggots crawl all over everything. She is right—there wasn't much forethought to our retreat.

The next few days are such a delight. Despite burning to a rosy crisp, Diane maintains her cheerful, witty nature, making us laugh. Every day we switch partners and canoes to change things up. I enjoy sharing all aspects of river life with them. To escape the incessant heat we go "pufda" swimming (that is, floating around in the river, wearing life jackets); we cook breakfast burritos and pineapple cakes for breakfast; stop in Ye Ole Tyme Saloon; play a rousing game of Skip-Bo each evening; and sleep under the stars when possible. Steve even brought fat juicy cuts of Agnes, the Black Angus cow I saw grow up on his farm. Tom made a green stick grill to cook her on. Poor Agnes. She's delicious.

I am pleased to see Tom's spirits pick up. He is happy and more at ease. At lunch, on our fourth day out, we have a chance to talk alone. We munch our PB & Js while Steve and Diane lie on the sand to catch a nap.

Steve and Nancy paddling by a barge being loaded

"You sure are chipper today." It is more my way of inquiring than a mere observation.

"Yeah"—he draws the moment out a little, then looks at me, then down at the sand. "That's 'cause there's no way around it. I've got to pull out."

I don't respond. He isn't perking up because of Diane and Steve breathing life into the trip again; he is motivated because he's come to a decision.

"Okay, if we call it quits in Atchison?"

What am I to say? No? How can I make him go on? I certainly can't continue without him. I sigh and look down at the sand. It's not the result I hoped for. Gulp. The most I can muster is "Why?"

"I gave this trip a year. It's been thirteen months."

"Yeah, but a lot of it, we spent sitting out in Driggs."

"I know. I know. I just don't have the drive anymore. It's a struggle for me every day. Packing and unpacking every single day—I hate it."

"But you seem much better. We're having fun now, right?"

"Only 'cause I see the end in sight. I'm burned out. Just ready to get on with my life." His rejected marriage proposals hang heavy in the air between us. He doesn't bring that up. He never has. For a few moments, we sit in silence. It doesn't occur to me to change my mind. I wouldn't be true to myself if I did. He looks at me again. "I feel terrible about letting you down."

"Naw, I understand," I say, not really knowing if I do but trying to make light of it. "I'm pretty well spent too."

I start packing up the jars and bread into the lunch backpack, mostly so he doesn't see my face. His mind is made up. I'm trying to hold back tears.

For the rest of the day, I try to resign myself to quitting. I get surges of anger, and I taste a bit of rejection in there too. Is this what love is supposed to be like? I think I love him. I certainly don't want him hurt. He says he loves me. Oh, why can't we get rid of all this emotional hogwash and just paddle?

We erect tents to escape mosquitoes that evening, and Tom and I have more time to talk privately. I don't say much. He has a lot to get off his chest. He says he is turning one of his favorite things—canoe camping—into something he hates. His arms ache a deep-down ache. He just can't go on. He says his main concern is losing me. I churn this all over that night since sleep evades me. Love, anger, failure, exhaustion—it is all too much to figure out.

After five days on the river, we arrive at a boat launch in Atchison, Kansas. I remember somehow squeezing all our equipment, Diane and Steve's equipment, four people and a dog into a Ford Escort Wagon with two canoes on top. I remember looking out the one unblocked window at the boat launch in Atchison that marked the end of our river expedition, vowing to return to this very spot one day to finish what we started.

CHAPTER 8

Once Again

Nothing is as real as a dream. The world can change around you, but your dream will not. Responsibilities need not erase it. Duties need not obscure it. Because the dream is within you, no one can take it away.

—Tom Clancy

Eleven Years Later

Phase II, Day 1 (March 29, 1997): The boat launch I remember so vividly from eleven years earlier was rather ugly and mundane—just a cement ramp off a riverside road. In a much less rambunctious river, trailered boats got backed down, parallel to the river, and fed into the downstream eddy the ramp created.

Preparing to launch. Photo courtesy of Roy DeWitte.

Today, only our lowly canoe gets prepared for launch. Tom and I load MW at the bottom of the ramp while Mom, Dad, and an occasional passer-by look on anxiously.

"That water is really running fast," Dad says as I return to his truck for another load. Mom and Dad volunteered to return us to the river in Atchison, Kansas a few months ago, when I announced my intention to complete our journey.

"Are you sure you want to do this?" Mom's worried look, which she's perfected through the years, says what's in her heart.

"Well, it is running fast," I stammer, "but we can do this." I want to convey determination and confidence, but my reservations come out instead.

My parents are good at seeing through my downplay of words. "We can stay here awhile longer and see if it changes," Mom suggests. The trailer is at a nearby campground, where we all stayed last night.

"That'll be great, Mom." I give her another hug. I say nothing about the nightmare I had.

I awoke this morning in a panic. I dreamed our canoe hit the prow of a barge. I experienced the terror of capsizing and being sucked underwater into the gullet of the behemoth. I kicked and fought for breath when I sprang awake with a gasp. As I sat there, chest heaving, bug-eyed, causing Tom all sorts of concern, I wondered if this was a premonition.

Joining flotsam for the spring flush on the muddy Missouri.
Photo courtesy of Roy DeWitte.

Yesterday I stood on the bank of the flood-swollen Missouri, watching the churning brown water race downriver. Limbs, branches, trash, and logs longer than MW bounced along in the current, sweeping past. Tom came up beside me. "It's fast, huh?"

"I'll say." I gave him my half-smile, eyebrows-raised glance of concern.

"We should make good time on it, though," he added, ever the optimist. Wordlessly, we watch yet another tree trunk race by, heading straight for a barge moored downriver. Barge prows are perfectly designed to shed debris expeditiously. I watched uneasily as the tree trunk crashed into the reinforced steel prow with a BOOM, then got sucked underwater with a swoosh and a slurp. That barge just gobbled it down, along with all the other debris coming its way. My eyes wide, teeth clenched, and mouth taut with dread, I turned to Tom. He understood my deep concern. I don't want to be eaten by a hungry barge. We intended to join that tree and many others in that chocolate-brown mess of an aquatic raceway tomorrow.

I Accept

Eleven years ago, Diane dropped us off from our expedition. Tom and I parted ways. I immediately suffered from his absence. My chest physically ached. I missed his touch, his reassuring presence, his confidence in me. Nothing felt right, until I relented.

He answered my call with "Hello?"

"Yes." That's all I said. He'd know my voice.

"What? Does that mean what I think it means?"

"Yes. But I want you to come here and ask me in person."

"Okaaaay!" The mirth in his voice made me smile.

Suddenly everything was right with the world. Contentment replaced anxiety. Joy replaced sadness. That day, a dozen roses arrived at my door. The next day, Tom arrived. I couldn't erase my perpetual smile.

We spent most of the next eleven years in a kind of heaven on Earth. I directed adult programming at Great Smoky Mountains Institute at Tremont. Tom worked for the National Park Service as an interpretive ranger in the park. Here we enjoyed fulfilling jobs, glorious surroundings, and special friends. And yet, as time wore on, the pull of an unfinished task exerted itself steadily and without mercy. I realized I could never be totally at ease again until we hit the Atlantic Ocean paddling.

Our canoe-themed wedding

I finally felt compelled to address that nag, that unfulfilled promise that I made to myself so many years ago: to cross the country by canoe—completely.

I felt excitement and anticipation as we quit our jobs, rented the house, stored the car and all our furnishings, and bid farewell to our dear friends to embrace river life again. The crush of saying goodbye was eased because our paddling route would bring us back this way. The Little Tennessee River borders Great Smoky Mountains National Park to the south, where Fontana Lake, which we had paddled before, is readily within reach. We could rendezvous, camp, and paddle together with our friends soon.

Getting a Feel for the Missouri

Phase II Day 1 (March 29) continued: The big dirty Missouri River has more hazards than just ginormous flotsam. Strange upwellings boil up in the middle of the river at random. Sometimes water even sprays into the air from sudden bursts of this roiling water.

Although no obstacle or creature ever shows itself as the cause, we dub this phenomenon "The Missouri River Monster." Whatever is under there, I don't want to be above its outburst. By hugging the shore, we can avoid the monster. But there, other hazards lurk. Submerged dikes jut out from the shoreline, encouraging the river to self-scour, keeping the central channel deep for navigation. These wing dikes usher oncoming water toward the river center, where it is flushed downstream with the rest of the torrent. This creates an intense whirlpool at the tip of each unseen dike. It only takes a small whirlpool to throw the bow around and send us into a pirouette. A big vortex could easily flip a canoe. We have miles and miles of this crazy swirling stuff to do.

With timely draws, confident braces, and balanced leaning, we navigate a thin line far enough from shore to skim the outskirts of the whirlpools but not way out, where the monster surges and sputters, hungry to devour a tiny canoe.

With one day under our belt, we camp on a levee downriver from Leavenworth, Kansas, with the federal prison in sight. As Comet Hale-Bopp streaks across Earth's path, I can't believe we've come all this way in such a short time. Even today, in just four hours of paddling, we bagged twenty-eight miles. After I climb into bed and settle down beside Tom, we listen to the coyotes howl in the distance. Dogs that sing—I love that. I can't help but long for Sirius, now too old for canoeing shenanigans, living in luxury at Tom's folks' house.

"Look—there's two people up there," Tom blurts out.

"I guess they're people," I say, squinting into the distance. "Hey, I think they're waving."

Tom realizes it first. "It's your folks!"

Sure enough. Who else would be waving so energetically? I can now make out Dad's Tilly hat and confirm the heartwarming sight of my doting parents.

We get as close as possible and pull into shore to greet Mom and Dad. The bank is too steep for a complete reunion, but we can get within speaking range.

Mom says, "We've been looking for you."

"I didn't know you were still hanging around," I answer.

"We happened into some folks who saw you and reported that

you were going along okay." For a moment, I wonder what age I must be when my mother stops checking up on me.

But there is no room for cynicism; I feel the warmth of their loving concern filling me with gratitude. "We found a park in Kansas City that went down to the river." It took a concerted effort for Mom to talk this loud. "But the road to it was closed because of toxic contamination."

"Yes, we saw it too," I shout.

She relays more details of their diligent detective work: people interviewed, maps purchased, roads explored. Now, Mom and Dad are satisfied that we can handle ourselves on this river.

They are a long way from their campsite, and it's getting late, so they head back to the trailer. They will leave for home tomorrow. I could never ask for better parents.

Workin' the Spring Floods

Phase II Day 3 (March 31): Weariness demands the end of a paddling day.

"Pull out by that round log," I instruct Tom, indicating a floating log jammed against the bank. Exiting this river is no easy feat. Steep banks close us in. Some are buttressed by a wall of sharp, slippery boulders; others have been carved into a curling wave shape by erosion. This prospect is encouraging, however. As we get closer, it becomes plain that the "round log" has four stiff limbs—and a tail—and is a stinky, bloated dead cow. Moving on.

This whole first week, we bump and jostle along with the flotsam. Bottles, tires, logs and sticks, and a sundry of trash race us downriver. Our objectives: try not to ram into too much stuff; steer clear of the foamy eddy monsters and whirlpools; give barges a wide berth; don't touch the water. If I splash my face or get my hands wet, I wipe it off with my bandanna right away. Toxic parks, dead cows, foamy suds—not a bather's paradise.

The impending spring floods have weighed heavily on Tom, but now, as we paddle our last day on the Missouri River, I smile as I listen to his frivolous chattering interspersed with airy and sputtery whistling. This uncharacteristic cheerfulness results from our recent inquiry with the U.S. Army Corps of Engineers and the U.S. Coast Guard about our prospects on the Mississippi River. We now know that we can be on and off this important waterway before floodwaters hit. But if we are deemed a danger to ourselves or others, the coast guard will not hesitate to pull us off the river. Terms accepted.

CHAPTER 9

America's Most Famous River

The face of the water, in time, became a
wonderful book—a book that was a dead
language to the uneducated passenger, but
which told its mind to me without reserve.

—Mark Twain

Dodging Barges

Phase II Day 16 (April 13): After we paddle the last seven miles, the
Missouri spits us out into the mighty Mississippi. As far as I can see
downriver to the right, the shoreline has barges docked two, three,
four, up to six abreast. Upriver is just the same. I'm reminded of a
busy truck stop on the New York State Thruway. As on a commer-

cialized city street, there is no curb to be seen—with one exception: directly across in Illinois. I can see the makings of a park.

Tom sees it too. "Hey, head straight across," he directs. "I want to get some pictures."

"On it." Like my mother taught me, I look both ways for traffic before proceeding across the street—ah—river. I point MW slightly up-river to compensate for the Mississippi's push and pump water to cross.

The Lewis and Clark Expedition launched from here

Spying a canoe-friendly spot, I nose MW onto the pebbly shore. Tom jumps out and hoists us firmly aground.

An inscription on a stone marker says this is the site of Camp Dubois—the winter training and send-off point of Lewis and Clark's expedition. From here they set out to explore the Louisiana Purchase and search for a water connection to the Pacific Ocean. We have now retraced much of their route. (By the way, after our visit—in 2004—a replica fort and visitor center was built nearby to accommodate visitors for the two hundredth anniversary of the launch of their expedition. But there was none of that when we stopped by). After reading the commemorative inscription, we pose for a photograph.

Then looking over the two mighty rivers, we assess our progress.

"Over four hundred miles in sixteen days," Tom sums up our achievement.

"The Missouri was really moving us along."

"The Mississippi will be our last chance to go downriver for a while."

"I know. Don't remind me."

"We'll only be on it for two hundred miles." I let him voice what I already know. "One and a half to two weeks should do it. Then it's uphill on the Ohio. That should be interesting." He trails off. Tom is concerned about the floodwater on the Ohio now. He's got to have something to worry about.

Industrial traffic, dockage, loading, and unloading facilities dot practically all of St. Louis's Mississippi riverfront. We are but a speck in a sea of massive vessels. With barges lining the shoreline, we are forced to paddle the main flow. Keen not to fulfill my premonition, I am ever mindful of them.

I sense water and flotsam getting swallowed at a more rapid rate as we pass one of the barges. We seem to be going by a bit faster too.

"Hey, this barge is moving!" I shout to Tom. "I'm giving it more room."

I steer MW further into the middle of the river. Passing the length of one and then another barge, we begin to hear the roar of a towboat.

Sure enough, it's churning up water, muscling those barges up-river ever so slowly. There is little difference between barges at rest and those on the move! I want to get outta here.

With St. Louis Harbor behind us, some towboat and barge traffic eases up. We encounter vessels every day. The winner is a tow of thirty-five barges being handled by two towboats.

Compared to the Missouri, the Mississippi seems to flow a tad quicker. The Mississippi is equally as filthy and clogged with debris since the Missouri contributes everything she has (which is a lot) to what the Mississippi already carries. Ol' Man River seems to have an unexpected playful side. It has fun flotsam. After two days on the river, we encounter a baseball, tennis ball, racquetball, football, basketball, a bat, and a plastic bounce-house ball. We also rescue a Canada goose decoy named Brad from the willows. Yes, Brad has his name and telephone number on his underside. Maybe we'll call his owner. We'll see. Tom ties Brad to the stern, giving MW a pull toy.

Dodging barge tows continues to be our primary pursuit down this hardworking river. One catches us by surprise around a bend. We get stuck on the deep outer curve with a tow bearing down on us.

We decide to stop and hang out, almost beached, in the shallow water. Our advantage: we can float in three inches of water—tows can't.

As the barges glide by, I examine every tiny rust speck on their hulls and consider touching one with my outstretched paddle, but don't dare. Heavily laden with cargo, the barges sit low in the water. When the fifth visible barge slowly passes, we begin to hear and ultimately see the towboat responsible for pushing this massive fifteen-barge tethered armada.

The whole river boils in the wake of the boat's noisy and amazingly powerful 6,000-horsepower engines, and we diligently brace against the bouncy ride it gives us.

CHAPTER 10

The Ohio

There is nothing insignificant in the world.
It all depends on the point of view.

—Johann Wolfgang von Goethe

A Mouse among the Cats

Phase II, Day 23 (April 20): I look downstream before departing the Mississippi for the Ohio River. The incoming Ohio water avoids mixing with the brown Mississippi River water as far as I can see. Eventually, the waters will mix, but I think Ohio doesn't want to. We approach this confluence with a sense of trepidation—certainly glad to be out of the path of impending floodwaters. But our current concern is—the current. We have no idea whether we can even paddle our little selves up against the springtime flush.

The Ohio is another major transportation artery servicing

America. It carries products and raw materials from city to city east of the Mississippi. Tom's concern is our ability to paddle against the flow; mine is not to get run over by a towboat.

We beach MW on a spit of stark, brown, slightly sloping land north of the confluence and disembark. A few steps in, Tom nods, purses his lips, and smiles. My shoulders slump, and I pout.

"Barges" is all I manage in a pitiful, disheartening tone. As far as I can see, the Ohio has no shoreline. It is completely lined with barges.

"Yeah, but look at the current"—he gives me a little elbow poke. "We can do this. No problem." His perkiness annoys me.

All along the Cairo industrial area, barges pack three to eight abreast on both shorelines. Some are even moored in the middle of the river. We are but a bug navigating a corridor of sleeping cats.

Barges and towboats and more barges and towboats—they never end! Toss in a couple of dry-dock marinas, loading and unloading docks, and that is the riverfront for Superman's city—Metropolis, Illinois. The port tug is working today, pushing a barge here, poking a barge there. We give him a wide berth as we pass. Not long after, I turn to see him bearing down on us. With rows of barges on both sides of the river, there is no place for us to pull over, and it's too narrow for him to pass, so our only option is full steam ahead.

"Pump water NOW!" I shout and kick it into high gear. After a glance over his shoulder, Tom, in the stern, joins me. I call for switches every twenty strokes, and we shovel water furiously in perfect synchrony. I know the captain can see us working our butts off to get out of his way—but where can we go?

After passing two moored barges, I see our out. "Beach!" I scream between heaving exhales. I nod my head in the direction of an opening between the row of barges, hoping Tom will see what I mean.

"Okay," he shouts and adjusts course.

Wind and waves are challenging, yes, but a tug on your tail is supremely motivating. We don't let up until we start to scrape the shoreline. I stumble out, feeling like a ragdoll, and yank MW up with my best, albeit wimpy effort.

Tom hops into the water, and together we heave her up to avoid the incoming wake. Once the harbor tug has passed, we look upriver to see a towboat pushing eight barges our way. We watch him expertly squeeze his tow between all the moored barges. There's no way we could navigate this corridor with him! If we didn't get crushed, we'd swamp in the furious sloshing of the wake bouncing back and forth between barge hulls. It would be scary beyond belief. As I lie flopped on the beach, I thank God for a strategically stationed landing.

The forty-eight miles on this river of trepidation takes us only three days to travel. We are feeling pretty darn proud of ourselves. We deserve a lake. And so it shall be.

CHAPTER 11

The Tennessee

The rivers flow not past, but through us,
thrilling, tingling, vibrating every fiber
and cell of the substance of our bodies,
making them glide and sing.

—John Muir

Sweating Out a Tornado

Phase II, Day 26 (April 23): I sit on the riprap below Kentucky Dam Lock, playing push-me-pull-you with MW. While I wait for our turn to lock through, the water level drops and rises several times as water is let out of or held back from the lock. Poor MW got beached on the rocks the first time the level dropped, but now I've learned to push her out with the paddle as the water drops or pull her in with the bow and stern painters when it rises. Finally, we get the short horn blast and green light. Under the gaze of a dozen spectators, we rise sixty-four feet in twenty minutes in the Kentucky Dam Lock.

Waiting on riprap for our turn to lock through

We are no longer within the realm of the U.S. Army Corps of Engineers. The Tennessee Valley Authority, or TVA, operates the locks and dams on the Tennessee River. This agency manages reservoirs and generates electricity for Tennessee and parts of six surrounding states. Like the Army Corps, it provides recreation by way of boat ramps, parks, visitor centers, and land management while facilitating navigation and flood management.

"Look at all the motorboats," I exclaim on this lovely spring day. "MW is in her element." Anglers, along with wave runners and all manner of personal watercraft play on Kentucky Lake. There is still some towboat traffic, but finally, small crafts rule.

"Motorboats make the worst wakes," Tom points out.

Not to be infected by his sour mood, I continue, "Yes, but I mean we are finally back in our realm. These are MW's kin. No more cat-and-mouse." I have indeed been looking forward to escaping commercialized rivers, and my chipper mood reflects my relief.

"Well, I think I can tell you now something I knew you would not have wanted to hear earlier," Tom said.

"Really?" I remark, sensing my good mood may soon be quashed. I stop paddling and turn around to look at him. "What makes you think I'd want to know now?"

"It's just kind of coincidental," he says.

"Well, what is it?"

"While we were still on the Missouri, my mom told me of a news story," he pauses. He has kept this secret for quite some time. "In Florida, a motorboat lost power and got sucked under a barge. Someone got the whole thing on video. It was on national news."

"Ohhh." I cringe. Goosebumps suddenly sprout all over me. Paddle across my lap, I turn to face forward again. "My dream came true," I mumble, horrified. I recall the nightmare that startled me awake in a panicky sweat as we set out on the Missouri. That *was* a premonition. This horrible thing happened to someone else. I shiver at the thought.

"Two people drowned. I think one of them tossed a baby aside at the last second." Does he have to make the story worse?

"Oh, geez." I am almost in tears now. I can imagine the scenario all too clearly. We have passed enough barges to know how they devour everything, big and small, under their prows.

"I didn't want to tell you then," Tom speaks softly.

I turn back and look him squarely in the eye, "I appreciate that." I sincerely do. We paddle in silence for a good while. I think about whether divine providence has indeed kept us safe. There never were any times when we truly felt endangered by the vessels. Some encounters were too close for comfort, but I never experienced the encroaching maw of a barge bearing down on me. Do I owe this to luck, alert and prudent paddling, or God's benevolence? I conclude that all three played a part.

Many days later, driven by an increasingly ominous-looking sky, we search for a sheltered spot to wait out the storm. Rising winds and choppy waves force us to pull out on a treeless island in the Tennessee National Wildlife refuge. After I haul MW securely ashore, Tom, in the stern, stays put and snatches his weather radio from his journal box. Putting the earbuds in, he listens intently while I survey a menacing sky.

"Oh, geez, I wonder what county we're in," he says, hopping out, grabbing the map out of its protective plastic zip bag, and unfurling it on the sand.

Feeling the contagion of his anxiety, I plunk down beside him. "Why?"

"There's a tornado watch for Decatur and Perry counties until seven o'clock. Here's Decatur," he says, circling the word with his finger. "And let's see . . . yup, here's Perry."

"Wait a minute," I interject, sticking my head closer to the map. "Where exactly are we now."

"Right about here." He pokes a spot confidently. "Straddling both." The ominous clouds and blue-grey color of the sky confirm the gravity of the situation.

"Great, just where I want to be in a tornado. We can seek refuge in our flimsy nylon tent." My flippant comment doesn't convey my nervousness.

"We'll just have to batten down," Tom concludes. "Where should we set up camp?"

I look around. "Well, not here. There's no protection." We shove off and paddle upriver with vigor, wind and waves be damned.

Soon I spy a copse of two- to five-inch-diameter trees. I figure these young trees can bend and sway and take wind gusts better than big stiff ones. A big tree could uproot and end up on top of us. Let's avoid that! My thinking is to situate us deep into this thick young forest.

"Here—pull in here." I tug the bow toward the landing, and Tom propels MW to my spot. With practiced efficiency, I hop out and heave; Tom hops out; we heave in unison and are firmly ashore. After a minute of discussion, we get to work, using every bit of rope we have—which is considerable. We turn MW over; we clip the packs and waterbags to MW's thwarts to weigh her down; we carve long stakes, which we sink deep into the mud, using them to hold down the lace-work of ropes we run across her; we tie her bow and stern painters to older, hopefully deeply rooted trees; we squeeze the tent in amongst the thick grove and erect it; we tie each tie-down to a neighboring tree; we zigzag rope across the tent ridgepole, securing it to trees and more long stakes. Our camp looks like a giant spider has gone berserk.

When our campsite is finally lashed down, the rain and wind that drove us to stop cease. The water grows calm. The air suddenly becomes still. Robust, dark, angry-looking clouds blot out the sky. This eerie combination turns the whole world purple. We both stand by the water's edge, eyeing the battle raging in the sky. Rubbing my arms, I settle my goosebumps. Surely a funnel cloud will emerge from this billowing purple shroud at any moment. We crawl into the spi-derweb-secured tent with the door open to keep an eye on the sky.

Coincidentally, the novel I'm currently reading is *Vortex* by Jon Cleary. The whole book takes place in a single day—the day a tor-nado touches down and destroys a town. I just so happen to be at the book's climax, when the tornado is demolishing homes, cars, and people. Like an idiot, I while away our time continuing to read about the characters I've come to know, now frantically running for their lives or desperately seeking loved ones. Between the book and reality,

I'm hyperalert. I pray a few prayers, put our fate in God's hands, and continue reading about the characters' fateful mistakes or fortunate actions. Who knows? Maybe I'll learn something soon to be useful.

At 8:30 p.m., headphones in ears, Tom announces that two tornadoes have touched down south and east of us by the Alabama border. "Hail, heavy winds, and dangerous lightning still pepper the forecast until midnight," he repeats. The rain starts for a second time, intensifying into a thunderstorm that rattles our tent and nerves. But it quickly passes. Stillness rules the rest of the night. I remember hearing Tom announce that the tornado watch had been lifted before sleep consumed me. The next thing I know, sunlight wakes me.

"Hey, what time is it?" I ask Tom, lying beside me.

"Six fifty-two," he replies.

"Nothing happened, huh?"

"We must be blessed," he says. I lean up on one elbow to see if this is actually my husband.

"Really?" Not at all the religious sort, I find this comment quite unexpected.

He shrugs. "Maybe prayers do work."

Other River People

Phase II, Day 36 (May 3): While eating our strawberry pancakes, we watch a towboat with nine barges filled with coal pass our site heading upriver—our direction. By the time we are underway, the towboat is still within sight. I'm not very competitive, but when Tom says, "Let the race begin!" I purse my lips, nod my head, and dig in. And so begins another day of sneaking up a torrent of oncoming water.

Using shore eddies, changing paddling sides often, and ferrying across the river to get on the inside curves are all in our playbook of strategic paddling. Our quarry is not only still in sight after two hours of paddling, but we have gained significant ground. We take the inside, shorter route at Swallow Bluff Island and gain even more ground. Then the towboat stops at a curve to let an oncoming vessel with an even larger load pass downriver, which gives us another advantage. In three and a half hours, we are not only fighting the current but our quarry's wake as well. Declaring ourselves victors, we stop for lunch so our competitor can go on his way without our bearing down on him anymore.

Although paddling the Tennessee River is hard work, we've had some choice campsites like the one next to a TVA boat ramp at Cravens Landing. This is no remote hideaway but a neighborhood. The friendly folks welcome us to the community and even invite us in if we need anything. Blackie, the neighborhood dog, escorts us down the street or back to our site. In the morning, a small crowd gathers at the boat ramp to witness for themselves that we can, in fact, sneak up this rain-swollen fast-moving river.

The best campsite comes two days later in Savannah, Tennessee. After the sports reporter for *The Courier* interviews us, he invites us to stay at his B&B. At Sulphur Springs Bed and Breakfast, we eat catfish, watch a ball game, hang out with the family, and sleep in a bed—truly revitalizing tonic. We even watch a video—*African Queen*—where Humphry Bogart and Katharine Hepburn get stuck in a boat together. They endure hardships and ultimately fall in love. How absurd.

In 1986, a man and his wife set out to travel by river to the Gulf of Mexico. They started by building a sailboat in Saltillo, Tennessee. The Tennessee River's stench and the sight of dead fish and clams washing up on the bank led Leaf Myczack and his wife Cielo to embark on a different mission—to become a sort of Lorax, speaking for the river. When their new sailboat, *Broadened Horizons*, was seaworthy, they spent their days—and years—plying the Tennessee River, bringing atrocities to the attention of city officials, media, TVA personnel, residents, state legislators, schoolchildren, and anyone else they could reach. Calling themselves the Riverkeepers, Leaf and Cielo adopted the Tennessee River to monitor, observing it from 1989 until 2004. They spoke out about shoreline development, industrial seepage, runoff of residential herbicide use, cutting of bank-stabilizing trees, and many other river insults as they made their voyages up and down the river.

Rivers worldwide have been, and still are, trash depositories, eliminators of effluent from industrial processes, disposers of non-point pollution, and receptacles for unwanted waste because rivers wash things "away." Here in the U.S., an increased outcry that there is no "away"—that there is always someone downstream—led to strengthening the Federal Water Pollution Control Act of 1948. With more stringent amendments, the law, passed by Congress in 1972, became known as the Clean Water Act. Even more than a decade later, violations were still rampant, but the Riverkeepers persisted in making noise and giving voice to the river.

I would love to run into *Broadened Horizons* and engage in a long conversation with the like-minded Riverkeepers. I am impressed with their devotion and bravery to speak up in opposition to financially influential developers and legislators swayed by big business. Although we keep our eyes peeled and scour marinas, *Broadened Horizons* eludes us.

Unlike these two Riverkeepers, who cultivated a long-term relationship with a single river, we have only a short-term encounter with the waterways we travel. But in this land, where energy is water and water is energy, we urge readers of the *Augusta Chronicle* to be prudent in their use of electricity in order to conserve water. We ask readers of the *Herald-News* out of Dayton, Tennessee, not to take water for granted—it requires our respect, attention, and care.

I hope there are at least some readers who say more than "That's nice" or "Wow" to our cross-country endeavor but rather take our water-conservation appeals to heart. We sprinkle in suggestions such as joining forces with a watershed council, organizing a river cleanup, joining your town's conservation committee, volunteering to remove exotic plant and animal invaders, and nagging your government officials to promote higher water-quality standards. Then we paddle on, never knowing our impact. I think the Riverkeepers do it right.

Eleven days later, my nose detects Decatur, Alabama, before my eyes. What a noxious place! The stench makes me feel sick to my stomach. We pass a chemical company spewing steaming water into the river. Thermal pollution is as real a threat to river life as chemical insults. We pass many recognizable corporate giants lining the riverfront. I regret not having a motorized backup so we could whiz by this awful place. There's work to be done here to salvage the river.

We press on to find shelter on the other side in Wheeler National Wildlife Refuge. Rumor had it, alligators are present in these parts. Being hypervigilant and imagining how an alligator might rip our tent to pieces or snap at a vital appendage, I am jolted by an explosion that jars me an inch out of my seat. I shriek. Wide-eyed, I hear a barrage of small arms fire. Then we listen to what sounds like a helicopter whirling.

"Are we under attack?" I blurt out. Tense about alligators to begin with, and now this. My heart is racing, adrenalin surging.

"Noooooo," Tom replies in a voice tinged with uncertainty. "Get closer to shore so I can read that sign." I begin to paddle again, angling close to the north bank, where we eventually make out: U.S. ARMY INSTALLATION, NO TRESPASSING.

Pausing my paddling, I pick up the map to examine the small print. "Ahh, yes. Seems we've passed the wildlife refuge." I turn the map sideways. "This must be Redstone Arsenal. It's an army installation." Relieved and satisfied, I return the map to its place on deck and resume paddling. "They must be practicing."

"Yup, drills." In a moment, a cloud of chlorine-scented smoke drifts down the river to engulf us. "Well, this is one no trespassing sign we're going to obey," Tom says with a cough. We put our backs into paddling upstream as fast as possible to get away from all the horrible happenings at the arsenal.

Lavishly Embraced

Phase II, Day 50 (May 17): Tom bolts upright. Bobbing on the bed, he exclaims, wide-eyed and with desperate realization, "We're on a DOCK!"

The jostling and outburst jolt me awake. I, too, sit up and quickly get my bearings. "No, sweetie, we're not on a dock." He puts one leg over the side of the bed, swinging it back and forth, feeling for water. He bounces three more times to rock the "dock."

Again, in a more panicky voice, "WE'RE ON A DOCK!"

Now I'm alarmed. If he's asleep, he sure is animated. "No, we're in a BED, not a dock!" I shout into his ear. With another push on the mattress he relaxes, finding me to be entirely correct. He falls back on the pillow with a huge sigh and looks over at me.

"Wow, are you awake?" I ask.

"Yeah, now I am," he says. "Gosh, that was weird."

"What was that all about?"

"I sorta woke up and looked out the window, then at the foot of the bed, and I swore I was on a dock," he says, sitting up again. "I knew the lake was receding, and I was afraid it would leave us high and dry."

"I know it has been a long time, but this is what we call a "bed," sweetie, a very luxurious bed." I console him with a wry smile. "Most people sleep on one." I give him a soft belly slap. "Now, c'mon. Time to get up. Fun day ahead."

Geography and conservation lesson.

We are lavishly resting in Joe and Linda's guest room in Huntsville, Alabama. I met Linda while working in the Smokies. This board-and-batten home they built themselves is *Better Homes and*

Gardens-worthy, adorned with quilts, antique tools, punched tin cupboards, and homemade furniture. For the next three days, we converse, shop, repair MW, and sightsee. We visit the Huntsville Space Center and the George C. Marshall Space Center, where we see a part of the international space station. Linda invites us to do a program at school for her students, which was a lot of fun. Can't forget to make our mark with the local media either. *The Huntsville Times* reporter got it right when she printed, "The Condons saw alarming pollution, passing places where chemicals were being dumped into western rivers." Somehow someone missed the mark about the alarming eastern pollution—namely here on the Tennessee River.

With a bagful of Joe's homemade biscuits, they deliver us to the dock above Guntersville Dam. "Get out of Alabama!" Joe affectionately calls after us as we paddle away. I have the newly signed "thank-you" paddle tucked in beside the gear and the warmth of their loving hospitality tucked inside me.

By now, the perfect paddle stroke is automatic. Plant, pull, feather; plant, pull, feather; plant, pull, feather. Through repetition, my muscles have learned to go about their business without much attention. The paddle is an extension of my body. MW goes precisely where I want her to go without much thought.

As we tolerate daily rain showers mile after mile, we support each other, endure each other, entertain each other, and vex each other. Sometimes we sing. Sometimes we play a game. Sometimes we share our observations. Sometimes we paddle in companionable silence. But it all happens as we plant, pull, feather; plant, pull, feather.

This stretch of the Tennessee River through northern Alabama and back into our home state of Tennessee is beautiful. The most picturesque part of Phase II so far is the Tennessee River Gorge, a twenty-six-mile section west of Chattanooga. Mountains rise over 2,300 feet on both sides of this narrow, twisting lake made by Nickajack Dam. As rain moves through, mist and clouds rise and reveal the rich hardwood forests of the Cumberland Mountains. The glassy-smooth lake doubles the majestic cliffs above.

On Memorial Day, we paddle through Chattanooga—a proclaimed "green" city. Peppered with trees, downtown is pleasant and attractive. A string of parks and walkways line the river, frequented by joggers and walkers. The nationally recognized Tennessee Aquarium perches on the shoreline, where steps invite people right down to the river.

We paddle by Maclellan Island. The whole island is an environmental-education center. Fishing docks, crammed with anglers, jut into the river. I love to see a city embrace its river. The real beauty is that Chattanooga used to be a filthy place. Dedication to the cause has brought about—dare I say these words together? —a lovely city.

We cook breakfast in rain. We paddle in rain. We lunch in rain. We establish camp in rain. We cook supper in rain. We go to sleep to the sound of rain. Sometimes the rain comes in the form of a tiny cloud relieving itself as it races across the lake. We cannot outrun these torrents despite our best efforts, but they give us fair warning. We hear a pounding waterfall getting louder and louder. We look behind to see a dark curtain stirring up the surface as it chases us down. No time to waste. Pull up the hood, cinch up the spray skirt, stop paddling, and hunker down while big, heavy drops give us a whooping. Within a minute, our punishment has ceased. We raise our heads to see the attack cloud continue on its way.

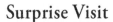

Surprise Visit

Phase II, Day 63 (May 30): After ringing the doorbell, a confused-looking man opens the door. We stand on the front step. As I explain who we are over the cacophony of three barking dogs, Bob's face lights up with delight. He wasn't expecting us. We've never met. All we know is Bob and Mary Lynn are former Tremont participants who, through the grapevine, invited us to spend a night at their lovely home on Watts Bar Lake.

I am over the moon with the concept of sleeping the night in a place called the "sunroom." We decorate every nook and cranny of the glorious sunroom with clothes, journals, raincoats, shoes, and other odds and ends that need to dry—which is everything.

I am delighted to see an article of mine, "A Sense of House," from *Walker Valley Reflections*, the Tremont newsletter, displayed on the refrigerator. Bob explains that this is precisely how they feel about their home and have had the article up for several months now. Wow, I'm on someone's refrigerator! It feels good to be an author.

We are soon in the presence of some inspiring environmental activists when Mary Lynn and her guest, Arthur, come in from a botanizing hike. The year before, Arthur tried to get a bottle bill passed in the Tennessee legislature but said the business lobbyists outnumbered the environmental advocates, and it failed. Arthur and Mary Lynn are trying again. They plan to put a slideshow together and ask us to be on the lookout for pro-bottle-bill photos. With free and easy conversation between environmentally conscious individuals, this lovely evening renews my mind and spirit. I go soundly to sleep, knowing the rain outside—of course, it's still raining—cannot affect us in the sunroom.

The next morning on the dock, preparing to head out, we load MW. I feel dry and renewed.

"The forecast calls for heavy rain and flash flooding today," Mary Lynn warns as we settle into our seats.

"Well, we're certainly used to that," Tom concedes, trying not to betray his utter disappointment in this bit of information.

"Our rain gauge recorded over five inches of rain this past week," Bob remarks.

With one final hand squeeze to Mary Lynn and a nod to Bob, I hope my sincerity comes across when I say, "Thank you for a wonderful break." Then we paddle away from our newfound friends and the luxurious sunroom.

Except for constant rain and tent puddles every night, paddling the rest of Watts Bar Lake is almost pleasant. During a break in the weather, we stop for a three-mile hike into Loudon, Tennessee for groceries. Upon our return to MW, the clouds threaten to compensate for their lack of attention. We shove off under a black sky just as a crack of thunder booms. Plops of rain start to pelt the landscape, and a sudden wind gust tells us we must find cover straightaway.

Our plan: paddle furiously until we get close to a park pavilion Tom spotted just around this bend, tie MW to the bushes to fend for herself, and race for the shelter. But another option soon presents itself—emerging into view from around the corner.

"I'm heading for the culvert," I shout over the sound of the wind, leaving no room for discussion.

"Good," I think he says. We don't let up until we are entirely within our little tunnel. Our cozy retreat is about four canoe lengths long, connecting our lake to a little pond. Rain, now heavy, blows in after us but can't quite reach. From our safe haven we watch the wind tossing branches and snatching spray off waves. I shudder with the thought of being out there: pelted by rain, bombarded by debris, blown broadside, and tossed by waves. How is it that we are so well provided for?

The Last Lock

Phase II, Day 67 (June 3): Tellico Dam and Fort Loudoun Dam separate the Tennessee River from the Little Tennessee River. Going from one river system to another requires passing through the Fort Loudoun lock. Today is our sixteenth and last lock of the trip. A reporter and a photographer from the *Knoxville News Sentinel* document this event. Mostly, I look forward to reuniting with my friend and boss from Great Smoky Mountains Institute at Tremont and his family, collectively known as the "Voorhi."

Getting the lockmaster's attention with the small craft pull cord.
Photo courtesy of Knoxville News Sentinel.

Entering Fort Loudoun Lock. Photo courtesy of Knoxville News Sentinel.

After locking through, we paddle onto Fort Loudoun Lake (that stretches northeast toward Knoxville) and through a channel connecting it to Tellico Lake on the Little Tennessee River. The reporter and photographer followed in another canoe. We pull into the boat launch, where Ken, Jennifer, Bonnie Jo, Woody, and Robin greet us with hugs and doughnuts. The reporter does his best to interview us amid the catchup chatter and stuffing myself with doughnuts.

Waiting to rise seventy feet. Photo courtesy of Ken Voorhis.

Paddling out of the last of our sixteen lockages.
Photo courtesy of Knoxville News Sentinel.

CHAPTER 12

One Last Climb—
The Little Tennessee

I do not think there is any other quality
so essential to success of any kind as the
quality of perseverance. It overcomes almost
everything, even nature.

—John D. Rockefeller

The Trick to Portaging Very Tall Dams

Phase II, Day 70 (June 6): Let me tell you a story about a little creature who helped humans question our self-ascribed authority over nature. You see, a population of small fish were in danger. They didn't know it. And people didn't realize it until 1973, when Dr. David Etnier, a University of Tennessee biologist, discovered this fellow—

previously unknown to science—swimming around in the oxygen-rich waters of the Little Tennessee River. But danger lurked in the form of the Tellico Dam, which was under construction. A completed dam would turn the flowing river into an oxygen-poor lake, making it uninhabitable by this fish, known as the snail darter.

Tellico Lake, on which we now paddle, was one of the most controversial impoundments of all time. By 1975 the snail darter was listed under the Endangered Species Act, signed into law the same year the snail darter was discovered. A second-year law student, his law professor and other dam opponents took the Endangered Species Act out for a spin, bringing a lawsuit against Tennessee Valley Authority that was building the dam. The case went all the way to the U.S. Supreme Court, which ruled in favor of upholding the Endangered Species Act and preserving the snail darter.

This, however, was not the end of it. Congress then grappled with the issue, TVA's cause being championed by Tennessee Senator Howard Baker and Congressman John Duncan. In 1979, a congressional vote on an unrelated bill contained an amendment exempting Tellico Dam from the Endangered Species Act; it narrowly passed. Two weeks later, President Jimmy Carter signed the bill into law. Two months later, the Tellico Dam floodgates closed, and the dam was complete. The lower Little Tennessee River spread out to become Tellico Lake.

Hold on—this story has a happy ending. This little three-inch fish with black vertical stripes suffered a setback but was not out of luck. Before the dam gates closed, the U.S. Fish and Wildlife Agency, Tennessee Wildlife Resource Agency, and TVA transplanted snail darters from the Little Tennessee to the Hiwassee River, where they still reside and are doing well. The Tellico population was indeed eradicated, but the little rascal has been found in other tributaries of the Tennessee and other nearby rivers. In 1984 the fish was upgraded from "endangered" to "threatened," a move supported by Dr. Etnier. Good for you, snail darter! And thanks to the people who saved you!

The regretful thing about Fort Loudoun Dam is that it is our final lockage. Not our last dam, though. It just means this is the end of commercial travel. Boats can continue on the Tennessee River all the way to Knoxville, but there is nothing up the Little Tennessee that warrants locks. The remaining dams will just have to be portaged the old-fashioned way. Boy, am I looking forward to that!

Our first order of business is to stop on the shores of Tellico Lake near the cute burg of Tallassee, basically a wide spot on a narrow road. It is named for the ancient town of the Overhill Cherokee, who inhabited this region in the eighteenth century. The historic Tallassee was located seven miles upstream but is now under Calderwood Lake. The important thing is, Tallassee has a post office, and this is where we had our Savannah maps sent.

The post office is a small space inside the hamlet's general store. What a treasure this place is! Cobweb-covered glass cases and dust-laden shelves display a meager selection of goods. The two bags of chocolate chips they carry are each a solid hunk of morsels. There is no syrup to be found, but a jar of homemade blackberry jam for pancakes will do. I blow off the dust and deem it acceptable. I peruse a box of "5 for $1" rocks, none of which look any more interesting than those we encounter in the river every day. I'm guessing it is the enterprise of the proprietor's seven-year-old. A red union suit on display with a yardstick through the arms hangs over a junky assortment of yard sale trinkets. All the T-shirts are black, each with one of two slogans: LAKE TRASH or FAST WOMEN AND HOT BIKES. I'm sure the glass-framed pair of holey wool socks has a story, but a photo of Elvis in karate garb tops the décor. Tom teasingly asks permission to pick an issue from the crate of outdated *Playboy* magazines, but I give him the "forget it, buddy" look. After making our purchase of jam, bread (still seems somewhat squishy), ice cream for me, and root beer for Tom, plus our maps, we hike further up the road to scout out our first dam to portage on this river.

Portaging—my favorite pastime

The Little Tennessee will assist us in paddling up the mountains with four impounded lakes. We must find our way around Chilhowee, Cheoah, Calderwood, and Fontana dams. All were built between

1916 and 1957 by Alcoa Aluminum Company to power its processing plant in Alcoa, Tennessee. Alcoa's electric company, Tapoco, owns and operates the three "C" dams. TVA operates Fontana, regulating lake levels all the way down. Beyond the last lake, it's a big mystery as to how far up a mountain stream we can paddle.

It takes about forty-five minutes to portage around Chilhowee Dam in two trips. We get out at the Dangerous Waters sign. Once we unload MW, we rearrange gear for portage, trade sandals for hiking boots and socks and consolidate equipment for as few trips as possible. I straddle the unwieldy bag, legs apart, back straight, crouching down, grasping the straps with crossed arms. On my silent count, I heave the bag up with a grunt and a little boost from my foot, swinging it around to my back as I scoot underneath. It's a rather nifty maneuver. With a couple of hops to get it perched just right, I cinch up the waist belt until it squeezes my hipbones. With a deep knee bend, I pick up the remaining loose gear—a water bag and fanny packs with water bottles. If I bend over too far, the deadweight sack would certainly shift forward, throwing me headlong into the ground. Now, that would be a sight. So, head up, bent only the necessary amount, I begin the quarter-mile trudge up the gravel access road to route 129 at the top of the dam.

The trick to portaging—and there are many—is to not think about it. Occupy your mind with something other than the agony your body is experiencing.

Body puts one foot in front of the other, time and again, which doesn't need too much attention from Mind. I'm not that good at it, as I stupidly occupy Mind trying to figure out how heavy my pack is. I think about dog food. I've hoisted forty-pound bags of dog food without much trouble at all. I've also picked up fifty-five-pound bags with a little more trouble. I've never carried dog food on my back before, but when I heaved this sack on my back, it is heavier than the heaviest bag of dog food I've ever managed. I'm going to guess a conservative sixty-five pounds, but it's probably more. Tom's overstuffed sack tops mine. I'll put his at seventy to seventy-five pounds. Any more than that sounds absurd, although it is quite feasible.

With this figuring done, I search desperately for something else to think about. I can't ponder my burning thighs or my tender hips under the tiny waist belt. No attention must be given to my back or shoulders as they submit their complaints. Think! Oh—I name the plants as I walk by. Then I start naming the states in alphabetical order. I'm to Massachusetts when I reach Route 129.

Not too far ahead, Tom has stopped at a decent put-in for MW. He bends over, hands on knees, head hung, wincing and breathing heavily. I catch up to him and hold his bag as he slips out of it. It clunks to the ground, and so does Tom. "Next time, I think I'll carry stuff instead of packing it inside," he gasps.

"You don't have to overload," I offer, bent over slightly to balance the weight on my back instead of my shoulders. I unclip the waist belt and loosen the shoulder straps. "I know you can do it, Babe. You don't have to prove anything to me." I brace myself, stand up and swing that blasted sack off my back. It too, clunks to the ground.

"Thanks, Babe." He twitches a little smile my way. "I'd help you, but I'm too beat."

"I know." I collapse onto my bag. "I think the waist belt helps, but it bites into my hips." I lift my t-shirt and peek under my shorts to see the damage in that department. My skin is red and raw.

After a few swigs of water and a little rest, now without burdens, we float down the gravel road. On the second trip, Tom portages MW by himself. I help him swing it up on his shoulders and situate his pullover for padding. I carry the heavy kitchen pack. This load seems heavier than the first but much easier to manage. It is an external-frame backpack designed to be carried, and has a much more agreeable padded waist belt. I pick up the paddles, take a few steps, turn around to survey the area making sure we don't forget anything, and follow the canoe with legs, already ten yards in front of me up the road.

Tom shouldering MW in yet another dam portage

Whether the canoe acts as a sounding chamber or Tom is actually that loud, I don't know, but I can hear every grunt, every groan, every complaint and swear. I help Tom take the canoe off for a rest and readjust his padding. He makes it to the top and our put-in. I don't have to work so hard to occupy my mind this trip. Just listening to Tom and empathizing with his pain somehow makes my aching legs, heaving lungs, raw hips, and pounding heart seem minor.

After paddling the glassy smooth water of Chilhowee Lake, we take out at the Calderwood Dam access road, unload, and anticipate a relaxing evening camp before commencing with another steep, torturous climb. We'll tackle that tomorrow. But security guard Raymond shows up. We are not allowed to camp here, he announces. My heart sinks. He quickly turns that around by offering to take us to the top of the dam. We latch onto his offer with a vengeance, as we know this portage could take us a good day and considerable trouble to do.

After watching us portage around Chilhowee Dam, Raymond got our story at the Tallassee store and was duly impressed. We ride every twist and turn of this steep road with gratitude in our hearts. I again thank God for angels like Raymond, who offer their help so willingly. This portage would have been excruciating.

Lugging gear down the mile access road to Calderwood Lake is comparatively easy but putting in is not. A steep embankment with loose shale and heavy undergrowth makes for a challenging put-in. I belay MW from the top as Tom clears a path and guides her to the water. I do the same for all the gear while Tom stays below to pack her up.

Finally on the water, I recall the Tallassee store fellow telling us how cold Calderwood water is. I can now test what I assumed to be profound exaggerations at the time. I plunge my hand into the beautiful green-hued water. Like touching a flame, my muscles react before my mind can tell them what to do. I jerk my hand out in an instant.

"Wow, that's painful!" I stuff my hand under my armpit to warm up.

Why people repeat what they see causes others discomfort, I don't know, but Tom has to do the same.

"Holy crap!" He yanks his hand out. "I guess swimming is out of the question." We both sit with hands under pits for a few moments. "I suppose this comes straight from the bottom of Cheoah Dam and doesn't get any sunlight."

Like Chilhowee, the steep mountainsides plunging into the green water here are clothed in small-leaved Rhododendron, now in bloom, and mountain laurel, whose blossoms have withered. I recognize red osier, hemlock, striped maple, and many other mountain-loving plants that hint at our upward progress. We are paddling 1,088 feet above sea level here on Calderwood. The Great Smoky Mountains are to our north and the Unicoi Mountains to the south. It is just us, the verdant mountainsides, and frigid clear green water. Small streams cascade into the lake from both shores. I look way up to see people at the overlook. We were there two hours earlier. Do those folks see us? Are they wondering how the heck those people in a canoe got way down here?

And so our ascent of the Smokies by canoe continues for two more lakes. Fans of the action thriller *The Fugitive* with Harrison Ford are familiar with Cheoah Dam, our next conquest. In the film, Dr. Richard Kimball (Ford's character) leaps off the dam's face, plunging into the surging waters below. What took him seconds to tumble down will take us excruciating hours to trudge up. But we climb, as we must, up to the road. Fortunately, John, a benevolent passer-by with a canoe trailer, who works for Nantahala Outdoor Center, helps us with our second load.

"Voorhi" to the Rescue

Phase II, Day 73 (June 9): Yesterday's dry spell broke our fifteen-day streak. The sky demons notice that they missed a day of rain and immediately remedy that. We cook a pancake breakfast in the vestibule, hoping the rain will let up. It doesn't. We huddle in the tent, reading and journaling, hoping the rain will let up. It doesn't. Eventually, we pack up anyway.

As I look out from under my drippy hood, I find Cheoah Lake quite serene. The water is glassy smooth, with a gentle covering of mist. An otter swims alongside us. Its curiosity satisfied, it submerges, leaving only a ripple. We hunker under our hats and hoods paddling towards Fontana Dam. The rain adds to my sense of solitude. The lake narrows, the current more insistent as we get nearer. At 480 feet high, Fontana Dam is the tallest dam east of the Mississippi. How are we ever going to portage this one?

The Voorhi sign our thank-you paddle

Questions swirl around in my mind: Will we intercept the Voorhi, our favorite Smokies family, today? Can we score a roof over our heads for one miserable night? Leaving telephone messages and not actually conversing left things up in the air regarding their earlier invitation to take a break at their cabin. Our workout is finally interrupted when the flashing of vehicle headlights parked along Route 28 causes me to peer out from under my hood. Despite the downpour, the Voorhi crew jump out: Jennifer, Bonnie-Jo, Woody and Robin all shouting and waving their arms. They found us! They came! Elation!

Over the next two days, our aching muscles recover over games of

"Robbers and Spies" with Robin and Woody, writing letters, swimming in the pond, and mending gear. One evening I sit on the couch, sewing new crotches into my underwear. I saved the sleeves that I cut off a T-shirt a couple of weeks ago for this very purpose. Young Bonnie-Jo walks by.

"You're sewing underwear?" I look up to see her looking at me as if I were eating slugs.

"Yup," I smirk with a shrug of my shoulders. "A couple of my undies need new crotches. Shouldn't everyone keep their panties in good repair?"

"Okaaaaayyyyy." She walks off slowly, with a sideways glance. I continue sewing. After all, I'm a river person. We are a frugal sort.

How Far Up a Mountain Can One Paddle?

Phase II, Day 75 (June 11): How far up a mountain can one paddle? We will find out at the upper reaches of Fontana Lake.

Even under cloudy skies, Fontana is a spectacular mountain lake. Ridge after ridge extends beyond both the north and south shores. Unlike Chilhowee, Calderwood, and Cheoah, this large lake absorbs some sunlight and is a reasonable temperature. Like them, it is clear and green. Wintergreen, wood betony, fire pink, spiderwort, yellow star grass, small-leaved rhododendron, mountain laurel, privet, hydrangea, and flame azalea are all in bloom, sprinkling bits of color here and there. If I were a plant, the Smokies is where I'd like to live.

This beauty, however, is rudely tempered by debris. Logs, foam floatation, an assortment of bottles, and a multitude of cans have collected in every cove. The irony of so much trash on such a beautiful, otherwise picturesque lake is too much to reconcile. We position ourselves in a couple of inlets to get some compelling photos to promote a bottle bill. This trash clearly demonstrates the need to make cans and bottles valuable.

The lake becomes more dissected with islands, long peninsulas, and wide coves at the far end, making the real channel hard to follow. Just beyond that, the "fun" begins. First we hear it; then see it: Class II rock garden rapids coming into view around the bend. MW noses her way up between the first few sets of rocks like a champ. In no time the going gets rougher. Tom, in the bow, hops out and begins frogging.

"Do you really think we can go *up* this?" I shout to Tom. Rapids like these are what people go down for a whitewater thrill.

"Sure," he bellows over the noise, "I'll pull MW up, and you paddle."

One of the zillion things I've become adept at on this expedition is adjusting my perception of what is possible. Most boaters finesse their way down rapids; we are muscling our way up. I mentally shrug off my doubts and pit my mind and body against the current.

I use my Norse paddle like a pole in the stern to plant against the rocky bottom and shove. Tom is frogging. That is to say, he is in the water, yanking MW up by the nose. Only if we are synchronized can we make progress, so when Tom shouts, "Heave," I push, and he pulls. Then, whether thigh or waist deep, he forces his way against the flow in front of MW, using her for balance, shouts the word, and we do it again. We progress two to three feet at a time with each heave. When the water gets over waist-deep, Tom scrambles in while I hold her steady, and we paddle frantically for a few feet until the next rocky rapid. A two-foot ledge necessitates my getting out as well.

In this manner, we paddle, frog, curse, and heave our way slowly up the shoreline, ducking and crashing through branches, squeezing MW through chutes, and tugging her over ledges. We even try poling our way up this torrent with poles Tom fashioned from saplings.

In this technique, you use a long pole to push the canoe upstream—while standing. Yes, people do this. Early trappers and explorers poled their way up shallow mountain streams. Today, folks pole as a sport. Apparently, people like us don't do this well. Tom lost his pole when it got wedged between rocks, and my attempts pushed MW off track.

We hope to get to Franklin, North Carolina, twenty miles from here, before getting out and crossing the Appalachians. Is the river this fast the whole way? If so, this is not a reasonable endeavor.

The lure of better conditions further on, not wanting to admit defeat, or just being inexcusably boneheaded made us persist in this folly again the next day. Due to three thunderstorms that traveled through last night, the water level and speed have augmented yesterday's already high water. This time I am out front, frogging in waist- to chest-deep water, which by the way, one should *never* do. What madness are we afflicted with?

After an hour and a half more of hauling MW up steep ledges, skirting overhanging trees, being slapped and scratched by bushes, slipping on rocks, plunging into neck-deep holes, and fighting the relentless current, we take a minute to catch our breath in a tiny shoreline eddy. Tom is now in frogging position and anchors MW from the bow with arms draped over her port gunwale. When I can talk, between gulps of air, I shout over the rapids, "Haven't we tried this long enough?" With Franklin still twenty miles away, and no sign of this river easing up, I've already deemed this a fruitless effort.

"I don't see the point in continuing," Tom relents. My countenance jumps for joy. "The water's so damned high. All this rain."

With Tom in the bow, me in the stern, we bring MW about and run whitewater the way it should be run. Down. In two minutes, we . pass last night's campsite—where we were an hour and a half ago. In ten minutes, we get poured out into the calmer water of Fontana

Lake. A angler placidly waiting for a bite in his skiff asks where we are going. I say we tried to go upriver. A raise of his eyebrows indicates I piqued his attention. He shakes his head and states matter-of-factly, "Too much water." He's right about that.

So tonight we sit, as we have every night lately, cramped in our sopping wet tent on this hillside, cooking supper in the vestibule while rain, thunder, and lightning torment us.

We eventually fall asleep looking forward to tomorrow—when our friends Marty and Kristen, coworkers from The Great Smoky Mountains Institute at Tremont, will come to pick us up.

CHAPTER 13

Final Push—
The Savannah River

It is good to have an end to journey towards;
but it is the journey that matters in the end.

—Ursula K. Le Guin

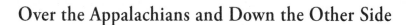

Over the Appalachians and Down the Other Side

Phase II, Day 79 (June 15): "You paddled *up* that?" Kristen asks,
with raised eyebrows, as we gaze down from the overlook. This is the
first of three stops where the four of us pour out of our portage car to
see if the river has gotten any easier to paddle.

"Yeah, well, not so much paddled…" Tom starts.

"More like pushed and pulled and shoved," I finish.

"How far did you get?" Marty inquires, peering at the river and then at Tom. It is difficult to gauge based on our tedious mode of travel.

"Well"—he was doing some sort of calculating in his head—"two hours the first day . . . an hour and a half yesterday . . . ten minutes to go downstream . . ." He squints a bit. "I'd say we did between a quarter-mile and a half-mile."

"WOW!" Marty and Kristen and I sing in unison. I suspect, however, that they remark on how much distance we covered. I ruminate on how little.

Exuberant with Class II and III rock garden rapids the whole way up the mountain, the Little Tennessee was not about to let us scramble up her.

The upper tributaries of the Savannah River are tapped for power production by Duke Energy. Canoeist's translation: dams. Jocassee Dam is 300 feet high and has three generators. At night, water gets pumped back up to Lake Jocassee to be used again. A commercial waterway does not extend this far upriver. Canoeist's translation: no locks.

Two days after our car portage over the mountains, we stop at Devil's Fork State Park to inquire how best to tackle our first portage on this river.

"You can't portage it," the park ranger states matter-of-factly.

"Excuse me?" Tom asks.

"It's a good way to spend a night in jail," he adds for effect.

Tom and I exchange skeptical looks. Fortunately, another ranger decides to call Duke Power, and Tom speaks with the person on the other end. I listen as Tom explains our expedition. Then Tom listens. Then, with a thank-you, he hangs up.

"Well?" I inquire. "How far is the portage? Can we do it?"

"We stay right here," he replies.

"Huh?"

"The manager is coming around with a truck to pick us up."

Our current portage difficulty solved, we find ourselves paddling Lake Keowee with a new name on our thank-you paddle. Blueberries are ripe, so we hug the shoreline and collect. Blueberry pancakes are on the menu for breakfast.

A similar scenario is played out at Keowee Dam, where we also get escorted, avoiding Oconee Nuclear Station and the hydroelectric installation. But first, we pay a visit to Duke Power's World of Energy educational center. After playing with all the interactive exhibits, I get a good look at myself in the bathroom mirror. I am mortified! My bodily injury tally is as follows: I have chigger bites on my toes, belly button, and waistline—many of which ooze; I have about a zillion itchy no-see-um bites scattered 'round; a myriad of mosquito bites in prominent and some curious places (I do pee in the woods an awful lot); several boils of poison ivy; a raw, red, bothersome scratch on my ankle thanks to a greenbrier just today; tender, red hips from carrying my drybag; finally, all my frogging bruises make me look like I'm breaking out in some weird disease. From the waist down, I'm a disaster. Allen, from Duke Power, graciously donated a can of insect repellent to us today. From the looks of me, it's too late.

Once we reach the southern end of Hartwell Lake, South Carolina is to our northeast and Georgia to the southwest. The Savannah River will continue to be the border between these states all the way to the ocean.

Finding us hitchhiking back from Hartwell for groceries and mail, Bryan stops to give us a ride. He makes a side trip to show us the Georgia Guidestones in Elberton: a fascinating shrine erected in

1980 by a group desiring a better life for humanity and harmony with nature. It looks like Georgia's version of Stonehenge. After touring and admiring the monument, Bryan doesn't have time to go on to Hartwell, so we thank him for his hospitality and seek our next ride on Route 77.

On the other side of the road, an old station wagon is backing out of the driveway. A woman yells out to us, "Come on."

The two kids in the front seat squish into the back seat to make room for Tom and me in front. The dashboard of our generous and bubbly driver is covered with wallet-sized portraits of her family that prevent any hope of seeing the gauges. She tells us about every single household we pass while en route to the Hartwell post office.

On our way home, we bump and bounce around in the bed of a pickup truck of two historical-restoration carpenters. Once at their destination, Elberton—our halfway point—Chris asks where we are going, and we tell him the usual story. They are so impressed that they buy us each a Mountain Dew and take us all the way to where we stashed MW.

Richard B. Russell Dam is a whopper. Once again, we avoid arrest and receive vehicle assistance from David, a U.S. Army Corps of Engineers employee. Here too, turbines can spin the opposite way to pump water back up to generate electricity again. David explains that because of blueback herring in adjoining J. Strom Thurmond Lake, they no longer reverse the turbines at night. The fish get sucked up and churned around, resulting in a massive die-off. Since these are commercial fish, they have clout. The situation, David tells us, is currently in litigation.

Blueback herring are anadromous fish, meaning they migrate from the ocean up rivers to spawn in fresh water. During this spring migration, they collect below dams—knocking on the door, so to speak—asking to pass. The fish avail themselves of fish ladders, where they occur, and sometimes get locked through where there are locks. This dam has neither a fish ladder nor a lock. We humans know how to complicate nature, that's for sure.

About the litigation: after fourteen years in the court system, a federal judge allowed the Army Corps to pump water back up to Russell Lake. To mitigate the adverse effects, the Corps is compensating fish, for instance, by oxygenating the water. The fish have responded in the only manner available to them: by adjusting. Each of these lakes we travel now has successfully reproducing landlocked populations of blueback herring.

Augusta

Phase II, Day 91 (June 27): The Augusta City Lock and Dam provides our next puzzle, but the Augusta Canal soon solves it. Completed in 1892, this canal facilitates transportation, provides mechanical power, and supplies drinking water for the city of Augusta even today. Perched atop a hill above the canal is the Savannah Rapids Pavilion. We trudge our little selves way up there for answers. There, we not only learn that the canal is indeed canoe-friendly but highlights historical points of interest for paddlers by way of an accompanying brochure.

Even more delightful is that a group is expected to paddle the canal today, outfitted by American Wilderness Outfitters, Ltd. This keeps getting better. Not only might we have canoe companions, but a company with the acronym of AWOL will assist us.

As we lunch at a picnic table at the bottom of the hill below the Pavilion, we are entertained by George from AWOL, outfitting

Kimberly-Clark employees. One employee, eager for her outing, told me that one in four people worldwide either wipes their bottom with, blows their nose with, or wraps their baby's bottom in a Kimberly-Clark product. Anyway, a thorough discussion with George determines our complicated plan. Somehow, he will outfit and lead his crew, transport me to the grocery store, rendezvous with Tom to pack our gear in his vehicle, pick me up, and deliver us back to the river. Oh, before all this happens, a reporter and photographer from the *Augusta Chronicle* will visit us.

At the bottom of the hill, Kimberly Clark folks are milling about, choosing partners, figuring out how to fasten life jackets, and measuring for paddles. Soon, AWOL George and his helper send canoes careening down the grassy embankment toward the canal and the Kimberly Clark folks below. I am thoroughly entertained, watching lively acrobatics as folks dodge canoes, bump into one another and attempt to catch the projectiles before they bowl someone over.

My attention is soon diverted to the parking lot, where a well-dressed man is trying to determine how to get down the hill. His suit, tie, white shirt, and dress shoes ring out "reporter." He awkwardly but effectively pinballs his way down from tree to tree. Robby, from the *Augusta Chronicle,* lands at our table, relieved to be on flat ground. After Robby brushes off his slacks and adjusts his tie, he asks many of the usual questions. We take advantage of the AWOL group preparing for their canoe trip to emphasize the benefits of keeping a river clean for recreation.

George stops by to confirm our complicated plan. In a minute more, Robby deems our interview over. I hope his next interview is on a flat surface, or he at least dons sensible shoes.

The canal is a delightful canoe trail. Tom reads the accompanying brochure as we whiz along past loblolly pines, rerouted streams, Spanish moss, Works Project Administration stonework bridges, remains of a Civil War-era gunpowder factory, and through the gate of a flood-control dam.

Our campsite tonight in the midst of Augusta is near a rowing facility. The sheriff cruises the area frequently, keeping an eye on us, as requested by our AWOL friends. Necessary or just cautious, I don't know. But it is reassuring.

AWOL Jim drops off a copy of the *Augusta Chronicle* in the morning. There we are, in full color in the Metro section: Tennessee Couple Canoes Country." We leave the hospitable city of Augusta behind us. I'd like to come back here someday.

With Augusta in our rear-view mirror, we have only 186 miles of alligator-infested river between the Atlantic and us. The serene river flows effortlessly along at 3 to 4 miles per hour, but it smells terrible, and churned-up suds form bubble pillows in eddies. Sandy beaches dot the inside bends, while slippery mud banks border the river elsewhere. We pull onto a beach to contemplate whether a heat-relieving swim is worth the risk. I bend over to examine the unmistakable tracks of an alligator. In a moment, Tom joins me.

"Everybody says they're shy," he says confidently.

"So I've heard." I'm still dubious.

"I'm hot. I'm going swimming," Tom says, deciding to take his confidence out for a spin.

"Right here?! With alligators *right here*?"

"They're not here now."

"How do you *know*?"

With a splash, Tom plunges over backward, disappearing into the murky water.

"Oh sheesh, don't splash! That attracts them!" I implore him, even though he is out of sight. Tom comes up, smiling. "You really are a jerk!"

I stand knee-deep and splash cool water over my hot face and arms, hoping it is not as polluted as it smells, keeping alert for suspicious wakes in front of me or rustles behind me in the vegetation.

Paddling once again, actual 'gators begin to make themselves known. "Hey, I think I see one," I exclaim in an excited whisper at my first sighting. I watch, heart a-flutter, as the fellow slowly turns towards us. I draw the canoe further away from his apparent trajectory. He sinks out of sight without a ripple.

"Where is he?" Tom asks from the stern.

"Too late; he submerged." I sigh. "He didn't seem to like the sight of us, so he went under."

By the end of what turns into a four-gator day, I am much more comfortable sharing the river with them. They do seem extremely shy. It is difficult getting any pictures of them at all. Soon, I can't get enough of them.

Independence Day on the River

Phase II, Day 97 (July 3): I am enjoying the serenity, admiring the reflection of light-green willow leaves in the still water, alert for more green-backed herons, great egrets, or gators, when an annoying motorized sound breaks my reverie. Soon, two guys speeding and whining up the river on wave runners slow to a stop near us.

"Where ya goin'?" the first fella asks without preamble. Our destination doesn't rouse as much of a reaction as the answer to the question, "Where'd ya start?" The conversation goes as many before until the larger fellow, Russell, shifts his considerable weight and tumbles off the wobbly machine with a sizable splash, emerging with a barrage of curses. He tries to pull himself back aboard with enthusiastic grunts and groans. Time and again, the machine tips over. The three of us find this a delightful source of amusement and interject with, apparently, less than helpful suggestions. Eventually, his fumbling gets too painful to watch. Tom gets a bright idea of how to help.

We paddle over to the front of Russell's watercraft. Tom tucks his paddle away and leans over to hold the front down while Russell clambers up the back. Russell, being a big boy, kicks and pulls and grunts. Tom struggles to steady his machine and I brace MW, who is bouncing like a rocking horse. Finally, Russell plunks back down into the water with a groan. Tom concedes this is not effective. Nor is it in our best interest. After all, we've come all this way from the West Coast and haven't dumped once.

At last, his friend gets the idea of helping. After two more failed attempts, Russell finally gets aboard. "Man, I'm too drunk to be out here!" Russell admits. "Say, why don't you guys come to our Fourth of July party tomorrow night? Me and my brother Bubba are put-tin' burgers on the grill. You're welcome to come!" He explains the location of his house as he slowly motors back and forth. Then, in a high-pitched whirr, the two of them, Russell and the quiet one, spin around and head back downriver.

"I guess Russell's starting to party a little early," Tom remarks.

"I wonder what he'll be like tomorrow."

"So, you want to go to his party?" Tom teases with a knowing chuckle.

"Oh yeah, a drunk dude with a brother named Bubba. Now there's an enticing prospect," I reply.

"Well, it was nice of him to ask."

I have to admit that all the folks we meet, including Russell, are very friendly. I just don't want to hang out with everyone we meet.

After this twenty-six-mile day, we pull into Blue Springs

Landing. We don't seek out Russell and Bubba, but instead meet Ruth and Charlie, owners of the air-conditioned bait shop. Charlie escorts us to Blue Spring State Park, where a pool of crystal-clear water was once the featured jewel. But, as Charlie explained, an earthquake altered the artesian well, so Blue Spring is now an algae pit.

We endure yet another nightly thunderstorm by the river, then wake early to the *vroom thup thup thup; vroom thup thup thup* of an angler trying unsuccessfully to start his motor. Ruth and Charlie come out to bid us goodbye and say they fretted for us last night during the storm that took out Blue Springs' electricity. I assured them we have weathered many storms and that electricity is only missed when you have it in the first place. More-doting grandparents would be hard to come by.

The river is abuzz today, the Fourth of July. Boats cruise back and forth, towing knee boarders or children in tubes. Bikini-clad girls ride the bow like figureheads. And, as always, anglers tool along in their jon boats, sometimes with leafy branches propped overhead for shade. One thing is clear: people love their waterways.

I can't help but recall the fearsome odor and froth of the river just downstream of Augusta, which I cringe to think was probably due to overflow of a wastewater-treatment plant because of all the rain. Now, 115 miles downriver, there is minimal aroma.

I sincerely wonder if our efforts have impacted people's thinking. Although enforcement of the Clean Water Act passed in 1972 has brought great strides in pollution control in our nation's waterways, there is a long way to go—as attested to by the odor and suds on the Savannah River.

Whether you are a backyard gardener spraying herbicides, a manager needing to dispose of manufacturing waste, a farmer applying pesticides, or a lawmaker, every adult decides how to dispose of and properly use potential water contaminants. Here are some mind-calibrating thoughts to consider:

- **Drinking water:** Municipal water gets treated and transported to your house at great expense. Don't let it run out the faucet, showerhead, or hose without being used. Well water from aquifers is equally precious. Don't use more than you need.

- **Plastics:** Plastics take a lot of water to manufacture and don't biodegrade. At best, some photodegrade (decompose in sunlight) and become smaller pieces, which enter an intricate food web that includes humans. Keep this in mind as you purchase and discard plastic containers and bags. Your purchases will likely still be around more than five hundred years from now. In other words, every piece of plastic thus far manufactured is still around today, in one form or another. Encourage manufacturers to seek alternative, biodegradable materials.

- **Resist bottled water:** Use tap water that is routinely monitored. The plastic in those bottles took much more water to produce than the water it holds. Practice the 3 Rs—Reduce, Reuse, and Recycle—in that order of importance.

- **Food:** Food takes a tremendous number of resources to grow, package, transport, and store. Eat it in a timely manner so it doesn't go bad. Be creative with leftovers. Eat lower on the food chain—raising farm animals takes a lot of water. Compost food scraps. Challenge and compliment yourself for "zero food waste."

- **Outside:** In your garden, use only native plants that don't require watering. Use drip irrigation or water by hand if watering is necessary. Be in tune with your environment: lawns don't make sense in the Southwest. If you are a lawn owner and must water, do so in the early morning or evening to minimize evaporation; turn the sprinkler off when rain will do the job; avoid spilling over onto sidewalks or driveways. Collect rainwater from roofs in barrels for outdoor-watering purposes. Use a spray nozzle on the hose to avoid wasting water. Use swimming pool covers to minimize evaporation. Fix leaks quickly.

- **Paper:** Depending on whether water is recirculated or not, it takes two to thirteen liters of water (one half to three and a half gallons) to produce one sheet of printer paper.[15] Go for paperless options. Get off junk-mail lists.[16] Recycle and buy recycled paper products. Use less.

- **In the workplace:** Make certain environmental factors weigh into decision-making as much as economic factors. Promote and practice the 3 Rs in every facet of business and manufacturing.

- **Farming:** Farmers think about water constantly. Some things they do or should be doing include growing drought-tolerant crops and those adapted to the region. If irrigation is necessary, install drip irrigation systems. Don't irrigate during peak sunlight hours. Build water-retention ponds. Enhance soil with compost and mulch to improve its water-retention properties. Plant cover crops to reduce evaporation and enhance the soil. Prevent runoff.

Incorporate water-consciousness into your lifestyle as if your life depends on it—because it does.

Ebenezer Creek

Phase II, Day 99 (July 5): We have established our finishing date. We've told our families and allowed them time to make their way down to Savannah, Georgia, to meet us. Before our announced Atlantic Ocean appearance, we find ourselves with time to dally, so we take a side trip on a Savannah River tributary called Ebenezer Creek.

Creeping through the blackwater of Ebenezer Creek

"This is so cool," I say in a barely audible whisper as we glide along. Like a battalion at attention, magnificent tree trunks support a canopy so thick no sun is allowed to enter. The darkness and the motionless black water create a primordial atmosphere. At any moment, a "swamp thing" could emerge and scare the living daylights out of me. A stillness this quiet is eerie, hard to fathom. Drops plunking the water from our paddles seem annoyingly loud. As far as I can see, forest and stream are one and the same in every direction. There isn't even a noticeable current.

I glance behind us, wondering how we'll find our way back, but whisk the thought away, not allowing the concern to overshadow the moment. We slip around tupelo trees whose huge buttresses support sixty-foot-tall trunks. Knees stand guard around bald cypress trees, providing additional support. The only missing element from this spooky movie setting is a rumble of thunder. Oops—as if my thinking makes it so—the grumbling of an impending storm sends a chill up my spine.

"We'd better search for a campsite," Tom's matter-of-fact voice is reassuring. Almost three miles up, we come upon a green patch of grass surrounded by towering pines that make for an inviting campsite. In a half-hour, when the rains come, we are ready to escape into our tent.

After the storm and dinner, I insist we go for another exploratory paddle in the forest. We glide slalom-style among the trees, cutting through the thin film of pollen now covering the water's surface. I am completely enthralled.

Ebenezer Creek is a blackwater river, meaning it is slow-moving water flowing through a forested wetland. With a preponderance of decomposing vegetation, the water is nearly black. The creek is also a backwater ecosystem since the Savannah River creeps in during high water, causing the flow to back up and come to a near standstill.

After twenty minutes, our blackwater fun is shattered by a gunshot upriver. My heart jumps a beat.

"What do you say we turn around?" I suggest. Tom has already begun the turn.

Faced with a lake of trees, motionless water, and uniform darkness, we might have had some difficulty finding our way back, but MW's undisturbed path through the film of pollen is better than a trail of breadcrumbs.

Fortunately, no one manifested from my fervent imagination disturbs us at our secluded site that night. We sleep well in the fresh aftermath of the storm.

The Last Campsite

Phase II, Day 104 (July 10): Now we paddle against the incoming tide. It is not nearly as strong as the West Coast tide on the Columbia.

I compare my paddling skills today to my abilities when we started eleven years ago. To say I've improved is an understatement. Expertise is inevitable after paddling nearly 5,000 miles. Draws, pitch strokes, pries—I did it all back then, but now finessing a paddle is as natural to me as walking. My upper-body strength has unquestionably increased but at the expense of my sit-in-the-canoe-and-do-nothing legs. They used to fly me around the track and over hurdles with ease. Now they complain when all I ask of them is to haul me and a backpack up over an occasional dam.

My evaluation of what is possible is forever altered. What riprap used to be too rugged, current too fast, lock too intimidating, waves too high, or wind too strong is now just a matter of practiced technique, endurance, and determination to conquer. Just because it's hard doesn't mean it's impossible.

Today we pass by the cities of Port Wentworth and Savannah, Georgia—possibly the busiest ports we've experienced. Farthest upriver is the industrial zone. Paper mills, chemical factories, and power plants line the riverbank, each accompanied by an appropriate stench. I empathize with anything aquatic that must endure this. In Port Wentworth, ships from Monrovia, Norway, and Panama are docked. One is being relieved of its cargo of containers. Towering overhead is a massive scaffold supporting a crane outfitted with a grasping mechanism. We watch as it grasps a container, hoists it up, swings around, and deposits it onshore. Behind the cranes stand towers of these containers. Eighteen-wheeler trucks hustle them away one by one. I think about how uncomfortably big they are on the highway. Here, they seem matchbook size.

After passing under the beautiful Route 17 cable-stay bridge, the harbor gives way to downtown Savannah. A large and attractive riverfront allows pedestrians to walk along and enjoy their river. Roads along the river are paved in cobblestones that were once ballast from ships that have come to port here through the years. Stopping at a public dock downtown, I go ashore to telephone the *Savannah Morning News*. The paper already has a reporter assigned to us, and she and a photographer will be down to meet us forthwith.

Audrey gets everything we have to say on her hand-held tape recorder. I tell her how nice it is to see Savannah embrace its waterfront for recreation. Tom plugs our clean-water message, listing practical habits folks can adopt. They promise to be at our arrival on Tybee Island tomorrow morning, bright and early.

Onward we paddle, past Old Fort Jackson, a remnant of the War of 1812. I'm captain today, and I opt for the southern channel rather than the main, northern channel to get a reprieve from the freighters. Saltmarsh surrounds us, and the land is flat. Finding a site for the night within easy striking distance of Tybee Island will be a trick. We must be close enough to arrive roughly at our appointed time, yet camp on dry ground.

"There's a clump of trees over there," Tom says, pointing to the left.

"Way over there?" In between are six- to eight-foot-tall grasses and marsh plants mired in mud.

"Do you see anything better?"

I scan our surroundings. With most campsite choices, there is often the possibility of something better a little further along. But here, the chances of a suitable site closer to the ocean drop with every stroke. Saltmarsh is taking over the landscape. "I guess we should try it," I reply. Getting there may be hard, but not impossible.

We pour on the speed to shove MW as deeply as possible into the vegetation until she stops. "I guess we walk from here," I say.

"I'll see what it's like." Tom hops out with both feet, his knees dropping out of sight before he stops sinking. Not to be deterred, he slogs into the reeds out of view, the mud-slurping sounds and mumbled curses growing fainter to my ears. In ten minutes he returns, lurching for MW's bow for support. Between gasps, he proclaims, "It's okay." I wonder what he would deem not okay. Crotch deep? Neck deep? So I too hop out, and we heave MW along, fully loaded. Just like frogging, using MW for balance, we take two or three steps ahead, stop, and heave MW forward, then slog alongside her some more and heave. No thigh exerciser can equal this. Add sharp, sticky plants that grasp clothes and scrape skin, and you have a miserable workout. After ten minutes, the mud thickens, and we only sink ankle-deep. We lighten her up by packing the gear out on our backs and hauling them to the site. This is a mid-calf deep exercise. Finally, we drag MW to our little island in the salt marsh and throw our exhausted selves down on firm ground.

"Geez, look at me," I say, pointing to the bloody scratches covering my arms. "Those plants are vicious!"

"You've got a lot more than me," Tom says, inspecting himself.

"Well, you've got hair to protect you."

"That's true. That's one good use for all my hair."

"Look at our legs," I now point out. We are coated in mud from the knees down.

"I guess we'd better find a place to wash off."

"So much for our showers last night."

"They'll take us, no matter what," he says of our waiting families. Everyone is there now, just a few miles away. Tom's folks are snug in a hotel, where they generously booked a room for us tomorrow night. I ache for that luxury right now. My parents and my brother and his family are at a nearby campground. On this final night of our expedition, our camp consists mostly of palmettos and a few big pine trees. It is a perfectly acceptable site, but it will be another booger to get out of tomorrow morning.

At supper this evening, we give God a special thanks for ushering us through some tight spots. We overcame wind, waves, storms, and even came too close to a tornado, but the blessings had them beat. My faith in the compassion of humankind has been reinforced through every phase of this journey. Friends and strangers invited us into their homes and lives. People went out of their way to usher us around impassable dams. Many gave us rides to town, a fish for supper, a cold drink, or just a friendly wave. Even accounting for the theft of our camera equipment by one selfish, misguided individual, I can still attest that good people prevail in this nation of ours.

I don't regret the end this time. This is nothing like pulling out in Atchison, where regret and failure put me in a funk. This is our destination. This is what we have sweated, cried, ached, and pushed to achieve. An overwhelming sense of accomplishment envelops me as I write in my journal. My throat tightens and tears well up as I reflect on what it took to get here.

As I ponder, I enjoy an orange sunset as it turns red and slowly fades over the salt marsh. I wonder where life will lead me now. A smile pushes away the tears when I think of the open book in front of me, exciting and new. I'm not a drifter anymore. Amid the many unanswered questions I generate, one truth makes itself evident. I feel as though I've discovered my life's work. I've found a meaningful purpose as an environmental educator. We've encountered horrible abuses of beautiful rivers. We've also seen the remarkable results of conscientious efforts to safeguard waterways and natural areas.

Rivers provide for our commerce, agriculture, electricity, drinking water, and recreation. They are crucial to the vast array of wildlife that lives in, on, and around waterways. The only thing that will safeguard the health of our waterways and, therefore, us is a well-balanced attitude toward our natural environment—what conservationist, educator and father of wildlife ecology Aldo Leopold calls the "land:"

> We abuse land because we regard it as a commodity belonging to us. When we see land as a community to which we belong, we may begin to use it with love and respect.

I want to continue nurturing that attitude of love and respect in my career.

Oppressive heat on a breezeless night is not the only thing robbing us of much-needed sleep. Anticipation of the 5:07 alarm (a compromise between Tom's 5:00 and my 5:15 request) keeps me wondering what time it is. Regular flashes of heat lightning flicker through the tent as if a marquee were just outside the window. Then there is the relentless scritch-scratching of seemingly millions of very busy crabs outside, climbing on the nylon and scurrying over the dry palmetto leaves. Top it all off with pent-up excitement about our last day on the river, and I am awake for hours. Tom doesn't fare any better.

Atlantic at Last

Phase II, Day 105 (July 11): My alarm eventually rouses me out of some lower level of consciousness. I don't waste any time getting up and moving. In the glow of our head-mounted flashlights, we pack for portage.

With the tide going out to sea, our fifty-yard salt marsh march is muddier than before. But by using MW for support to pull up my legs after every slurpy step, it is still possible. By 6:06, we are floating down the Savannah on the outgoing tide, dangling our legs overboard to rinse off the mud.

The morning is calm and quiet and cool—it begins with dignified slowness. At times like these, I wonder why I don't get up earlier to enjoy such moments. I paddle in silence as I try to soak in the feeling surrounding me. The sun glistens off the water and dots the small white puffy clouds. A couple of shrimp boats ply the waters around us. It is otherwise still and serene. I feel a sense of camaraderie with the shrimpers. We are the dawn club. Others, wise enough to experience the break of day, must share this sense of exclusivity. Those who come later will not have known of this special serenity. It is the secret of the dawn club, and today, I am a member.

In a few minutes, we pass under the bridge leading to Fort Pulaski National Monument. During the Civil War, this Confederate fort was pummeled by a new invention of the Union Army—the rifled cannon. Visitors can now see the holes blasted in the masonry and understand why the Confederates had no choice but to surrender. Beyond the fort, we paddle past a small, white brick lighthouse that marks the end of the Savannah River. The north channel joins the south channel here, both emptying into a small bay. We watch a large container vessel exiting the river. Across the bay to our right, we see Tybee Island's North Beach Lighthouse. In 2002, Tybee Island Historical Society painted the Tybee lighthouse to its present black-white-black daymark, but here in 1997, the white base–black top lighthouse hails the end of our voyage.

A light breeze picks up, stirring just a slight wave action.

"Look at the ocean. It's so calm," I remark to Tom.

"It shouldn't be any problem to land," he says. A few days ago, we discussed the prospect of paddling out into an ocean of waves. We made a plan. We would ride the river straight into the surf to get beyond the breakers. We would travel the swells parallel to land until the landing point, wherever that might be. Then, we'd do an about-face and ride the waves right into shore. Once we hit the beach, the bow person would have to make a quick exit and pull MW up before a wave crashed over her stern. We would be in public view, so it would have to be good. To our relief, the ocean this morning couldn't be more delightful.

Nose pointed into the ocean, we aim to round a sandy point on the southern shore. As we get nearer, I see two figures. Yes, they are people, and now there are more. It's my family! Dave, Frances, Stephanie, Robbie, Mary, and Tom's dad Paul. They wave, yell, jump up and down, and take pictures. They wave us around the point to the lighthouse. Around the bend, I see my dad. He waves us on further south.

As we paddle, the welcome committee scurries to the rendezvous point. Then I see it—a banner marking the finish line. From out in the ocean, I can see a big white sheet hung between two poles: CONGRATULATIONS, YOU MADE IT across the top, and PADDLE FOR WATER: PACIFIC TO ATLANTIC on the bottom. In the center is an outline of the United States with our route traced across it. Everywhere in between, reporters, friends, and even family not present have signed their congratulations. Our moms and reporters flank the banner. We turn MW and ride the gentle waves toward shore.

**Riding gentle Atlantic Ocean waves ashore on Tybee Island, Georgia.
Photo courtesy of Roy DeWitte.**

I feel like a celebrity amid the hugs, congratulations, photos, and interviews. When things calm down, Tom, I, and our supportive families gather in front of the banner. We raise our paper cups to toast a successful trip with—what else?—clean, clear, delicious, magnificent-tasting water.

We made it! Photo courtesy of Paul Condon.

Toasting success with nothing but wonderful water!
Photo courtesy of Paul Condon.

Wednesday, July 9, Tom's journal entry:

The trip is nearly over. I almost regret its ending, but I look back with joy. Not only have I completed a remarkable feat of physical endurance, but I have won the love of the most wonderful woman I have ever known. That is the greatest treasure I have from this voyage.

Saturday, July 12, Nancy's journal entry:

Friday, July 11th was a fantastic day. It ranks up there with my wedding day. I'll never forget the greetings, congratulations, the banner, and the excitement. I smile at the memory. Not only do I feel a great sense of accomplishment, but I completed it with the love of my life.

The author and her husband. Photo courtesy of Paul Condon.

Some Paddling Vocabulary

River Words

Confluence—The junction of two (or more) rivers.

Downstream "V" —A tongue of water flowing between two obstructions in rapids. Generally, the way to go.

Eddy—A spot in a river where water runs countercurrent to the main flow. Occurs behind obstructions or curves in the river. The void created downstream of the obstruction draws water in to fill the void so water goes in the opposite direction. The **eddyline** is the boundary between the main flow and the eddy.

Flatwater—Still or slowly flowing water.

Hydraulic—Backflow, usually created below a shallow falls where water surges backwards to fill the void below the ledge. Strong ones can toss objects or people around and around for a long time. Definitely avoid!

Inside of a curve—The shorter distance of a river bend; often shallower with slower water.

Jetty—A human-made structure that sticks out from land into water. Usually made of boulders.

Outside of a curve—The longer distance of a river bend; often deeper and with swifter water.

Pillow—An unimposing bulge in whitewater formed by a rock barely submerged. To be avoided. Definitely not soft like a pillow.

Standing wave—A wave that stays in one place, made by an obstacle or converging currents.

Strainer—A sieve of brush or tree branches in a river through which water flows freely, but large things like debris, canoes, or people cannot. Very dangerous.

Lock and Dam words

Dam—A structure across a river or stream to hold back water.

Dike—A raised embankment to prevent high waters from inundating land; a levee.

Lock—A chamber allowing vessels to bypass a dam, bounded by upriver and downriver gates (doors). Water (and vessels upon it) rise when a valve is opened by the lockmaster, allowing water from the upriver reservoir to enter. Water lowers when the downriver valve is opened, allowing water out of the lock.

Lockmaster—The operator of a lock.

Riprap—Quarried boulders piled up to reinforce a shoreline from erosive forces such as waves. From Day 1 we become competent at disembarking on these rocky embankments.

Spillway—A channel allowing for the passage of water around or over the dam or levee.

Tainter valve/Tainter gate—A type of floodgate controlled by an operator that regulates the flow of water. It is opened or closed to raise and lower water levels in locks.

Canoeing words

Belay—A climbing term, meaning to secure a rope to a person (or canoe or something else) going down or up a steep slope.

Blade—The flat part of the paddle that pushes the water.

Bow—The front of a boat.

Crossbow draw—A draw on the opposite side from the one you're paddling on, with no change of hand position. This is a temporary stroke helpful in whitewater to draw the nose away from an obstacle.

Draw—A stroke in which you reach the paddle out to your paddling side and draw the water directly toward yourself. This moves the canoe sideways.

Feather—To slice the blade of the paddle through the wind upon the return of a stroke.

Ferry—To maneuver a canoe across the current by using the current to push the boat across the flow.

Floatation Chamber—The enclosed area at the front and back of a canoe filled with foam or air to aid in buoyancy.

Frogging/Frog—To get out of the canoe and walk, pulling it along with the painters or gunwales.

Grip—The handle part of the paddle gripped by your top hand.

Gunwale (or Gunnel)—A railing that tops the edges of the sides of a canoe or other boat.

Hull—The bottom of the canoe or any boat.

Line/Lining—To tug a canoe through rapids or around rocks by pulling the line/painter.

Low Brace—To make use of the paddle as an outrigger to steady the canoe. Reach the paddle out to the side as far as able and lay the blade flat on the water surface, putting weight on it.

Open canoe—A small, lightweight boat, narrow at both ends and open on top—like ours. Canoeists use a single blade paddle. Compare to a kayak that is decked and is propelled with a double blade paddle.

Painter—A rope attached to the bow and/or stern of the boat.

Pumping water—Our made-up term for "full speed ahead;" paddling furiously.

PFD—A Personal Floatation Device, otherwise known as a life jacket. We affectionately call ours "pufdas."

Poling—To make use of a long pole to wedge on the bottom and push the boat forward in shallow water.

Portage—To carry a canoe and gear from one waterway to another.

Put-in—A site where the canoe is put in the water.

River left—The left side of the river, heading downriver. Going up-river, *river left* is on your right.

River right—The right side of the river, heading downriver. Going upriver, it would be the left bank.

Shaft—The long pole part of a paddle.

Stern—The back of a boat.

Sweep—A paddling stroke that turns the nose away from the paddle. Plant the blade forward as far as possible, make a wide arc with the blade, sweeping until your paddle is at right angles to the boat. On an imaginary clock in front of you, a sweep goes from 12:00 to 3:00.

Take-out—A site where the canoe is taken out of the water.

Thwart—A cross brace that adds strength to an open canoe.

Acknowledgments

Writing a book and a cross-country canoe expedition have a lot in common: hard work, perseverance, encouragement, and a huge amount of help. I'm truly grateful to Beth Giddens for her professional guidance and encouraging words. I am so amazed you stuck with me all these years! Thanks to my supportive beta readers who willingly shared their expertise: Chris Wrabel, Heidi Colonna, Jane Condon, Louisa Gluck, Marsha Ramah, Sonja Wastvedt, Sue McDowell, and Susan Middleton. I'm so fortunate to be the beneficiary of such generosity.

And to my editor, Margaret Harrell, who encouraged me to be more right-brained. Your keen sense of storytelling helped make this book a more enjoyable read. I couldn't ask for better. Only I am to blame for any quirky faux pas herein.

My talented designer and formatter, Dan and Darlene Swanson from Van-garde Imagery, who worked their magic to transform my manuscript and cover into a beautiful book. I am grateful to my cousin and talented artist, Kathrine McDowell McGough for the rendering of our paddling picture. You got the artistic talent in the family. And I can't neglect to thank the team at Self-Publishing School for ushering me through the procedure, allowing me to share my adventure and message with the world.

The folks mentioned in this book are but a sampling of the open-arm reception we received from so many individuals on our expedition. A cold drink, a lift to town, a night under a roof, a fish supper—I am forever grateful and humbled by the many acts of kindness extended toward a couple of bedraggled river folk. I'd list you by name, but my editor laughed at the prospect of the world's longest acknowledgments page. That being the case, please know that you made a difference in my life. I now know that no matter how divisive our country may be in other matters, kindhearted souls are at its core.

My deepest thanks to the generous companies whose equipment kept us safe and supported our cause. This expedition could not have succeeded without your help. Cascade Designs, Eastman Kodak, Extrasport, Grade VI Expeditions, Hi Tec Boots, JanSport, Katadyn Water Filters, Mitchell Paddles, Norse Paddle, Patagonia, Pelican Products, Sawyer Canoe.

A special, long-awaited thanks to my friends Diane Tunney and Steve Porter. You came to our rescue and toted us home, saving a couple of emotionally spent wayfarers. Nothing I can do will adequately repay your kindness, but it will never be forgotten.

Although reluctant to let me go, my family rallied: delivering us to the river for Phase II, creating a memorable landing, praying ardently, sending packages with cookies. I hope I made you proud. Tom's family covered our ongoing expenses and made leaving civilization possible. I'm privileged to be a part of the Condon clan. Apologies to both sets of parents for putting you through such turmoil. To save you from too much worry, I didn't tell you about the dangerous parts—until now.

Endnotes

1   History.com editors, "Lewis and Clark Expedition," March 16, 2021, https://www.history.com/topics/westward-expansion/lewis-and-clark.

2   Meriwether Lewis, April 9, 1806, entry in *The Journals of the Lewis and Clark Expedition*, ed. Gary Moulton (Lincoln, NE: University of Nebraska Press/University of Nebraska-Lincoln Libraries-Electronic Text Center, 2005), https://lewisandclarkjournals.unl.edu/item/lc.jrn.1806-04-09#lc.jrn.1806-04-09.01.

3   William Clark, October 31, 1805, entry in *The Journals of the Lewis and Clark Expedition*, ed. Gary Moulton (Lincoln, NE: University of Nebraska Press, 2005), https://lewisandclarkjournals.unl.edu/item/lc.jrn.1805-10-31#lc.jrn.1805-10-31.02.

4   Richard Brooks, "Which Language Has the Most Words for Snow?" Dec. 19, 2015, https://www.k-international.com/blog/which-language-has-the-most-words-for-snow/.

5   Paul Lindholdt and Lilian Seitz, "Hanford Nuclear Site," HistoryLink.org, Oct. 26, 2020, https://www.historylink.org/file/21101.

6   US Dept. of Energy, "About Hanford Cleanup," March 21, 2021, https://www.hanford.gov/page.cfm/AboutHanfordCleanup.

7   Jackie Skaggs, "Creation of Grand Teton National Park (A Thumbnail History)," Jan. 2000, https://www.nps.gov/grte/planyourvisit/upload/creation.pdf.

8   Water Resources, "Irrigation Water Use," United States Geological Survey (USGS), March 1, 2019, https://www.usgs.gov/mission-areas/water-resources/science/irrigation-water-use?qt-science_center_objects=0#qt-science_center_objects.

9   International Assessment of Agricultural Knowledge Science and Technology for Development (IAASTD)," *Agriculture at a Crossroads: Findings and Recommendations for Future Farming*, "Water," June 2016, https://www.globalagriculture.org/report-topics/water.html.

10 United States Department of Agriculture (USDA) National Agricultural Statistics Service, "Chapter 1, Table 10 – Irrigation," 2017, https://www.nass.usda.gov/Quick_Stats/CDQT/chapter/1/table/10/state/US/year/2017.

11 USDA, *Census of Agriculture 2017*, "Irrigation and Water Management; Results from 2018 Irrigation and Water Management Survey," https://www.nass.usda.gov/Publications/Highlights/2019/2017Census_Irrigation_and_WaterManagement.pdf.

12 Dave Bjorneberg, "Some Information about Irrigation," USDA - ARS - Pacific West Area, Northwest Irrigation and Soils Research Laboratory, 1997, https://www.ars.usda.gov/ARSUserFiles/20540000/k12/irrigation.htm.

13 Alyson McCann, "Drip Irrigation," URI Home*A*Syst Water quality Program – College of the Environment and Life Sciences, Aug. 5, 2014, https://web.uri.edu/safewater/protecting-water-quality-at-home/sustainable-landscaping/drip-irrigation/.

14 USGS, "Geographic Names Information System: Missouri River," https://edits.nationalmap.gov/apps/gaz-domestic/public/summary/756398.

15 P. R. Van Oel and A. Y. Hoekstra, "Abstract: The Green and Blue Water Footprint of Paper Products: Methodological considerations and quantification," 2010, *Value of Water Research Report Series No. 46, UNESCO-IHE*, Delft, the Netherlands, https://research.utwente.nl/en/publications/the-green-and-blue-water-footprint-of-paper-products-methodologic.

16 Amy Loftsgordon, "How to Get Removed from Mailing Lists and Email Spam Lists," Dec. 31, 2019, https://www.nolo.com/legal-encyclopedia/how-to-get-removed-from-mailing-lists-and-email-spam-lists.html.

Made in the USA
Monee, IL
29 October 2022

16791451R00208